Your Phobia

Understanding Your Fears Through Contextual Therapy

Your Phobia

Understanding Your Fears Through Contextual Therapy

by
Manuel D. Zane, M.D.
and Harry Milt

American Psychiatric Press, Inc.

1400 K Street, N.W.
Washington, D.C. 20005

Cover Design by Sam Haltom
Text Design by Tim Clancy and Richard E. Farkas
Typeset by Unicorn Graphics
Printed by Fairfield Graphics

Library of Congress Cataloging in Publication Data

Zane, Manuel D., 1913–
   Your phobia.

   Includes index.
   1. Phobias   I. Milt, Harry.   II. Title.
RC535.Z36   1984   616.85'225   84-12454
ISBN 0-88048-008-4

Contents

A Note to the Reader   *vii*

Foreword by Manuel D. Zane, M.D.   *ix*

Foreword by Harry Milt   *xiii*

1   The Phobias and Contextual Therapy   **1**

2   The Simple Phobias   **33**

3   The Social Phobias   **61**

4   Agoraphobia   **75**

5   Causes and Treatment of Phobias   **103**

6   The "Anatomy" of Your
    Phobic Reaction   **135**

7   Mastering Your Phobia   **149**

8   Recruiting Your Helper   **175**

9   The First Meeting with Your Helper   **203**

10 Gaining Control Over Your Phobia   **241**

11 Organizing a Mutual Support Group   **267**

Index   *279*

A Note to the Reader

YOUR PHOBIA: UNDERSTANDING YOUR FEARS THROUGH CON-TEXTUAL THERAPY is one in a series of books for the general public from the American Psychiatric Press, Inc. By selecting authors who are recognized leaders in their fields, we attempt to provide the general public with authoritative, up-to-date information on some of the prevalent problems of today's world—depression, drug and alcohol abuse, and phobias, for example. Some other books in this series include a glossary of psychiatric terms and a guide for families of psychiatric hospital patients; other appropriate topics will be added as the series continues to grow.

Each of our books for the general public is the result of many years of professional experience on the part of the authors. However, you, the reader, should keep in mind that there are often *several* valid approaches to psychiatric care and that all of these approaches may not be fully represented in a single book. Some approaches may be more appropriate than others, depending on the situation and characteristics of the individual involved and the nature of the problem. If you, a family member, or a friend are troubled with an emotional or behavioral problem, we recommend that you seek professional psychiatric help, either from a psychiatrist in private practice in your area or from a local hospital or mental health clinic. You and your psychiatrist can then evaluate the problem, decide whether some form of treatment is necessary, and explore the various psychiatric therapies that are available.

For many readers, the information provided in a book is sufficient to answer their questions and may perhaps even calm some anxious feelings concerning a potential mental health problem. For some readers, though—particularly those who have been troubled with a potentially serious emotional problem—a book can be the first step toward finding professional help. One of the primary goals of American Psychiatric Press, Inc., in conjunction with the American Psychiatric Association, is to inform the general public about mental health. This book helps to fulfill that goal; however, the opinions expressed in this book are not necessarily those of the American Psychiatric Association, and no endorsement should be implied.

Shervert H. Frazier, M.D.
Editor-in-Chief
American Psychiatric Press

Foreword

By Manuel D. Zane, M.D.

When, in the late fifties and early sixties, I started to treat increasing numbers of phobic people, I found my psycho-analytic understanding to be of very little help. Because of the urging of one of my highly accomplished agoraphobic patients and my unusual experiences as a psychiatrist working with physically handicapped people in rehabilitation medicine, I be-gan to venture with my patients into their phobic situations. Thus, with them I walked in the streets, into open parks, and into crowded department stores; rode escalators, elevators, trains, buses, subways, and ferry boats; went onto rooftops; drove in traffic, on highways, and over bridges; ate in restau-rants; sat in churches and the movies; visited pet shops; etc. From these diverse experiences with many, many phobic peo-ple, I gathered entirely new information about what causes a person's phobic behavior to arise, get worse, get better, or disap-pear. New ideas then emerged about the processes that caused these observed changes. Instead of searching the highly illusory past, which is basically the psychoanalytic approach, I explored the role played by the current context: the thoughts, feelings, expectations, and imagery inside the person and the social and physical environments outside.

I soon learned that many of the ideas and methods of the treatment that evolved, which eventually I called contextual therapy, bore many similarities to some also being advanced independently by Dr. Claire Weekes in Australia, by Dr. Arthur B. Hardy in California, and by Dr. Isaac Marks in England. We were all employing some forms of treatment that involved direct exposure of the phobic person to the phobic situation and utilizing, when needed, the help of paraprofessionals and other people. What is most important, in my mind, about these new developments is that an opportunity emerged for psychiatric professionals, working closely with paraprofessionals and phobic people, to observe directly what made the phobic reaction get better or worse and then to study, understand, and treat the processes by which fear in a phobic situation becomes overwhelming or becomes controlled. For me as a psychiatrist, this was a new direction: to explore concrete investigations of actual phobic experiences rather than to rely on theoretical explanations.

At this time, as a clinician who is actively involved in treating many phobic people, what seems to me to be central to the development of phobic disturbances—as this book will emphasize in great detail—is the role of the human imagination. Typically, phobic people, like the artist or the writer, possess an exceptional, innate ability to vividly experience and feel that which is imagined. Alone and ignorant of the disturbing effects this ability can cause in an individual, a person with this fabulous gift can develop a serious problem when he or she is unable to differentiate bodily reactions to *imagined* dangers from reactions to *real* dangers. The assistance of an objective person is essential to help the individual make this distinction. Otherwise, for example, a little dizziness arising from some stressful situation may seem to become, through use of a vivid imagination, an actual brain tumor, with all of its shattering and gripping implications, and a harmless skipped or rapid heartbeat can become a certain harbinger of imminent death, with its chilling and commanding connotations. In treatment, a phobic person therefore needs help to learn, believe, and accept that these distressing feelings and symptoms derive merely from frightening thoughts and imagined dangers, and that they hold no more real threat than exists in a scary nightmare. Thus, despite compelling feelings of danger, phobic people must gain corrective information from new experiences obtained by entering their phobic situations, so that they will, in time, be able to recognize and accept that their feelings of danger in the phobic situation are from imagined and not from actual dangers.

To get this experience—and to stop being the helpless victims of unrealistic beliefs of danger that are fabricated largely from past private imaginings—phobic people need assistance. We have written this book to help phobic people develop the information they require and learn to react more realistically in their phobic situations, and for readers who are interested in this area—including professionals—so that they may better understand the theory and application of contextual therapy.

This book emphasizes repeatedly that phobic people must be encouraged and helped by others to enter the phobic situation over and over again in manageable steps and to learn, by getting more and more new information, that the fantasized dangers constructed by their brain, though felt keenly, are harmless. At the same time we anticipate that all who work with and gain an understanding of phobias will come to appreciate more deeply our inescapable dependence on one another if we are to use our imagination—which has been called "the principal business of the human mind"—to free and enrich rather than to distort and constrict our lives.

Foreword

By Harry Milt

When I first considered writing a book with Dr. Zane on the phobias and contextual therapy, I regarded it as just another professional task, albeit one of major proportions. Most of my writing during the previous twenty years had been on subjects in the area of psychiatry and mental health. Since I already had a good, comprehensive, theoretical knowledge of the phobias, I presumed that I would just need to do some more research and bring this knowledge up to date. But contextual therapy? I had never heard of it. A psychiatrist friend, Dr. Ralph Crowley, had heard Dr. Zane speak on the subject once or twice, and he suggested that Dr. Zane might have something new.

With this introduction I approached Dr. Zane and proposed that we write a book together on phobias and contextual therapy. "What," I asked him, "*is* contextual therapy?" When he had finished explaining, it appeared to me that I was hearing about merely another wrinkle on a method already widely in use in the treatment of the phobias—the method known as "in vivo" or "exposure" therapy. At first; Dr. Zane had a hard time convincing me that contextual therapy was really a new approach, one which concentrated on the phobic process itself, teaching the phobic person to control it, understand it, and ultimately to master it. It was a new theoretical concept. He then invited me to sit in on an eight-week clinic in contextual therapy at the Phobia Clinic of the White Plains Hospital Medical Center, to meet the patients.

My own conception of the phobias was a mixture of Freudian and behavioristic interpretations. It may seem strange to the reader that I was able to reconcile such supposedly antagonistic theoretical views into a unified hypothesis. Yet, we tend to forget that psychoanalytic and behavioral therapy both strive to get the patients to unlearn maladaptive behavior patterns and to learn new, appropriate, and useful ones. One method deals with the antecedants and the consequences; the other with the consequences alone.

But I found as I began to learn about contextual therapy that neither of these two approaches was sufficient in the treatment of the phobias; that the key to the problem lay in the phobic experience and the phobic process itself. As I sat in the clinics and listened, I was able to relate to what was going on on a personal basis: I had had my own encounters with phobias—elevator phobia, phobia for heights, airplane phobia, and a little bit of agoraphobia. This made it easier for me to become involved and to absorb what I was hearing and observing.

I was astonished by the utter simplicity of the concept and by the aptitude and speed with which the clinic patients were grasping it and putting it into practice. I was astonished, too, to see how quickly some of the patients were improving in just a few weeks. Further, I found myself applying what I was learning to areas of my own life—situations where I was experiencing anxiety, stress, dejection, and fleeting episodes of phobic reaction. I was in fact becoming increasingly enthusiastic about contextual therapy. Perhaps this feeling comes through in places in the book where the writing is especially intense.

I have faith in this book and its capacity to help people who are suffering from a phobia or phobias. I hope it will bring relief to others as it has to those who have already been successful using contextual therapy.

The case histories used in this book come from my interviews with patients, from tape recordings of contextual therapy sessions, from the accounts of professionals working with phobic patients, and from my own experiences. All case histories have been disguised to conceal the identity of the original subjects.

CHAPTER ONE

The Phobias and Contextual Therapy

P HOBIA IS A STRANGE DISORDER—insidious, mysterious, bizarre. In some it affects only a limited part of daily life. In others, it infiltrates almost every aspect of living, leaving untouched only the few basic things one does in order to survive.

The symptoms may come on gradually over the years, giving first one warning, then another, then another, or they may strike seemingly "out of the blue," as the afflicted so commonly say, fulminating to full-blown proportions in a matter of months or even weeks.

Some who suffer from phobias actually know their misery by its name. Most haven't even heard the word, or, having heard it, do not realize that a phobia is what they've got. They know only the dread, the mental torture, the deprivation that comes with the ailment, the separation and isolation from life and other people, the loss of pleasures they once enjoyed, the narrowing of their lives into little islands of safety out of which they dare not venture, the awareness that even within these little patches of safety, phobic terror may suddenly strike.

Some texts refer to the phobias as one of the "minor emotional disorders." But anyone to whom a phobic person has revealed himself, divulging his fright, his feelings of helplessness and desperation, and the damage the ailment has done to his life, will wonder what some people could mean by "minor."

A flutist whose fine talent has won her a seat with a leading American symphony orchestra sits at home with window shades drawn, terrified to venture out or to let anyone come in. She fears that even the sight of another person will bring on an attack of choking and suffocation, and that if this happens, she will die. Her father speaks with her over the telephone, does her grocery shopping, knocks on the door, and leaves the packages and departs. She tries not to think of the first attack, but her memory keeps on bringing it back to torture her, vivid in every detail—the sudden wave of nausea, dizziness, feverish malaise; the fright that she might faint; the feeling of being hemmed in by the other members of the orchestra and their instruments in the constricted, half-dark pit; the flight from the pit through the small, narrow door even as the conductor was signalling her next passage.

A policeman with twelve years on a big city force, a hero who has been decorated for bravery, sits on a park bench dejected, bewildered, and frightened, searching desperately for some understanding of the mysterious malady which came upon him suddenly, several weeks after he was rescued from an ambush. He is terrified to go out on an unguarded height or even to look up at the roof of a building for fear he might have a compulsion to go up and jump. Only the captain of his precinct knows about his problem. His fellow officers have been kept in the dark. He is too embarrassed to tell them about his plight, afraid they will react with rejection and contempt. Tall, vigorous, powerful, handsome, he cannot tolerate the thought that he might be viewed by his buddies as a frightened, cowering weakling. He fears he is going out of his mind and that "they might have to come for me, put me in a straightjacket, haul me off to the looney bin, and give me shock treatment."

An attractive young woman of twenty-four, known for her vivacity and keen enjoyment of life, recounts how she has broken off her engagement, rejecting the entreaties of her fiance. "How can I possibly marry him," she asks, "when I've been reduced to something no man could possibly want—a frightened child who is terrified to be alone, to answer the telephone, to drive in my car, to go shopping, to go to a movie, to be in a restaurant, even to look out when it is raining. We used to go dancing until the early hours of the morning. We loved to go to the theater and restaurants. We had many friends and we had a great time together. What good am I to him now? I can't leave the house by myself, I can't travel. We can't go anywhere any longer. I used to be involved in drama and I had to quit that. I had to quit my job. Now I'm a helpless hermit."

At age thirty-three, a pilot who had flown Air Force jets at fifty thousand feet and at supersonic speeds, who had gloried in putting his craft through the most intricate and dangerous maneuvers, accepts with hopeless resignation and despair his dismissal as a flying instructor. He still cannot believe the unbelievable thing that happened to him. "I was cruising along at five thousand feet without a thought or worry in my head when I happened to look down and I became aware of the height, something that had never happened to me before in all my years of flying. But there it was, a sickish feeling in my mouth and stomach, a fright, an awful feeling that unless I got the plane down right away, I would jump or go out of my mind." Getting hold of himself, he had managed to keep control of himself and the plane, and make a safe landing. But from then on, he would not go up in a plane again nor even venture onto any sort of height.

A priest walks sadly by his church and the rectory which had been his home for more than twenty years and wonders whether he will ever be able to go back there again, to regain his role as pastor of a devoted congregation. He does not know what will happen to him, now that he is separated from a vocation which has been his life. The crisis had been long in coming. First there had been the difficulty in speaking in public, an ordeal which had begun even when he was still studying for the priesthood, and which had progressed slowly over the years until he could no longer deliver a sermon. Then came the time when his hands began to shake as he was distributing Communion. One day, his hand shook so badly that he dropped the chalice, spilling the wine over the altar cloths, the rail, the floor. Horrified at what he regarded as a desecration, he would not permit himself ever again to say mass or give Communion, nor even to come near the altar.

A young salesman, whose aggressive and successful performance had won him an executive sales post by the time he was twenty-nine, wonders how long it will be before his chief discovers his problem and he is compelled to relinquish his position. The instant he wakes up in the morning, he finds the dread waiting for him, the dread that he will have to take a prospect out to lunch, or that he will be asked to lunch by a colleague. "I can picture myself sitting in the restaurant," he says, "and then that tightness in my throat, that gagging and nausea, and I see myself vomiting all over the table and over my lunch companion." His problem—the nausea and fear of vomiting—had come on suddenly one day, without warning. It left, then returned, intensifying to the point where he could no longer eat anywhere in public. Dates with his girlfriend were cancelled because he could not take her to a restaurant or to parties. Then it began to happen to him even when eating at home. He has lost forty pounds in two months and now worries constantly about his health. He fears he will no longer be able to get by with excuses at work and that the confrontation will come very soon, costing him his career.

A thirty-two-year-old mother sits in her living room, on a wooden kitchen chair, weeping hysterically. She thinks she's on the verge of a nervous breakdown because of "this terrible thing about bugs." She points to the chair on which she is sitting and explains she is afraid to sit on an upholstered chair or sofa because there might be bugs in the seams or under the cushions and they might come out and crawl up on her. When she wants to fix something to eat for herself or her children, she dashes into the kitchen, grabs something from the refrigerator and dashes out again. She is afraid she might see a cockroach crawling out from under the sink. In the bathroom, she examines the crevices and joints for "silverfish." In her bedroom she searches the floors, the corners, the cracks in the wall for bugs that might come crawling out. There is no room in the house where she feels safe. The only time she loses the fear of bugs is when her husband is at home. Her husband says he just doesn't want to come home after work, because he cannot stand the tension and the hysteria. He cannot tolerate having his wife "get on me for nothing." But he will not stay away for fear she "might do something crazy."

A securities analyst, thirty-five years old, awakes, gets out of bed, and peers out the window, tentatively, in her hospital room, to see what the weather is like. She breathes a sigh of relief when she sees the sun is shining and that there is no wind. Even here, in the hospital, where she has had to come during the worst of her panic attacks, she does not feel entirely safe from wind, thunder, and lighting. Had it been raining when she looked out, or even windy, she would have quit her room and gone to another room in the hospital's interior, one without windows. Developing slowly over the years, this problem had become impossible. The first splatter of rain on a window would make her anxious and tense. A flash of lightning or clap of thunder would send her running from her office hysterical, to hide in the windowless rest room or board room. It would be hours before she could return to her work and concentrate, or even speak on the telephone. It had become so bad that even the scene of a storm on television or a picture of a storm in a newspaper would send her into hysterics. Finally, it had become necessary, during the height of the rainy season, to send her for a few days to a hospital. It was the only place where she felt safe.

Eight people, men and women, with lives and vocations as different as one could possibly imagine. Yet all have one thing in common. They suffer from the ailment called *phobia.*

Phobia? What is phobia?

Take any book on phobia and you will find, in all likelihood, a list containing such items as these:

Acrophobia—fear of heights; *claustrophobia*—fear of closed-in places; *agoraphobia*—fear of open or public places; *mysophobia*—fear of dirt or germs; *zoophobia*—fear of animals.

Some lists go on and on with as many as 100 items or more. Each item is made up of two elements—first the Greek or Latin word for a particular situation, object, condition, or creature with the suffix "phobia" tacked onto it. Then follows the definition, introduced by the phrase "fear of."

But if you ask phobic people to describe what they feel when confronted by the phobic situation, object, or animal, you will only occasionally hear the word fear. More often you will hear words such as terror, horror, dread, and panic. If you press them further they will tell you that even these words do not describe adequately the intensity of their experience, and add such expressions as, "It was so bad I couldn't stand it." "I thought I would go berserk." "I thought I would go out of my mind." "I though I was going to start screaming." "I thought I was going to faint or die."

What they feel is not just fear, but total emotional disorganization, a sensation that they are "going out of control," that they are at the edge of final irreversible disaster. The difference between normal fear and phobic fear or panic is not just quantitative; it is also qualitative. Phobia is not just very strong, or very intense fear. It is an entirely different experience.

Normal fear is a reaction to a definite perceived danger, real or conjectured. The cause of the fear is identified and the response is more or less controlled. In phobic fear the danger is not apparent, not recognized. All that is sensed is an overwhelming dread, without any apparent cause. The response is uncontrolled, mounting quickly to the level of unbounded panic.

Let us take an instance of an understandable fear reaction as it might occur in ordinary life. John Jones, storekeeper, has just finished counting his day's receipts and is getting ready to close up shop and go home. This has been a good day and he is feeling cheerful and relaxed. Suddenly, a tough-looking stranger walks in, hand stuck in his pocket, and announces, "This is a stick-up." Instantaneously, Mr. Jones realizes his life is in danger and experiences a sharp stab of fear. His body reacts automatically. Every organ—brain, heart, lungs, glands, nerves, muscles—mobilizes for a maximum effort to escape from this danger. In his mind, Mr. Jones reviews the possibilities. Refuse to cooperate? Run to the back room and yell for help? Reach for the baseball bat under the counter? Cooperate? There is only one safe choice. Cooperate. So, the brain, nervous system, and other organs interact to produce a smooth, unprovocative compliance. But since the danger is not entirely over, the bodily mobilization persists, manifested by a pounding heart, a sick feeling in the gut, dryness of mouth, perspiration, light-headedness, shortness of breath, dizziness, and a weak, trembly sensation in the limbs.

In the following few seconds, the holdupman collects his booty and flees. Once the danger is over, Mr. Jones no longer feels fear. His body begins to demobilize, and the physical sensations subside.

Now let us look at another fear reaction, somewhat different from the one we have just observed.

It is late at night, and Mary Smith, age thirty-five, has just gotten off the bus on her way home, after an evening's visit with her ailing mother. The streets are dark and deserted, and only two or three lighted windows can be seen along the entire length of the street. As Mary starts on her three-block walk to her apartment building, her mind is far away, absorbed with concern about her mother. Suddenly she becomes aware of footsteps behind her, and in an instant she has a sense of possible menace. She looks back and sees a man coming toward her, about twenty-five feet behind. A series of thoughts flash through her mind. This man might be the slasher the police have been hunting for. Or it could be a drug addict after her money. It might be a rapist. Or it might just be an innocent person out for a walk. Responding to the more threatening of these possibilities, her brain signals danger and fear, and the other organs mobilize accordingly. Ms. Smith feels the physical sensations representing the initial stage of this mobilization— the beating heart, trembling of the limbs, shortness of breath, and the others. With lightning speed, her mind reviews the alternatives. Should she run? Should she scream? Should she stand there and fight the man off? Should she run to the nearest house and start pounding on the door? Should she turn around and find out if the man is really following her? Intermingled with these lightning speculations, a series of images flashes into her mind. She "sees" herself being mugged and choked from behind, being dragged off into an alley and raped, being stabbed and left to die in the gutter. The mental review of the various possibilities and consequences sets off a chain of differ- ent bodily reactions, each designed to achieve a different goal— run, scream, turn around and attack, fight back, flee, submit. The result is momentary disorganization, confusion, indecision, paralysis, and panic. But still she is able to hold on. Out of this confusion and chaos, a clear choice emerges and a firm decision is made. She decides she will hurry her walk, keeping an eye on the nearest lighted ground floor window. If the man pursues her and threatens her, she will start running and screaming and race for the house she has targeted. Once this decision is made, the body mobilizes around a "get ready to run and scream" pro- gram. Reorganization takes place, the confusion clears up, the feeling of panic subsides. Fear and its physical correlates persist until Ms. Smith reaches the safety of her home. Out of breath, trembling, she unlocks the door, locks it behind her, and col- lapses in a chair, weeping but safe. As she sits there, her system reorganizes once again. The "fear alert" is no longer needed, nor are the corresponding physical preparations. Breathing be- comes regular, muscular tension eases, the heart beat slows down, the stomach relaxes. Fear has done its job. It has helped remove this woman from a possible threat to her safety, even her life.

In phobias, too, a variety of fear-triggered bodily responses take place. Patients describing an attack of phobia report dry- ness of the mouth, perspiring, forced and rapid action of the heart, difficulty in breathing, tension, light-headedness, flushing, weakness in the limbs, and other subjective sensations reflecting the body's mobilization to get away from a source of danger. *But what danger?*

The man in our first illustration was in real danger of being shot and killed. The woman in our second illustration believed she was in possible danger of being raped or murdered, not at all an unrealistic concern. These we can understand. But what was the danger to the flutist whose case we described earlier? She is not being threatened by anyone. The members of the orchestra and the conductor are colleagues and friends, and they are carrying musical instruments, not guns or knives. Yet her body mobilizes as though in response to a real danger, and she flees from the scene in a panic.

The Air Force pilot who suffered a panic attack in his plane attests that nothing in the situation threatened his safety. He hadn't the slightest fear that his plane might crash or explode ... nothing except a bewildering and terrifying awareness of height, a dread he might jump, a panicky feeling of having to flee the situation by landing his plane.

The young woman whose dread of storms and wind forced her to hide out in a hospital says she is "frightened to death" by the elements, but knows she is not in any real danger—except, possibly, for the exceedingly remote chance that she might be struck by lighting.

Similarly, one could not possibly construe any realistic threat to life or limb in the case of the woman with the phobia for bugs, or the priest whose shaking hands spilled the Communion wine, or the man who was afraid he was going to vomit, or the policeman who feared to look up at tall buildings because this might arouse an impulse to run to the roof and jump.

This—the absence of an identifiable, manifest threat to health, safety, or life—is characteristic of all phobias.

But if the phobic person is not fleeing from a real danger, then what *is* he fleeing from?

We need only to listen to phobic people as they tell about their reactions in the phobic situation.

Louis T. (elevators): "I saw myself trapped in this elevator with no way to get out. I couldn't breathe and felt I was going to suffocate. I wanted to scream. My skin was all pins and needles and I felt my eyeballs were going to pop out. The feeling was so terrible I couldn't stand it."

Esther R. (heights): "The second I walked out on my balcony, and looked down, I started to feel dizzy and faint. My heart started racing and pounding and my legs felt shaky and weak. I had this frightening thought that I would jump over. I panicked and ran back into the room. My friends wondered what was wrong with me."

Emil T. (moths): "Just seeing that fuzzy thing fluttering around and flying up against the window literally made my skin crawl—I could feel it. I could see this loathsome thing flying through the glass window, and flying into my face. It was terrible. I had to run out of the room so I would no longer be able to look at it. I felt I would go berserk."

William F. (train): "As soon as the [subway] train started moving, I got that closed in, trapped feeling, and I started to breathe deep, but couldn't get enough air into my lungs, and I gasped for breath and thought I was going to have a heart attack. My head felt like it was going to explode, with rockets going off like the Fourth of July. It got worse and worse until I thought I was going to die. I held myself together until the next stop and then I ran out."

Louise C. (darkness): "I was in the bathroom in this huge building and it was one of those rooms with no windows. Then suddenly the lights went out. I was in absolute, total darkness—not even a glimmer so I could see the door, or any way to find it—absolute black. I even thought I had gone blind. I panicked and started screaming, 'Get me out of here, get me out of here.' The feeling was so awful, I thought I would go crazy."

Maria D. (store): "I was poking around in the dress racks of a big department store and suddenly I got this dreadful feeling that I was lost in a strange place, and I didn't know where I was and I would never be able to get out. The dress racks were set up like a maze, and the more I scurried around looking for the exit, the more lost I got. I was terrified. My heart was racing and I was perspiring. I held myself together to keep from flying apart. I felt sick to my stomach, and there was a dullness in my head. My legs were so rubbery, I had to lean up against the wall. I started weeping and I heard myself saying 'Momma where are you; Momma where are you?' My mother has been dead for 15 years."

What we hear in case after case is a recital of uncontrollable, frightening bodily reactions, thoughts, and images; of dread, terror, and panic; of a state of mind so unbearable as to make the victim think he is going crazy, going berserk, going to faint or die. It is this from which the phobic person is fleeing—the distressing, frightening bodily reactions and thoughts and images, and the unbearable feelings and sensations they produce. This is followed by wild, headlong flight to get out of the range of the phobic situation—the stimulus which set off this reaction.

This phenomenon is in perfect accord with the *original* definition of the word phobia. This word derives from the Greek word "phobos," which is defined not as fear, but as panic-fear, terror, flight. The meaning emerges even more clearly from the account of an ancient Greek custom: the warriors of ancient Greece would paint the image of the deity Phobos on their battle shields to strike terror into the heart of enemy soldiers and send them fleeing in panic. And it is illuminating, too, that the word panic is derived from the name of the Greek deity Pan, who, in addition to his musical proclivities, had the power to inspire abrupt and inexplicable horror.

In summary:

It is not simply fear that the phobic person experiences, but rather feelings of dread, terror, horror, and panic.

These feelings are provoked, not by a recognizable, manifest threat or danger, but by the distressing, terrifying thoughts and images and the distressing bodily reactions aroused by them in the phobic situation.

The distress produced by these feelings is so unendurable that the individual is driven to flee from that which triggered it—the place, object, animal, or insect constituting the "phobic situation."

In discussing the process we have just described, some authors refer to it as the "fear of fear." While this formulation may be useful as a simplified explanation of what takes place in phobic flight, we prefer to use the longer explanation that the phobic person flees to free himself of the unbearable feelings and sensations brought on by his reaction to the phobic situation. But flight does not end the process; it is, in fact, only the beginning. Having fled from the phobic situation, that person will henceforth avoid it at all costs, because he does not want to subject himself once more to the unendurable distress he has experienced. This—dread and avoidance of a situation in which there is no recognizable, manifest danger—is the benchmark of the phobias.

HOW AVOIDANCE SPREADS

Some phobias produce only limited avoidance and may not cause much change in a person's life. Others are complex and may result in an elaborate avoidance pattern, in which first one situation, then another, then another is avoided, until ultimately, to use the words of one patient, "you are a prisoner inside your own four walls, cut off from everything and everyone on the outside." The dramatic nature of this development is illustrated in the case of Nancy H., who tells just how it happened.

It all started with an airplane flight four years ago. I was twenty-three at the time. Planes had always bothered me, but I managed to get by with Valium and travelling with a companion—never alone. This time, I was in Texas for a few days with my friend Anne. While down there I developed an infection that made me quite sick, and required minor surgery. The doctor suggested I wait a few days before flying back, because I might not react too well on the flight. I decided to wait but Anne had to return home, which meant I would be flying alone.

The following morning I took off for the airport. It was hot and sticky and the airport lounge was crowded and noisy. The thought of getting into a plane, jammed in and hemmed in by a lot of people, upset me. I decided it would not be so bad in first class, so I dashed out and changed my ticket. Finally we boarded, but the moment I sat down and fastened my seat belt, I knew I would not be able to make it. I felt suffocated and breathless. I tried to open the air valve but nothing came out. All kinds of frightening thoughts were going through my head. What if I became sick while we were on our way, thirty-five thousand feet up in the air? There would be no way to get out. I would become hysterical. I would start screaming and run up and down the aisles. Then, when I heard them closing the hatch, I knew I couldn't stand it any longer. I unhooked my seat belt, found the stewardess, and told her I was sick and had to get off. Apparently they have a routine worked out for this kind of situation, because she put her hand on my arm and tried to calm me with soft talk. All the time she was talking, I felt the plane taxiing and picking up speed, and then I just went nuts. I ran to the cockpit and burst in. I was hysterical and weeping and begged the captain to stop the plane and let me off. He must have seen that I was desperate because he told the copilot to radio the tower and

ask for permission to turn back. When the plane turned around
and the captain announced he had a sick passenger, the other
passengers looked at me like I was some kind of freak. I was
profoundly shaken and mortified by the recollection of how I had
behaved.

Later in the day, I left for home by train. Needless to say, I
have never gotten on a plane again. But the plane was only the
beginning of the avoidance chain reaction. Next it was bridges.
What was strange about that was that I never actually had a
panic attack on a bridge—I just started avoiding them. That
meant I was blocked off from access to the east, west, and south
of where I lived. There were bridges in every one of these directions. North was the only place I could go. Then, just as relent-
lessly, as though somebody had set up a schedule and was
pressing one button after another, there followed the avoidance
of tall buildings, then elevators, then driving by myself, then
driving altogether.

It got to the point where I was afraid to walk out on the street,
so I avoided going out, and then I was terrified to be by myself,
so I gave up my independence and moved back in with my
parents. That made a prisoner out of my mother because I could
not be alone. She couldn't go out to visit with friends, go shopping, go to a movie or anything. The most I would let her do
would be to go out for about fifteen minutes to a half hour. If she
stayed longer, I began to panic. I would pace up and down, from
one room to another, and get the feeling that I was going to
explode out of my skin. I just did not understand what was
happening to me. I had been taking Valium, but when my
mother went out, the Valium did not help. Then I took to swallowing a fast drink of vodka to hold down the tension. I didn't
combine the two and I was afraid of becoming addicted. But the
feeling I got being enclosed by those four walls, being all alone,
was so bad that sometimes I didn't care whether I would become
an addict or even if I would die.

However disruptive the tactic of avoidance may be in the life
of a person, it does serve the purpose of giving him immediate
relief by taking him out of range of the phobic situation or
object. But it is possible for the imagination to be so powerful as
to block off even this avenue of escape.

Connie has a phobia for anything that has to do with violence. She cannot tolerate hearing about, reading about, or
viewing pictures of war, violence, bombs, explosions, accidents,

revolt, or physical conflict. When she reads a word such as "tank," "bomb," "explosion," or "battle," she can actually visualize the tank in combat, the bomb exploding, soldiers shooting each other or using their bayonets on each other. Hearing words of this kind on the radio or in conversation produces the very same kind of reaction. Just the sight or sound of the word is enough to create a train of vivid images and to put her in a state of distress, panic, and despair.

To the greatest extent possible she avoids reading newspapers, listening to the radio, and watching television, and in this way she is able to avoid or block out the words and pictures that generate the frightening images in her mind. But even this does not offer her adequate protection, since the words to which she is sensitive cannot be screened out of ordinary conversation. There are times even when the troublesome words and images "pop" into her mind without any sort of identifiable stimulus from the outside, and the only way she can keep from being overwhelmed is to try to distract herself with some activity or reading matter she knows will contain no references to violence or combat.

THE REACTION IS SUDDEN, TOTAL

Many people experiencing the phobic reaction for the first time remark on the suddenness of the attack, the speed with which it develops, and the totality with which it dominates their mind and emotions.

Yet, when viewed in the context of the system's reaction to other threatening situations, these characteristics are not so difficult to understand. Think, for example, of a time when you were out driving and a child darted out in front of you, or of the time you were trying to pass a truck and saw another car coming head-on toward you at sixty miles an hour. Your system reacted in a split second before you were even conscious of what was happening. Your eyes picked up the danger signs and flashed them to your brain, where they were interpreted as life-threatening. Instantaneously, your entire system was dominated by a comprehensive reaction designed to save the child (in the first instance) and your life (in the second). In a tiny fraction of a second, signals were being flashed from your brain along a neural network controlling glands, circulatory system, respiratory system, and musculature of arms and legs. In another tiny fraction of a second, your hands and feet were executing maneuvers to avoid hitting the child or, in the second illustration, to avoid colliding with the other car. All this was happening automatically, reflexively, entirely out of conscious control. Had your system been dependent on a conscious appraisal and decision about what you should do, the accident(s) might never have been averted. Fortunately for us, we are "programmed" so that, in situations we perceive as dangerous, our body systems react with an instantaneous, total, and automatic response. All that we are consciously aware of are the "stab of fear," the dryness of the mouth, the pounding heart, the tension and trembling of the limbs, the perspiration in the palms and the armpits, and other physiological reactions.

Sir Charles Sherrington first drew attention to this phenomenon, noting that when a situation is perceived as injurious and dangerous, it captures the mind's attention and the body's reaction "to the exclusion, for the time being, of all else." All organs react to the one danger automatically—there is no choice. The more dangerous the situation is perceived to be, the more quickly, totally, automatically, and involuntarily does the entire system respond.

And so it is with the phobic reaction. A situation sensed by the phobic person to constitute a threat—even though *no* actual danger is perceived or recognized—sets off an automatic reaction of the entire system, which in turn generates a chain of frightening thoughts, images, and secondary bodily reactions. Instantaneously, the mind's attention and the body's reactions are captured "to the exclusion, for the time being, of all else." The response is automatic, comprehensive, and consuming.

But there is this essential difference between the system's reaction to a realistic threat and its reaction to a phobic situation: In responding to a realistic threat, the system has available a store of practical, proven programs, each one designed to mobilize an organized maneuver which removes the individual from the threatening situation. Braking and twisting the steering wheel can get you out of a possible automobile accident. Turning on your alarm or phoning the police can get rid of an intruder. Calling your doctor, taking your medicine, and staying in bed can save you from the dire consequences of life-threatening pneumonia.

But when it comes to phobic dangers, the system simply lacks effective programs with which to counteract them. This, the lack of effective programs or tactics to deal with the imaginary phobic dangers, is one reason why the phobic response is so chaotic and exaggerated, why it is made up of dread, terror, and panic rather than just ordinary fear.

But there is still another reason. When a person enters the phobic situation, or anticipates entering it, the imagination produces not just one set of frightening thoughts and images, but a rapid-fire barrage of many. Take the case of the policeman who shrinks from elevated structures for fear he might ascend them and have a compulsion to jump. As he looks at a roof or tower, or even thinks about doing it, a kaleidoscope of threatening thoughts and images flash through his mind almost simultaneously. He sees himself running up the stairs of the building, pushing aside people who try to stop him. He sees himself running to the edge of the roof and jumping. He sees his body hurtling through the air and landing with a thud on the sidewalk. He feels his heart racing, his head "expanding," his stomach knotting. He feels himself in a vacuum, and the world seems unreal. He wonders why he is having these weird thoughts. He has an impulse to "turn himself in" at a mental institution. He thinks, "Maybe I ought to turn around and run home." He wonders what his wife will think as he comes racing in "wild-eyed." He feels the perspiration trickling down his armpits. He thinks, "What a coward I am." He cringes at the thought that his buddies might find out. He has palpitations and believes he is going to have a heart attack. He wonders what will happen if he faints dead away on the sidewalk, or worse, out on the street and a truck runs over him. He is terrified that this "crazy thing" that's got hold of him will never leave and he'll be "a nut" all his life. He feels he cannot stand it any longer and might as well jump off a roof. Then he bolts for home.

If the system lacks the means to cope with even one of these imaginary threats, consider how much more unprepared it is to deal with a whole barrage firing all at once, and how disorganized it becomes while attempting to mobilize a host of conflicting survival reactions. This nearly total disorganization is reflected in the chaos and panic experienced while in the phobic situation.

DEFINING "PHOBIA"

Toward the beginning of this chapter we posed the question: "What is a phobia?" Having completed our exploration, we can now answer that question.

Phobia is a disorder in which the individual reacts with irrational dread and panic in a harmless situation, flees to rid himself of the unendurable sensations and feelings aroused in the situation, then avoids it and similar situations, henceforward, to avoid the anticipated recurrence of this extremely painful experience.

The phobic reaction, which is automatic, pervasive, and out of control, is produced, not by the perception of any realistic threat, but by a barrage of frightening thoughts, images, and bodily changes triggered by the phobic situation.

The system reacts in an exaggerated and chaotic way to the imaginary threats and dangers because it has no effective way to deal with them. The chaos and disorganization intensify and reach a point of panic as the system attempts, unsuccessfully, to react to a barrage of imaginary threats which are hurled at it practically all at once.

HOW WIDESPREAD ARE THE PHOBIAS?

It may be of some comfort for phobic people to know that the disorder from which they suffer was known and written about as far back as two thousand years ago. Several references to phobic subjects appear in the writings of Hippocrates, the father of medicine, including the following:

> He would not go near a precipice, or over a bridge or beside even the shallowest ditch, and yet he could walk in the ditch itself.
>
> When he used to begin drinking, the girl flute-player would frighten him; as soon as he heard the first note of the flute at a banquet, he would be beset by terror. He used to say he could scarcely contain himself when night fell; but during the day (when there were people about him) he would hear this instrument without feeling any emotion.

Shakespeare wrote, in *A Merchant of Venice*, of "some that are mad if they behold a cat." And Robert Burton wrote at length about phobias in his well-known *Anatomy of Melancholy* (1621). Following is an excerpt from this work:

> Montanus speaks of one that durst not walk alone from home, for fear that he would swoon, or die. . . . A second fears every man he meets will rob him, quarrel with him, or kill him. A third dares not venture alone for fear he . . . should be sick. . . . Another dares not go over a bridge, come near a pool, rock, steep hill, lye in a chamber where cross beams are for fear he be tempted to hang, drown or precipitate himself. If he be in a silent auditory, as at a sermon, he is afraid he shall speak aloud unawares, something indecent and unfit to be said. If he be locked in a close room, he is afraid of being stifled for want of air, and still carries bisket, acquavitae, or some strong waters about him, for fear of being sick; or if he be in a throng, middle of a church or multitude, where he may not well get out, he is so misaffected.

Thus, we have evidence from these writings that phobias as we know them today were known throughout ancient and modern history and in many parts of the world.

From other evidence we can conclude that there must be millions of people in the United States suffering from the phobias in every part of the country: in big cities, towns, and villages; in remote mountain areas and remote rural areas; among the poor, the middle class, the rich, the educated, and the uneducated; among Catholics, Jews, Protestants, and members of other religions; among professionals, business people, artists, and working men and women.

Exactly how many there are would be hard to say. Judging from conversations among professional people at their meetings and conferences, one would get the impression that this is one of the most common disorders which they encounter in their work. There are no comprehensive surveys to confirm or refute this impression; in fact there are no comprehensive surveys at all on the extent and distribution of the phobias. There are some reliable estimates, however, based on a count of the phobic patients who come to the offices of physicians, psychiatrists, psychologists, and psychiatric social workers, either in their private practice or in the clinics and hospitals in which they work. According to these estimates, there are between five and eight million people in the United States with a phobia severe enough to have a seriously disruptive effect on their mental health and daily functioning. There are estimated to be another fifteen million to eighteen million whose phobic problem is more limited than that, affecting them to a significant extent, but not disrupting their lives too severely.

What does *seriously disruptive mean*? How bad does a case have to be to fall into that category? We would say that every one of the illustrative cases we have discussed so far in this book would come under the *seriously disruptive* heading. *"Significantly but not seriously disruptive"* would cover those cases in which there is a phobia for just one or two specific situations and where the avoidance of these situations does not have a severe impact on the individual's life, overall. Here are some cases we would put in this latter category:

Roger P. has a phobia for elevators at present and formerly had a phobia for planes. When he had the plane phobia, he simply avoided that means of transportation and either used trains or avoided long distance trips. He recalls cancelling vacations that involved flying and taking cruises instead. On business trips he would take a train, even on cross-country trips. Being an executive, he could regulate his schedules and make up for lost time by taking along work on the train. When his elevator phobia erupted, he handled it by having a trusted colleague accompany him every time he got into an elevator. He was never free of anxiety in an elevator, always anticipating that it might stall and trap him, but the presence of a colleague or friend helped keep the anxiety at a manageable level.

Flora L. gets a feeling that she's unable to draw in enough air and that she may consequently suffer a heart attack whenever she goes into a theater, movie, concert hall, or classroom. This has compelled her to cut down the occasions when she finds herself in these situations, but she does not have to avoid them entirely. If she can take a seat in the rear and at the end of the aisle so she can exit easily if she feels an attack coming on, she finds she can tolerate staying there.

Elena G. has a phobia for birds; as a result, she and her family have had to move out of a suburban area into an area of high-rise apartments. This has been troubling to her children and husband, who loved the home and setting in the suburbs. In their new home, the only birds the family sees are occasional seagulls coming in from the bay, but they fly at too great a height to trouble Mrs. G. When her husband and children visit relatives in the country, she stays at home. The family has also had to give up taking vacations together in the mountains and at the seashore. The children are sent to camp, and Mr. G. takes vacations alone.

George B. gets panicky when he has to drive over a lofty, long bridge or on an expressway. As a result he has to take a circuitous route on back roads, and crosses the river about fifteen miles upstream, where the river narrows and there is only a small bridge to cross. He is more comfortable when driving with others and occasionally gets a ride in with a neighbor. He still suffers when driving with somebody else while crossing a bridge or using an expressway. But he is able to handle his feelings and can keep from "going out of control."

Louise T. has an unusual phobia for high-pitched musical instruments. She avoids this by staying away from concerts and movies. But at home, avoidance is much more difficult. The television and radio are in the family room, and when anybody turns on the television or radio, she has to go into an upstairs room so she will not hear the music. The children may listen to their radios in their rooms, but have to use their headsets.

HOW PHOBIC PEOPLE FEEL ABOUT THEMSELVES

Phobic people commonly express great distress about the fact that they can have such "weird, irrational fears." They think it is abnormal. Yet, there is nothing abnormal about it at all. The ability of the human mind to create dangers which are imaginary is a universal phenomenon.

Primitive people have always created demons and evil spirits which they imagined controlled their destiny and the forces of nature; some superstition-ridden populations still do so today. They devise rituals, incantations, magic, and spells to control these creatures of their imagination.

Little children create giants, witches, ogres, "boogey men," ghosts, and other frightening specters. With the help of understanding parents they learn, very gradually, that these are imaginary, and rule them out of their real world.

But the tendency to create imaginary threats and dangers does not vanish forever with the passing of childhood. It is retained throughout life and asserts itself at different times in different ways—sometimes harmlessly, as when we allow ourselves to believe in invasion by creatures from outer space, witchcraft, or

vampires; sometimes more seriously, as when we allow ourselves to magnify the significance of minor illnesses, setbacks,
and losses and interpret them as major disasters.

And so it is within the normal capacity of our minds to create
the dread that we might jump from a height, fly apart, be
trapped in an enclosure, not get enough breath and suffocate,
drive off a bridge into the river, "be lost" in a shopping mall,
vomit in a restaurant, or be annihilated by the forces of nature.

The fact that we can create and experience these imaginary
threats and dangers as adults simply attests to the creativity of
our imagination—nothing else. We also have the capacity to
compare these imaginary dangers against criteria of reality, to
establish for ourselves that they are "in the mind" and cannot
harm us. In the phobic person, this capacity is weakened but
never lost, and one of the purposes of contextual therapy, which
we describe in this book, is to restore it to its original strength.

Phobic people tend also to feel alone and isolated, to regard
themselves as different. It is an experience to observe them and
listen to them when they come together for the first meeting of
an eight-week phobia clinic at the White Plains Hospital Medical Center in White Plains, New York. (The same things happen
at the first meeting of virtually every new series of phobic people who attend the phobia clinic, and so it must be assumed that
the reactions are characteristic.)

As they enter the room where the session is being held, the
patients move in separately, keeping apart, having little to say to
each other, acknowledging each other with a perfunctory nod or
an impersonal "Hi." You see them glancing furtively at each
other, "sizing each other up." You know from experience with
earlier groups that each one is wondering what the other people
are like, what kinds of phobias they have. As they take their
seats, each one seems to be knotting himself or herself up into a
compact little mass, as though to leave as little surface as possible exposed to some invisible danger.

The coleader of the group (a paraprofessional aide and a
former phobic patient herself) makes the introductions. The
members of the group are told that theirs is not a unique problem, that there are millions of others with the same or similar
problems. Then, as they begin to relax a little and lose the
worried look on their faces, each one is asked to tell "What
brings you here? What is your phobia? What help are you seeking in this group?"

The first one begins shyly and hesitantly, in a low, barely

audible voice, and tells about her phobias, how they began, what precipitated them, how they developed and spread. All are listening intently to the speaker, and one senses that they are identifying with her. She tells them about an experience she had, and all around the circle heads nod in agreement as though to say: "Yes, yes, that's exactly what happened to me. That's my phobia you're talking about. That's the same thing I've got." They continue to recite their story, one after another, and the mood becomes more and more relaxed. Then about half-way around the circle, the person speaking says (and this happens almost invariably): "You know, when I registered for the group I didn't know what I was going to find; I didn't know what to expect. I thought I'd find a bunch of nutty people like myself, all with some real serious mental problem. And what I found is something entirely different. You are all very nice, normal people—not all the way normal, but you know what I mean. You've all got phobias, just like me, which have messed up your life but you are anything but crazy. And I guess, neither am I. And now I see there's nothing unique or different about me, and boy, what a relief that is."

Taking this cue, the group leader remarks that it is the nature of phobic people to feel separate and different and to isolate themselves; each one thinking that he or she is the only one with this problem, that no one else could possibly have the same "weird," "bizarre" feelings and thoughts that he or she has, or do the same "crazy things."

Further, the group leader adds, people who are phobic tend to be especially sensitive about what other people think about them, to imagine that everyone is watching them. Which, of course, she adds, is not so. "People are too busy with their own lives and taken up with their own worries and problems to pay much attention to anybody else, especially to a person who is looking and behaving perfectly normally so far as any outside observer can tell. People cannot read your minds, your thoughts, your emotions. . . . Phobic people suffer terribly but they seldom let on by look or deed what they're thinking or how they're feeling."

One of the things phobic people fear most, she explains, is that they will do something embarrassing in public. (All around the room the heads are nodding vigorously in agreement.) "They are afraid of making a show or a fool of themselves, of being subjected to ridicule."

As the sessions move along, a noticeable change takes place.

The members are no longer shy about being phobic. They speak
freely about their phobias and other "hang-ups," and they relate
what happened when friends learned from them, for the first
time, about their phobias.

Maureen, a girl of nineteen, tells a particularly touching tale.
Maureen has been homebound for months, unable to go anywhere by herself, not even for a one block walk from her home.
Occasionally, she ventures out very briefly, accompanied by her
mother, and they walk a block or two together. Maureen gets
"attacks where I can't breathe and I'm afraid I'll pass out in a
strange place where nobody knows me, and they won't know
what's wrong with me or where to bring me." When her mother
leaves for work in the morning, Maureen stays in bed as long as
she can, sleeping, dreaming, spinning fantasies. "The longer I
stay in bed" she explains, "the less time I have to wait until my
mother comes home and I can feel safe again." After dinner,
when it is dark, Maureen will venture out in front of her apartment building and "hang out" with some of her girlfriends.

"Whenever my friends used to ask me to go someplace, I
would give them excuses about having to wait for my mother,
or help her cook or do the laundry, and they would believe it.
After I came to the clinic, here, for a few weeks, I got up my
courage and decided to tell them. Last night Maria was there
and she asked me to go to the movies with her and I told her I
couldn't go. So she asked me why not, and I just said, 'Because
I'm afraid to go. I've got agoraphobia. I'm afraid that if I go
someplace I won't be able to breathe and I'll pass out.' Do you
know what Maria did? She put her arms around me and started
to cry and said, 'You big dummy, why didn't you tell me before?' Later some other girls came over and they started to give
me a hard time about not going anywhere with them and Maria
became angry and yelled at them and told them, 'Let Maureen
alone. She just doesn't want to go.' But then Maria and I decided that I should tell the others, too, and I did, and they all
came over and hugged me and said, 'Say, look. If you want to
go someplace and you're afraid, we'll go with you and if something happens to you, we'll take care of you and we'll take you
home.' I started to cry and I told them I was glad they knew
and understood and wanted to help, but I wasn't ready for that
yet, but that we would do it as soon as I felt brave enough. I let
them in on something else, too. They knew I was going to the
hospital every Wednesday [the "hospital" is the White Plains

Hospital Medical Center where the phobia clinic is located] and when they used to ask me, I told them I was going because I had an ear infection. Now I didn't have to lie to them any longer. I could tell them I was going to the phobia clinic."

"Most people do understand," the group leader interjected, when Maureen had stopped speaking. "They understand and they accept more than you'd ever expect. Most people are good, kind. They don't want to hurt you, and when they know that you've got a problem and that you're hurting you'd be surprised how they will rally around you. What Maureen just told you is not unusual. It's happening all the time. And, if it hasn't happened to you yet, it will, you'll see. But don't expect them to read your mind. You've got to let them know. Certainly I understand that it isn't easy, especially when you imagine that they'll think you're crazy when you tell them. But it isn't they who are thinking that. It is you. It is the way you are seeing yourself. So, it is you who have to change first; it is you who have to accept yourself and your phobia and know that it's a problem, maybe a different problem than other people have, but still only a problem. Some people have stomach problems, some people have marital problems, some people have a problem with alcohol. You've got a phobia problem. Once you see it that way and once you accept it yourself, you'll have no difficulty telling it to your friends. And the point needs to come where you do tell your friends, because if you don't, all your energy is going to go into making up excuses and keeping secrets. And you'll be cutting yourself off from friendship and help. But even worse than that, you will be doing something that will actually stand in the way of your getting better. When phobic people get these different anxieties and fears about all the terrible things that can happen to them, they keep these thoughts and feelings to themselves, never giving themselves a chance to check them out with others, and to learn how baseless they are. The more they keep these thoughts and feelings locked up inside themselves, the more exaggerated and terrifying these thoughts and feelings become. Opening yourself up to others, and letting some of the light of reality come into the darkness, is an essential step in the process of recovery."

Members of the group responded enthusiastically to these suggestions and said they would follow Maureen's example and tell their friends, as well as those relatives from whom they had been keeping their phobia secret.

"But what do you do," one of the group asked, "when someone is unsympathetic, when they know already and they're still
unfriendly and critical, and even blame you?"

"This is something you have to expect," the group leader
replied. "There are all sorts of people in the world. Some people
think—with all the best of intentions—that if they are stern
with you and lecture you, that it will help you to get yourself
straightened out. They just do not understand the nature of
phobias; they do not understand that this is something over
which you have little control, that it is making you terribly
unhappy and ruining your life. And then, of course, there are
some people who are just very self-centered and lacking in
feelings of concern and compassion. That's their personality and
you can't hope to remake it. That's probably the way they are
with everyone, thinking they're better than everybody else and
looking for a chance to put themselves above other people. But
you have to know that it is they who may be having a problem.
Fortunately, people like that are in the minority. There are more
of the other kind. Trust them—*and remember, you are not alone.*"

The message "you are not alone," sounded by the group
leader, and reiterated by us, here, is meant to be doubly reassuring.

First, it is intended to give heart to those who still feel that
they have to struggle with their misery, alone, and that nobody
can understand them or really cares. Second, it is intended to
convey the information that a remarkable change has taken
place in the past several years in public awareness about the
phobias.

It may be something of an exaggeration to say that you can
hardly pick up the newspaper or magazine today without reading an article about the phobias. But that is the impression one
does get today, bolstered by the sudden eruption of radio and
television programs on the subject on local outlets all over the
country and on the major networks, as well.

Why this sudden awakening? No one can say for certain, but
conventional wisdom has it that the media weren't talking about
phobias twenty years ago, because there wasn't very much to
report.

Then, all of a sudden, things began to change. In the late
1960s a new approach emerged in clinical practice to the treatment of the phobias. Earlier methods concentrated on attempting to relieve the patient's phobic anxiety by treating him *outside*

the phobic situation, in the hope that his fear would be reli
sufficiently so that he could confront the phobic object or p
without running away. The new approach concentrated on
bringing the patient *into* the phobic situation, a little at a time,
helping him to remain there without fleeing. This was called "in
vivo" or "exposure" therapy.

Then, in the 70s, as the clinics, hospitals, and private practi-
tioners using the method began to release accounts of their
successes, the newspapers, magazines, and broadcast media began to report them with increasing frequency. Today they are a
standard part of public knowledge about medical and scientific
developments. For people who are troubled with phobias, this
new public interest should be very encouraging because it
means that more facilities will be established to treat people
with phobias, and more research will be undertaken. It means
also—and this is of even greater importance—that as public
knowledge about the phobias increases, public attitudes will
change and people with phobias should encounter greater tolerance, sympathy, and understanding from employers, co-work-
ers, and family members. And this, in fact, is already happening.

Where does contextual therapy fit into this picture?

Contextual therapy came into being at about the same time
that the "exposure" or "in vivo" techniques were being introduced, and in that respect might be considered to be part of the
new wave that has revolutionized the treatment of the phobias.

Like these other exposure treatment methods, contextual therapy is based on the concept that it is necessary to help the
patient enter the phobic situation in a step-by-step procedure.
But, in addition—and this is its unique contribution—contextual
therapy concentrates on the phobic reaction itself. It enables the
patient to reduce its intensity, at first, and then, through his own
control, to bring it to a level where it causes little discomfort or
none at all. The phobic person is taught to observe his phobic
behavior *in its context*, that is, in the place and at the time that it
is happening. He observes and scrutinizes his own thoughts and
imaginings, what he is feeling in his body, what he is afraid is
going to happen, how he is reacting to what other people are
doing and to what is happening around him. He is taught to
observe the fluctuations which occur in the intensity of his phobic reaction (his terror and dread) at the very time that they are
taking place, while he is in the phobic situation. And he is

taught to see how these fluctuations are affected by what is going on inside of him (in his mind, his body, and his imaginings) as well as by what is going on outside of him (in the environmental setting of the phobic situation). He is helped to observe these factors and to understand the process which produces changes in his phobic reaction. This puts control of the phobic process, and consequently of his phobia, in his own hands.

The phobic person learns, through contextual therapy, that his phobic dreads and terrors are mainly products of his imagination, and that he no longer needs to submit to them as in the past. He acquires alternate ways to deal with them—techniques which undercut the phobic process and free him from its hold.

A Closer Look at the Phobic ("Phobogenic") Process

Phobic patients report that what they become aware of first when a phobic attack is triggered are the thoughts and images of the "terrible thing" that might happen to them. "I'll drive my car through the rails into the river." "I'll jump off the roof." "The bugs are going to crawl all over me." "I'll never be able to get out of this elevator." "I'll vomit all over everbody." "I'm lost and I'll never be able to find my way back." "I won't be able to get enough air and I'll suffocate." "I'll never be able to make it to the next exit on the expressway." "The snake is going to slither up and curl itself around my neck." "I'll see the lightning flash and I won't be able to hide from it." "I'll disappear under the water and die."

They then become aware, almost simultaneously, of the bodily changes taking place inside of them—the racing heart, shortness of breath, weak and trembling limbs, dry mouth, perspiration in different parts of the body, tightness around the head, prickling sensations in the skin, nausea, lightheadedness, and feelings of unreality.

Next comes the "I can't stand it" part of the reaction, experienced as, "It is so terrible, so unendurable, so unbearable that I'm going to faint—or scream—or go out of control—or go berserk—or die." At the core of this feeling, there is a sense of total disaster, of irreversibility and finality, of "the end." So distressing is this experience that it generates an overwhelming, uncontrollable impulse to flee.

But this does not end it. Having fled the phobic situation, the individual is beset by new fears. Is this going to happen again? Is there something seriously wrong with him? Does it mean he is losing his mind? How is he going to be able to keep this from his friends, fellow employees, employer, family members? What will they think when they find out? How will this affect his relationships, his job, his future? Should he go see a doctor? A psychiatrist? His priest or rabbi? Should he tell his wife (or she her husband)? Should he just wait for it to go away?

When next he goes into the phobic situation, or anticipates doing so, or even thinks about it, he is beset not only by the memories of the unendurable distress he experienced in his first encounter, but with all these additional anxieties as well.

This takes place in an escalating and expanding chain reaction. As the individual enters the phobic situation or imagines doing so, the system reacts with an involuntary distress reaction. This automatically evokes frightening thoughts and images, which in turn produce more frightening bodily changes followed by still more frightening thoughts and images. This intensifies the feelings of fright and disturbance even further and so the reaction spirals upward until it becomes so intense as to create an unendurable state of mind, and the feelings: "I'm going to faint," "I'm going to go berserk," "I'm going to go out of my mind," or "I'm going to die." This incremental spiralling from a reflex fright reaction into a massive phantasmal horror which blots out all sense of reality and generates an uncontrollable impulse to flee, we call *"the phobogenic process."*

This understanding of the phobogenic process—gained through study of the way people react in the context of the phobic situation—provides the key to the treatment and control of the phobias.

We have seen that the phobogenic process develops as the system focuses on and responds to the frightening, overwhelming thoughts and images which come flooding out of the imagination. The only way to prevent them from developing is to intervene against this preoccupation.

This is done by helping the patient to shift his attention *away from* this realm of frightening fantasy, *and into* an active involvement with the real, familiar, and reassuring elements in his surroundings. Since it can be very difficult to respond to and remain attentive to external stimuli while in the grip of intense imaginary fears generated by the phobogenic process, additional steps are necessary. The phobic person is helped to concentrate on some small activity, some achievable tasks which he can perform. Absorption with effective achievement of these small tasks automatically compels the system to reorganize itself around involvement with reality, and concomitantly reduces involvement with the realm of fantasy and imaginary dangers. Deprived of its essential fuel—the frightening fantasies—the phobogenic process weakens and ultimately comes under control.

How is all this achieved? Through a variety of techniques and tactics which are provided by contextual therapy.

It does not matter whether the patient has one simple, specific phobia, such as a phobia for cats or heights or elevators, or whether he has such a complex condition as agoraphobia. And it does not make any difference what the specific phobia may be, or what the different elements may be in the agoraphobia. The principle is exactly the same in all cases—gaining an understanding of what goes on in the phobogenic process, and applying a variety of strategies to control it. The specific techniques and tactics may vary from case to case, depending on the individual, and from situation to situation, depending on the nature of the phobia. But—to repeat—the basic principle and approach are the same in all cases and situations.

The tactics and techniques to which we refer are the ones described in this book. These will enable you to stay in your phobic situation, endure your "unendurable" feelings, cope with them, and handle and control them so you will no longer have to flee and avoid the place, object, or animal which provoked them. These tactics and techniques will be set down and followed through step by step in Chapters Seven through Ten. These instructions will take you from your first elementary venture into your phobic situation right through to the point where you will have in your possession all the tools you need to navigate confidently on your own.

Will contextual therapy work for you? It has worked for thousands of others at the White Plains Hospital Phobia Clinic and in other treatment locations where this method has been applied. Recently, a follow-up study was completed involving three hundred twenty-seven patients who had been treated at the White Plains clinic. On a six-month follow-up review, about ninty percent had improved significantly, utilizing the knowledge and techniques they had acquired at the clinic. A four-year follow-up review showed that there had been very little slip-page. About nine out of every ten had maintained their gains.

Years ago, when contextual therapy was still a new method, and when there was some uncertainty about how successfully it would work, we were startled to hear patients say, after only a few weekly sessions of treatment, such things as: "I walked all around the block yesterday—and I had not been out of my house for two years." "I got on the bus last night and rode for about a mile, all by myself. That was my first time in a bus for five years." "I was able to sit in the same room with the cat without getting hysterical." "We took a drive over the George Washington Bridge, and we had to go over the expressway to get there. Before I started treatment, you couldn't have dragged me there with wild horses." "I thought I would never go up in a plane again, but last Saturday, I took a trip to Washington and on Monday I flew back again. My therapy aide was with me, both ways, but in a few weeks I'm going to try it alone." "I went shopping at the mall and we were there for more than two hours. I went into one store after another, and it was scary and I had lots of anxiety, but I did it. That was the first time in eight years."

Today, such statements as these no longer surprise us. We have become accustomed to them; we expect them. And we expect that many readers of this book, too, will have similar successes a few weeks after they have put into practice what they learn in this book.

But people are different, and the problem which has to be dealt with is complex. Hence, for most people much more work and practice will be needed. Nor should anyone expect a smooth and unchanging course. There will be ups and there will be downs, which are normal in any learning process. And there may be temporary reverses, imposed by the life stresses which people ordinarily go through. But, over the long run, the trend will be one of continued improvement and progress, the rate depending on the individual and the circumstances.

When patients at the White Plains Hospital Phobia Clinic first start their series of eight weekly sessions, they are told something like this:

> Contextual therapy is not a panacea. We are not telling you that you're going to be cured in eight weeks. We are not even promising you that you are going to be cured in *any* length of time.

What you are going to get in this clinic are hope, tools and techniques, an understanding of your phobia, and some successes in breaking out of your phobia. But you must understand that this eight-week clinic is not the end. It is just the beginning. It will give you the understanding and the techniques which you can continue to apply weeks and months after the clinic has ended. A few of you will be able to apply easily, quickly, and automatically what you are going to learn and acquire here. Most of you, however, will find it necessary to work consistently and for some time, gradually freeing yourself of your phobia. Some will need to keep applying these techniques over and over again as episodes of the phobic reaction recur. But you will always have with you what you have learned here, to use it, should you need it.

To the readers of this book, we offer the very same prospects. This book is not a panacea. We do not promise that you will be "cured" after you have read this book, gained an understanding of the phobogenic process, and are able to put into practice the techniques this book will offer you. But we do give you the assurance that as you learn the principles and strategies of contextual therapy, and apply them diligently in practice, significant improvements are going to come. For a few, progress will come quickly, in weeks. For some, progress will come a little more slowly—in months. For a few, it may take years of effort—and perhaps even the help of a psychiatrist—to consolidate control over your phobia. But all of you will have available for the rest of your lives what you have gained from this book to use it as you may need it; even to transmit it to friends or relatives who may need help in dealing with their own fears.

There is still another benefit—a very important one—to be gained from contextual therapy. Over the course of the years, many, many patients have come back, unsolicited, to tell us that there have been major improvements not only with respect to their phobia, but also with respect to their life as a whole. They report basic, positive change in outlook, in self-esteem, in assertiveness, in self-understanding. We hear such remarks as: "I am a changed person." "I can't recognize myself." "My friends tell me there has been such a change in me." "My family tells me I am so much easier to get along with." "I have seen great improvements in my work." "I have ventured into areas that used to frighten the life out of me." "I am no longer so timid and apologetic." "Life doesn't frighten me the way it used to." "I don't fly off the handle the way I used to; I can feel it coming and I'm able to control myself." "I am much more patient and understanding." "I get along much better with my children." "I get along much better with my husband." "I get along much better in my office."

We trust that just as this has happened to people who have been treated by contextual therapy, it will happen to readers of this book as well.

HOW CONTEXTUAL THERAPY WAS STARTED

Contextual therapy was originally developed from observation of physically handicapped people. In the course of his psychiatric work with disabled patients, Dr. Zane, the coauthor of this book, was called upon to investigate a phenomenon for which the rehabilitation therapists could find no explanation. A patient would be doing well, when, for no apparent reason, his progress would come to a halt. The interruption would be accompanied by various symptoms such as severe trembling, fits of rage, spells of hopelessness, and verbal abuse of the therapist.

At the beginning of the investigation, Dr. Zane would have the patient come to him in his office at the rehabilitation center, and he would attempt to gain some insight through the traditional methods of psychotherapy. But nothing came out of this that would clarify the picture. It then occurred to Dr. Zane that he might gain more meaningful information by learning what was going on outside and inside the patient (the external and internal contexts of the reaction) at the very moment the disruptive reaction was taking place. This would have to be done, not by interviewing the patient in the office, but by observing him in the exercise room, and by questioning him about what he was feeling, thinking, and imagining at the time.

Working with several patients in this way, Dr. Zane was able to put his finger on a key factor in the problem. The intense emotional reaction and the interruption in progress came at a point where the patient was experiencing intense feelings and thoughts of insecurity, self-doubt, or failure. These might be coming from pressing family problems, unrealistic expectations and evaluations of the progress being made, unspoken dissatisfactions with the rehabilitation program, or inability to come to terms with the disability. In a delicately balanced organism, these thoughts and feelings had the power to create fear, disorganize muscular coordination, and undo emotional control. Simultaneously, another key principle was disclosed: When the patient was brought out of the mental preoccupation with his frightening thoughts and feelings, and helped to reassociate himself with comforting and familiar elements in the environment, the symptoms would go away. It was the frightening thoughts and images that were blocking muscular coordination and emotional control. Enabling the patient to shift from this preoccupation to the familiar realities in the surroundings compelled the system to reorganize around objective, realistic functioning.

In 1971, Dr. Zane introduced this method, to which he had given the name "contextual therapy," into the treatment of phobic patients at the newly established phobia clinic of the White Plains Hospital Medical Center. Since its original application at this clinic—of which Dr. Zane was then, and still is, director—the principle of contextual therapy has eventually been adopted as the basis of treatment in many other treatment facilities.

THE REST OF THIS BOOK

In the next few chapters we are going to talk about the different kinds of phobias, the way they develop, the ways they have been viewed in the past, and the different methods that have been used and are being used to treat them. If you wish, you may skip these chapters and move right ahead to the actual techniques and practice of contextual therapy, starting with Chapter Seven. It is our advice, however, that you do not jump ahead and that you take the time, instead, to read slowly and carefully through the next several chapters. This will help you to gain a better understanding of your phobia and will undoubtedly answer many of the questions which may have been troubling you.

CHAPTER TWO

The Simple Phobias

BEFORE PSYCHIATRISTS AND PSYCHOLOGISTS began to make a serious, in-depth study of the phobias—and that has been just in the past twenty years—it was a common practice for books and articles on this subject to compile lists of the various phobias, using the method we have already described of giving the Greek or Latin word for the particular phobic stimulus and tagging the word "phobia" onto it. We are going to give you a sample of about twenty from one of these very long lists to illustrate a point. Here are some of the names with which most readers will be familiar:

Acrophobia—fear of heights
Claustrophobia—fear of closed-in places
Agoraphobia—fear of public places
Mysophobia—fear of dirt and germs
Xenophobia—fear of strangers
Zoophobia—fear of animals

But here are a number of others which will undoubtedly be unfamiliar:

Aurorophobia—fear of northern lights
Barophobia—fear of gravity

33

Blennophobia—fear of slime
Cryophobia—fear of cold
Cyclophobia—fear of bicycles
Diabetophobia—fear of diabetes
Dikephobia—fear of justice
Gallophobia—fear of things French
Geniophobia—fear of chins
Kopophobia—fear of exhaustion
Leukophobia—fear of the color white
Methyphobia—fear of alcoholic beverages
Mnemophobia—fear of memories
Patriophobia—fear of heredity
Peladophobia—fear of bald people
Panophobia—fear of everything
Phasmophobia—fear of ghosts
Photoaugiophobia—fear of glaring lights
Scabiophobia—fear of scabies
Tuberculophobia—fear of tuberculosis
Uranophobia—fear of heaven

Why some have found it necessary to compile such lists as these eludes us. Following this pattern, one could readily take the Greek word or Latin word for every noun in the English language, add the word phobia to it and thus have an endless list of phobias—but to what purpose?

Perhaps the only value this practice may have is to draw attention to the fact that a person can become phobic to almost anything, depending on his experience and his imagination—any object, creature, place, situation, color, sound, sight, smell, word, person, name. We will explore later some of the various explanations accounting for individual fixation on one phobic stimulus rather than any other. For the present, however, it is enough to note that while there may be tens of thousands of phobic stimuli, there is only one phobic reaction.

Culling the literature for unusual phobias, Dr. Isaac Marks, author of *Fears and Phobias*, reports cases of phobia for loud noises, for "going through a door if noises could be heard on the other side," for reading books or letters, for outer space, dolls, fuzzy textures.

Joy Melville, a British writer, advertised to solicit letters from people with phobias and received a number of very interesting replies. We take the liberty of quoting a few excerpts from some of these letters which appear in Melville's book *Phobias and Obsessions* (Penguin Books).

"My fear has to do with churches. I have nightmares about them."

"My phobia is the sight of canal locks."

"Mine is a fear of dolls. They terrify me, especially the eyes. And this also applies to tailors' dummies and ventriloquists' dolls."

"My little girl of seven has a morbid fear of buttons."

"Since childhood I have had a fear of homemade cakes, biscuits or pastry . . . though shop and factory-made ones are perfectly acceptable."

"As far back as a young girl, I have had an inward fear about eyes."

"I have a phobia about traffic lights. Confronted with them I just die and cannot move one foot in front of the other."

"I fear all things under water, such as pier structures and the underside of bridges."

"I cannot bear to see a mass of pips. I can't cut open a melon, tomatoes, or pepper without my skin crawling and having to leave the kitchen."

"I have a fear of foam baths. I could not bring myself to step into a bubble bath; I must be able to see the water clearly."

"I have a morbid fear of ships. A few months ago a car firm used a ship in an ad. It caught me unawares as I was reading through the paper and I nearly died of fright."

"My fear is of looking in a mirror or in any reflecting surfaces."

"I have a phobia for balloons. If I am in a room with an inflated balloon, I become sick and if I didn't leave, I would probably faint."

Unusual phobias such as these seldom come to the attention of professionals working with phobic patients. The phobias for which people seek treatment have to do with more familiar objects and situations, generally related to some significant aspect of their daily functioning.

Authors differ to some degree on the classification of different phobias. In this book, we will follow the classification adopted by the American Psychiatric Association, grouping the phobias into three categories: simple phobias, social phobias, and agoraphobia.

Each of these three groups will be discussed in great detail, later. For the time being, they can be distinguished by the following definitions.

Simple or specific phobia: Dread of a specific object, situation, activity, animal, or insect.

Social phobia: Dread of situations where the individual may be observed by others in such acts as eating, speaking, writing, vomiting, or urinating. The underlying feeling is one of intense embarrassment and humiliation because the thing which the person is doing might make him or her "look silly," "foolish," "dumb," or "inadequate."

Agoraphobia: Dread of being alone, or of being in public places, separated from the safety of a known person or known place.

THE SIMPLE PHOBIAS

The simple phobias, sometimes referred to as the "specific phobias," include those in which the phobic stimulus is a specified situation, object, creature, activity, or experience. All the unusual phobias we have just finished describing would fall in this category. However, there are many others which are better known, including phobias for *heights* (acrophobia); *closed-in places* (claustrophobia); *the natural elements,* such as water, snow, lightning and thunder, wind, storms; *animals and insects,* including dogs, cats, mice, frogs, snakes, spiders, bees, and moths.

Heights

Some fear of heights is not uncommon. It is natural for most people to get uneasy feelings about standing at the unprotected edge of a lofty precipice or near the edge of a tall building. While the likelihood of falling over is not great, it could happen. Therefore, fear and avoidance are understandable, and, when they occur, are regarded as normal and acceptable.

Now, contrast such controlled reactions in the face of a possible, real danger with the terror some people experience when they stand at the edge of a height which is protected by a guard rail or even by a heavy link-chain fence, or when they stand in front of a window and look down into the street below, or when they are gliding up along the side of a hotel in an elevator whose walls and doors are made of heavy, thick glass. Despite the absolute absence of a real danger, they automatically react with fright, and as they look out and down below them, they even imagine and feel themselves to be falling. It is a fear they do not understand. It upsets them that they are having it. They try to push back and halt this instinctive reaction, but find they cannot do so. The initial burst of fear has triggered the phobogenic process, impelling them to flee, despite the insistence of the reasoning brain which tells them "there is no way you will be able to fall."

One of the most remarkable instances of acrophobia that we have ever come across is that of the tree trimmer, who climbs to the top of trees seventy-five-feet tall and taller every day, supported only by the cleats in his boots and a belt slung around the tree. Yet he experiences acrophobic terror when standing in front of a solid glass window, in his father's twenty-second story office. Another is that of the pilot whose case we discussed earlier. He is the one, you will remember, who has piloted jets ten miles up and taken them through every kind of a wild maneuver, yet experienced an awareness and a dread of the height while cruising along at a mere five thousand feet. A similar case is that of the steel worker who had been working on exposed steel girders for years without giving a thought to the possible danger of the height until one day, after being buffeted by a strong gust of wind, he was startled into awareness of the elevation and peril and fled the scene, refusing to go up again, even in the building's protected areas.

Some people who have acrophobia will experience the dread even in an enclosed building. They cannot see to the outside, yet react to their awareness of the elevation alone. Others have this reaction in the balconies of theaters, or on escalators and staircases no more than one story in height.

In many cases of acrophobia, patients report not only the irrational dread of the elevation, but also a dread that they "might go out of control and jump over." This may happen even when the elevation is protected by a solid, shoulder-high wall.

Some people with a phobia for bridges say that as their car ascends the slope of the bridge and they see the panorama of land and river spread out beneath them, they panic and "freeze." Some bridges which are unusually long and lofty have so many such incidents in the course of a year that police are routinely assigned to patrol the bridge to help drivers they find in this predicament.

Others with bridge phobia report experiencing a dread that they might drive their automobile through the rail and plunge into the river. They say they can actually see their car smashing through the rail, hurtling out into space, tumbling over and over, and crashing into the dark depths of the river with themselves—the drivers—trapped inside, their lungs filling with water. One writer who had this problem said he even visualized a large newspaper headline: "Auto Dives Off Bridge: Driver Drowns."

Dread of heights may be present in airplane phobia, too, but most often it is only one element in a complex reaction. Some people with airplane phobia stress mainly the height problem. Others stress their fear that the plane might crash or catch on fire. When challenged with the statistical argument that the risk of dying in an automobile accident is much greater than that of dying in a plane, they respond by saying, "But in a car, I feel that I've got control, that I can do something about it. In a plane it is out of my hands. There is nothing I can do. I am helpless." There are cases, also, where either or both these elements (dread of heights and dread of crashing) may be combined with an additional element—dread of being in an enclosed place, "boxed-in" or trapped. Also, some people with airplane phobia have a concern about "not getting enough air and suffocating." One patient, in fact, reported that she had no anxiety at all during take-off, flight, or landing. It was only after the plane had finished taxiing and the cooled air supply had been turned off that she was seized by a panic to get out of the plane immediately because of a fear that she might suffocate.

Enclosed Places

This phobia is experienced in a wide variety of closed-in situations arousing the dread of being trapped and not being able to get out. It may be speculated that this has as its basis a reaction which is in large part instinctive. Certainly we see it in animals as they are caught in an enclosure from which they cannot escape—a frantic running about and trying to find some means of egress. Whatever its origin—whether the arousal of a primitive fear or the result of some forgotten frightening experience in which the individual was closed in or trapped—the phobic reaction is one of intense distress and an overwhelming impulse to get out. First comes the surge of inexplicable dread. Immediately, the familiar surroundings become strange and threatening, and the normal reassurance that comes with being in familiar surroundings is lost. This sets off the phobogenic process, and dread escalates to terror and then to panic. Relief comes only with egress or escape, and from that point an avoidance pattern develops for that and other enclosed places.

The phobic reaction to enclosed places, according to people who have this problem, is experienced most intensely when the enclosed area is small, and when the means of escape are restricted or blocked. The elevator seems to be the situation in which this dread of enclosed places is experienced more than in any other. This is understandable when we realize that the elevator is, essentially, a box with thick, solid metal walls, floor and roof, sliding up and down in an enclosed rectangular shaft anywhere from a few stories to one hundred stories or more in height. People with elevator phobia say they dread the thought that they might be trapped in an elevator as the result of a power failure or some other mechanical mishap. The idea of being "sealed in" in this solid box with "no exit" is almost more than they can bear. The rational knowledge that they would not be trapped for long, and that surely someone would come to get them out, does not make enough of a difference. The thought of being closed up without any exit creates such strong feelings of fright that it blots out any rational intervention. One person with an elevator phobia used this illustration to convey the unbearable nature of this feeling. "How would you feel," she asked, "if you were locked into the trunk of a car, unable to move your arms and legs, not even able to get enough air." Another used this illustration: "How would you feel if you were placed in a five-by-five box where you couldn't even stand up, and you were buried ten feet beneath the earth, with just an air hose letting in the air." While neither of these images is sufficient to create more than a mild discomfort for most people, just the mere thought or image has power to set off a terrifying phobogenic reaction in people with claustrophobia. It isn't even necessary for them to have had an actual experience of being trapped in an elevator, or locked in a trunk, or buried in a box. Their imagination is able to create the horror as though they had actually lived through it.

Some people with the dread of enclosures will not venture into a stairwell for fear that the door would lock behind them, and that every door on every floor would also be locked and they would be unable to get out. The idea that they could easily bang on the door and attract somebody's attention does nothing to relieve the dread. There are others who will not pull closed the door of any room in their home which has a spring latch. One patient reported that "I never close the door of my bathroom when I go in. I always put a little stool in the door opening, so there's no chance it will snap shut and trap me in that little room." That she could open a window and yell for help does not alleviate this feeling. "What if none of the neighbors was home; what if they couldn't hear me; what if they couldn't get into my apartment—nobody has a key?"

Dread of enclosed places manifests itself very commonly with respect to all modes of mass transportation—planes, railroad trains, subway trains, and buses. It is only now, when so many more people are making their way to phobia clinics and other treatment services, that we are beginning to learn how many people there are who will not ride on a plane, train, or bus, and who have eliminated these modes of transportation from their lives, making whatever miserable adjustments are necessary.

When asked why they refuse to ride in these conveyances, they give replies such as these: "I'm afraid I won't be able to get out." "I'm afraid something will happen to me while I'm in there." "I'm afraid I might faint or have a heart attack." Some who have a phobia for trains say, also, that they cannot stand the speed, the surge, the powerful force of the train when it hurtles along "like a demon that's going faster and faster and could go out of control."

The dread of enclosed places shows up in numerous other ways in the daily life of the afflicted. We have already mentioned those who will not go into a church, movie theater, concert hall, or meeting hall unless they can sit in the rear and at the end of the aisle. Others will not enter any enclosure in which a large number of people are present, such as a restaurant, a cocktail lounge, or a room where a party or celebration is taking place.

One can easily realize how disastrous this can be in the lives of people who have done a great deal of socializing. Even for people who do not socialize much, having to miss such functions as birthday parties, anniversary parties, weddings, christenings, or a Bar Mitzvah can create a great deal of distress. In addition to being deprived of the pleasure of getting together with friends and relatives, those who have this problem also suffer strains in relationships because they are too embarrassed to explain why they are staying away. An excuse about "not feeling well" or having "to be away on business" may work once or twice. Beyond that it can only arouse the suspicion that the absence is deliberate and that the absentee doesn't really care whether or not offense is given. In addition to suffering the separation and loss of social contact, the phobic person is left with a feeling of inadequacy, dishonesty, and intensified fear.

Even sitting in a barber's chair, hairdresser's chair, dentist's chair, or a doctor's waiting room will arouse in some claustrophobic people the unbearable feeling of being trapped.

For some people who have claustrophobia, the aversion is aroused by just one or two specific situations which play a relatively minor role in their lives. The aversions can, on the other hand, be pervasive, producing catastrophic dislocations and undermining self-esteem.

Stanley L. had had a phobia for closed-in places from the time he was eleven, but he did not know it then, and didn't realize it until very much later.

My parents had taken me to a street fair in New York's Little Italy. It was all colorful and exciting. There were these stalls with Italian candies, pastry, and food. Overhead there were these arches of colored lights. The crowd was cheerful, laughing, talking, moving about. I was stuffing myself with food and having a great time. My parents moved from booth to booth and I tagged along. But, little by little, the crowd got thicker and by dark, it was just a solid mass, body-to-body, the entire width and length of the street, block after block. You had to fight your way through just to move a few feet, and people were pushing and tugging trying to go in different directions. I got scared and I could see my father was becoming nervous. Then he grabbed my arm with one hand, and my mother's hand with the other and started to bulldoze a path for us to get out. I could hear him say: "Let's get the hell out of here. It's dangerous. If somebody starts a stampede, we'll all get crushed to death." It was impossible, we couldn't move a foot. Then there was a sudden, hard push from behind us, and before I knew it, they had broken my father's hold on my arm, and I was being swept along with the crowd. I was terrified. I was kind of little for my age, and I was squeezed between those legs, bellies, and backs, unable to breathe, and I thought I was going to suffocate. I could hear my father and mother screaming, "Stanley, where are you?" and I was crying and shouting "Mama, Daddy," but the crowd just kept pushing me along. Then I felt a strong hand grab me by the arm and I heard my father's voice cursing and shouting. This time he just smashed his way through with his fists to where he had parked my mother behind one of the stalls. I was crying, my mother was crying. It was just awful.

This emotion-packed memory stayed with Stanley for a while and then faded. But as he grew up, he found himself being sensitive to crowds, and working out ways to avoid them. He wouldn't go to ball games or the circus with his father or his friends. He had to ride a subway to get to school and if one train was crowded, he would let it pass and wait for one less crowded. When he got a summer job, he solved the problem of crowded subway trains by getting up an hour earlier. He would not sit in the rear seat of a two-door automobile nor between two people in the front.

"I just couldn't bear the feeling of being squeezed in. I didn't know I had a phobia or that anything was wrong with me. I was just avoiding situations that made me uncomfortable the way other people avoid tight shoes or tight pants."

But when he graduated college and went to work as a writer, he found that he no longer had the options and freedom to choose where or when he would or wouldn't go. "It was amazing," he said, "how skillful you can get in creating excuses for not going someplace without telling people you're phobic." But it was not always possible to foresee a problem and find ways to avoid it.

There was this time when I was taking my girlfriend to the theater. I had tried to get orchestra tickets on the aisle, but it was a hit show and the best I could get were mezzanine seats in the center front row. I had planned to get there early so I could get used to it and get hold of my anxiety. But my girlfriend didn't want to hurry and I couldn't explain. On top of that the taxi got caught in traffic. The lights were just beginning to dim when the usher showed us to our seats and we had to squeeze in, bumping knees and stepping on toes. No sooner had we gotten to our seats, when I started to feel dizzy and gasp for breath. My hands were sweaty and shaking and I knew I had to get out. So I just whispered to my girlfriend, "I'm feeling sick. I have to get out. You stay, and meet me outside after the first act." People turned to look at me as I squeezed out and raced up the stairs. The rest is too painful to recount, but that was the beginning of the end of that relationship.

My next bad episode came about a year and a half later. I had found another girl. It was a whirlwind affair, and we got married. My parents had a very good friend who owned a publishing firm in San Francisco and were able to work it out that I could go to work there as an editor, provided I made the grade. It was a prestigious firm and a beautiful opportunity. If I did well, I had a chance to move up to a top editorial position. It was a dream. The publisher's son was coming to New York on business and we arranged an interview. It worked out superbly. We took to each other personally and he was happy with my credentials. Since he was going to be in town for a few days more, I asked him to have dinner with me and my bride of three months. I thought about a very elegant restaurant but decided against it because I didn't want to appear to be trying to impress him. So I decided instead on a Middle Eastern restaurant that had just opened and gotten rave reviews. I tried to reserve a table in a nice location within sight of the door, but couldn't. The demand for any old table at all was just too great. It was a lovely restaurant, attractively decorated, and I was feeling quite pleased with myself until I saw the captain leading us toward the rear and around a corner. It was a bad table near the kitchen; also, the door to the street was out of view. I began to feel anxious and had an impulse to bolt, but held on. After we had our drinks it eased off, and we all enjoyed our dinner. But while we were waiting for the dessert, the anxiety hit again, but this time, much more intensely. My wife, who knew about my problem, saw my distress and reached out for my hand under the table. Just then a new party was being seated at the table next to us and I overheard one of them say something about the maitre d' having to lock the door, because there were so many people outside insisting on getting in. The locked door did it. I leaned over, told my wife I was getting out, asked her to explain, and bolted. A few minutes later they came out and joined me. I was terribly embarrassed, not knowing what to say. But they were both smiling and do you know what this young man said? He said, "Don't let it trouble you; I understand. I have a phobia for bridges myself."

That got me off that hook, but it wasn't long before I was on another one. The chief editor of the division in which I would be working wanted me to come out and spend a few days there so we could become acquainted. That meant I would have to take a six-hour trip on a plane. I hadn't ever been on a plane before. I became anxious just thinking about it, but I had no way out. It was a once-in-a-lifetime chance; if I didn't go I'd be throwing away a career. So I booked a seat in first class, figuring that the luxurious setting, food, wine, and service would counteract my anxiety. But the minute the reservation was confirmed, my anxiety hit me in a wave. For days, I couldn't eat, I couldn't sleep, I couldn't concentrate on my work. I was cranky and quarrelsome. I drank more than was good for me.

When I awoke the morning of the flight, I felt that this was the day I was going to my execution, instead of to a new career. I was depressed and could barely drag myself around. My wife practically had to push me to the door and shove me into the cab. I was in a daze during the entire cab ride to the airport and I checked in feeling like a zombie. I stayed in a daze until we boarded and then my depression broke into an acute anxiety. By the time I reached my seat, I was in a state of panic. I couldn't stay. I had to get out. I got up, told the stewardess I was getting off, got to the counter, told them to retrieve my bag, and didn't even wait for it. When my wife opened the door for me she didn't even seem to be surprised. She didn't say a word, poured me a drink, and stayed behind when I went up to my bedroom. I closed the door, sat down, and wept.

It was this devastating episode that finally brought Stanley into therapy.

Other Specific Situational Phobias

Not much attention has been paid, in the literature or anecdotal reports, of people who have what might be called a phobia for depths. However, the cases are frequent enough to warrant their being mentioned. Some phobic persons will not enter a room or space located under the surface of the earth, such as basements, caves, or even apartments that are just a foot or two below sidewalk level. The phobic feeling, in such cases, is also that of being trapped and unable to get out.

The very opposite feeling—that of being too exposed—is experienced by people who have a phobia for open spaces which lack fixed, solid, reassuring boundaries—such places, for example, as parking lots, bodies of water, fields in the country, airfields, open expressways. These people say they need to have the protection of walls, trees, buildings, and other enclosures. Otherwise they have a feeling of limitless space and this makes them extremely anxious. The feeling is exemplified in an extreme form by a man who has a fear that he might walk to "the edge of the earth and fall over." Another patient says she is terrified by the mental image of the earth whirling about in limitless space.

It is possible for opposing phobic tendencies to exist in the same person. There is, for example, the man who had an intense phobia for closed-in places, such as elevators and airplanes, yet would not move into a contemporary home in which the walls had been eliminated between living room, dining room, and kitchen, leaving a very large area, unbroken except for one or two table-height barriers, and exposed on all sides by large expanses of glass. His explanation: "I can't stand the openness; I need the comfort of enclosure that walls give you." He would live only in a home with the traditional arrangement of a living room, a dining room, and a kitchen and with just a few traditional windows in each.

Dread of the Elements of Nature

A phobia for lightning and thunder, or storms of any kind, is a rather common phenomenon. Those who have this problem agree that they do not fear, specifically, being struck by lightning or in any other way being harmed by a storm, and of course they know they cannot be hurt by thunder. It is rather the feelings of "wildness," "vastness," "power," "force" of the elements, as exemplified by tornados, hurricanes, and mountainous seas, that provokes this terror. A harmless gust of wind or splatter of rain, a solitary bolt of distant lightning or thunder, a moderate fall of snow has the power to generate in some phobic people the same terror as might be provoked by the realistically terrifying hurricane, tornado, raging storm at sea, tidal wave, or blizzard.

For Albert J., the mere sight of falling snow—just a calm, gentle fall of snow, of the kind which brings delight to most people—had the power to trigger a full-blown phobic reaction. In most cases the reaction cannot be traced to any specific incident in the past, but this patient was able to make that sort of connection.

> I never did like driving at night or in the rain, and this time I had both. To make it worse, it was a very cold night, the rain was starting to freeze, and we were driving through the mountains. I

knew it was dangerous so I slowed down, clenched my teeth, held my breath, and prayed we would get through it safely. Then it happened. We were going around a curve on a downgrade. As we came around the other side my headlights picked up an iced-over stretch and I felt the car skid. You never think straight in a situation like that and reflexively I jammed on the brakes. We went into a sharp skid and started spinning around. When the car came to a halt, it was facing in the opposite direction. Luckily, there was no other traffic. I got out quickly with my flashlight to figure out our position. When I flashed it behind the car, I could see the solid ground for about two feet, and then the beam went off into nothing. We had come to a stop within twenty-four inches of a three-thousand-foot drop, with only a few small rocks standing in the way. I almost collapsed. From then on I wouldn't drive in bad weather, and when I was dating my wife, I refused to come get her or go out on a date if it was snowing or sleeting.

It did make good sense for me just not to drive in bad weather, and I didn't. But it's gotten much worse than that. If I'm in the office and it starts to snow—even just a flurry—I grab my coat and drive home. If it even looks like snow before I start out for work, I just don't go out. If snow comes up suddenly when I'm on my way to anyplace, I turn right around and head for the garage. At present, I can't even stand to listen to weather reports. If there is any mention of snow, ice, sleet, or storm, I get a terrible anxiety attack and stay shaken up for hours. Spring, summer, and early fall, I'm alright. But once cold weather sets in, I'm a wreck. All I can think about is snow, ice, sleet, skids, crashes, fallen high-voltage lines, smashups, every kind of calamity. If it is sunny in the morning, fine; if it's overcast my anxiety takes off like a rocket. That goes on throughout the winter and doesn't stop until late in April, when there's just no longer any chance of snow.

Christmastime is the worst time of all. Everybody else is talking and singing about a white Christmas, with sleigh bells jingling in the snow. But me—I'm praying to God that He doesn't let a flake of snow come down. I get so tense and irritable that my wife and children can't stand me. I've even heard the children complain that I spoil their Christmas, and I can imagine them thinking and saying to each other that they wish I would go away someplace during Christmas and leave them to enjoy the holiday with their mother and grandparents and aunts and uncles. I am even thinking of changing jobs and moving my family to the South where they never have any snow.

The power to inspire a phobic reaction is not limited to just those elements of nature which have the potential to be realistically frightening and harmful. On the contrary, the most beautiful and benign elements can be potent trigger stimuli for the phobogenic process. There is, for example, the woman who says she is terrified by the sight of a rainbow, the case of the man who is terrified by the sight of towering trees, and the teenage girl who would be sent into phobic flight by the sight of a flower garden. The frightening thoughts and images in the case of the phobia for the rainbow and the phobia for trees produced dizziness and faintness and thoughts that "something terrible might happen," but no inkling of what this "terrible thing" might be. In the case of the child with the phobia for flowers, the reaction took the form of a feeling of "crawliness," light-headedness, nausea, palpitation, and prickly skin.

Phobia for Water

Phobia for water is quite common, but it takes many different forms illustrated by these comments from a number of patients.

> It isn't water as such—like water in a river or in a bathtub—that bothers me. It's the feeling of moisture in the air, like in humid weather or when there's a fog or a mist . . . even steam coming out of a kettle or moisture condensing on a window.

> It's water that's pouring or spilling that gets to me. Looking at a lake or the ocean doesn't bother me. But show me water coming out of a spigot or a shower and I'll have to run out of the room. That's why I can't do any cooking, and why my mother has to fill the tub for me. A fountain out in the open is just as bad, or even water trickling down a rock from a spring or after it has rained in the country.

> I won't go within miles of a lake or a river—and the ocean, that's absolutely the worst. If we go driving anywhere, I have to get a detailed topographical map from the county, and if there's a lake or a river, even a small one, I don't go. I won't go to a movie unless somebody has seen it first and assures me there are no bodies of water in it. TV I just don't watch, unless it's one of those police or comedy programs where I know they aren't going anywhere in a boat. It isn't the boat that bothers me; it's the water.

In the case of this last patient, it is just the thought or the sight of a large body of water that can set off the phobic reaction. With others, the body of water will cause a phobic reaction only if it is viewed from a height, as from bridge or tower or airplane.

In still other cases, it is actual immersion in water which is intolerable. Some will not get into a bathtub or swimming pool. Others will not go into deep water in a lake, river, or ocean because of the "darkness and mystery" of the depths, or because "one could drown there." Some swimmers will not venture beyond their depth even in quiet waters even though they are capable, should the need arise, to swim in quickly to shallow, safer depths. This is essentially a morbid fear of drowning and is sometimes alleviated when the swimmer is within sight or sound of someone who could come quickly to the rescue in case of trouble.

Phobia for water may remain restricted to a specific situation or it may generalize to many situations. Such was the case of Doris F., whose phobia began, she believes, with a frightening incident that occurred while she and her husband were out sailing.

We were out in a sailboat off Seattle. It was a rough, windy day, but my husband is a good sailor. Then, a sudden, dark storm blew up and whipped up the waves into a rough, angry sea. I was frightened and my husband looked worried too. Then a big wave hit, caught us broadside, and turned us over. We were wearing life jackets and we both were able to hold on to the hull. We clung there for about half an hour and the storm blew over. A passing boat picked us up and hauled in our boat. My husband insisted that we were never really in danger, being so close to shore, but I would not go out on the boat again. A year passed and sailing was just put on the back burner. Then one day, we were crossing the bay on a large ferry boat—one that also carries your car. I was standing at the rail looking out when the panic hit. It had nothing to do with a fear of drowning. The water just looked very menacing, and I felt frightened. I felt I couldn't breathe and started gasping for breath. My head felt tight and heavy, and I became dizzy and felt I was going to fall over. I moved away from the rail toward our car, but my legs were weak and I thought I would never make it. My hands were wet with perspiration. My husband was frightened when he saw me and asked what was wrong. All I could say was, "I have to get off. I have to get off." He sat me down inside our car, put my head on his shoulder, made me close my eyes, and tried to comfort me. But the feeling did not go away. When we got to shore I was weeping.

Then this feeling spread to tunnels, bridges, and planes. I'm sure it all had to do with water, because when it's just a roadway over land, it doesn't bother me, and when the flight doesn't take us over water, I don't feel any anxiety. Tunnels give me an uneasy feeling because I have this ridiculous notion that the river could crush the tunnel and drown us all. A tunnel through a mountain is alright.

Up until about six months ago I could manage, in spite of these fears. But now it is getting impossible. If we have to go away anywhere, I get in a state worrying about having to fly, or drive over a bridge, or go through a tunnel—whatever it happens to be. By the time we take off I am a nervous wreck. Then, after we get where we're going, the whole vacation is spoiled because I start worrying right away about the return trip and I stay in a miserable state throughout the entire vacation or visit. Going to Toronto from Lake Placid we had to cross over that big bridge. I think it was the St. Lawrence River. I was in torture all the way up, and then I didn't enjoy a second of the visit—which always had been a great pleasure—agonizing about having to cross the river and the bridge coming home. Recently we spent a lovely week with friends in New Jersey and had another weekend set up for New York, but the idea of the tunnel under the water was terrifying, and I didn't spend a peaceful moment. Now we have a condominium in Florida where we go in the spring, but I'm afraid we aren't going to get there this time. I think that what I've got is turning into agoraphobia.

Phobia for Blood

Aversive reaction to blood is rather common. Some people "cannot stand the sight of blood" because it is associated with the loss of blood, and in its ultimate consequence, death. These people are frightened to submit to the drawing of blood for a blood test, and some may even faint when they see the blood coming into the vial. Others find the sight of blood "revolting" since they associate it with slaughter, and may become nauseated and weak at the sight of bloody meat in the butcher's showcase, or observing someone eating meat that has been cooked "rare." It is not often, however, that the aversion for blood takes the form of an intense phobic reaction, as in the case to be described.

According to the patient, Tony B., his phobia developed as the consequence of a traumatic incident when he was only eight years old. He and some other boys were engaged in rough play, and Tony was hit with a rock. When he started to bleed quite profusely, the other boys fled. Still bleeding, and terribly frightened, Tony ran to the home of a neighbor. (His mother was away, grocery shopping.) When his mother returned and didn't find him at home, she became upset and started to look for him. She found him at the neighbor's house, and when she saw him, with a deep, ugly cut on his forehead, and traces of blood still showing on his face and in his matted hair, she reacted with an outburst of fright, and fainted.

After that, he himself was unable to stand the sight of blood. The aversion developed slowly and spread, insidiously. The sight of blood on anyone else caused him to become faint. A pin prick on his finger or a scratch which showed even a minute sign of blood would throw him into a panic. If he actually cut himself to the point where blood would flow, he would faint. Eventually, he could not even tolerate having sharp knives or other sharp instruments anywhere around. He threw out his razors and took up an electric shaver, but even with this he did not feel safe. He would stay away from any situation in which he was likely even to see cutting implements such as knives and saws. The sight of a meat slicer in a delicatessen would cause him to panic. Eventually, he was unable to tolerate movies, television programs, newspaper accounts, or conversation having to do with mayhem, violence, or gore. He was unable to go anywhere where anyone was sick, and even the thought of surgery would "drive him out of his mind."

This situation worsened and reached its peak when he was twenty-five, and it was then that he came for contextual therapy. As difficult as it may be to believe this, this young man was giving blood at a blood bank two months after the beginning of therapy.

Animal Phobias

People with phobias for animals or insects make up only a relatively small proportion of the total number of cases coming to the attention of professionals working in this field. It is believed, however, that they are much more numerously represented in the general population and that the reason so few people with these phobias come for treatment is that, in most cases, the animal or insect can be avoided without causing too much disruption in the afflicted person's life. Most patients with this phobia are females.

Animal phobias—true phobias, not just ordinary fear or shyness for animals—are not uncommon in childhood. Many boys and girls have this problem, but most outgrow it. Those few who do not outgrow it become the adults with animal phobias. Patients report, almost without exception, that their phobia for the particular animal or insect had its onset in childhood, most often before the age of eight, occasionally between the ages of eight and fourteen, and seldom after that.

Cases of childhood animal phobia must have been quite commonly known in the days of Sigmund Freud, since he gave this account of them in a work published in 1913:

> The child suddenly begins to fear a certain animal species and to protect itself against seeing or touching any individual of this species. There results the clinical picture of animal phobia which is one of the most frequent among the psychoneurotic symptoms of this age and perhaps the earliest form of such an ailment. The phobia is as a rule expressed towards animals for which the child has until then shown the liveliest interest and has nothing to do with the individual animal. In cities, the choice of animals which can become the object of phobia is not great. They are horses, dogs, cats, more seldom birds, and strikingly, very often very small animals like bugs and butterflies. Sometimes animals which are known to the child only from picture books and fairy stories become objects of the senseless and inordinate anxiety which is manifest in these phobias. It is seldom possible to learn the manner in which such an unusual choice of anxiety has been brought about.

Why phobias for animals or insects persist into adult life with some children, and disappear after adolescence in others, is one of the many unanswered questions about these phobias.

A search for clues in the background and personality of patients with these phobias is disappointing. Research discloses that a substantial proportion of these patients had been shy, fretful, anxious, fearful children. But an equal number had been quite normal and without any unusual fears—other than the phobia. It has also been disclosed that, so far as could be told, there was nothing unusual about the families in which these children grew up, and that by and large these families were quite well adjusted. However, it must be noted that these questions have not as yet been explored very intensively, nor with adequate scientific controls. It is known that, at the time they come for treatment, a large proportion of patients with phobias for animals and insects are anxious, insecure people. Whether these characteristics are the cause or the result of the phobia, research has still to determine.

In most cases, the phobia is restricted to one particular animal or insect, and generally this is the only type of phobia with which that person is afflicted. There are a few cases, however, where the phobia for an animal or an insect is part of a larger syndrome, such as agoraphobia or social phobia.

Insects. Crawling insects have the capacity to inspire, in some people, loathing, revulsion, and aversion, and spiders especially so. People with a phobia for spiders use such words as "ugly," "sinister," and "evil." These associations arise, no doubt, from the way in which spiders have been pictured in children's story books, and even in books for adults. The fact that spiders spin a web to entrap other insects and that they then come and feed on their helpless prey is enough to stimulate frightening imagery with feelings of revulsion and fear in most people, young and old. This factor is exaggerated by people who have a phobia for spiders. They say they can actually "see" and "feel" the spider closing in and pouncing. They may not visualize themselves as the victims, but they are able to identify with the helpless fly or other trapped insect. The reaction to the sight of a spider, or even to a picture of one, is intense, extreme. Here are some of the comments people with this phobia have made, in describing what has happened to them: "I become paralyzed with fear." "My heart starts pounding and I get hot and cold all over." "If the spider moves toward me, I freeze and can't move away." "My stomach sinks and I get clammy all over." "My fingers get numb and I can't feel anything. Then I feel that my head is floating away separate from my body."

Other crawling insects such as ants, beetles, and roaches are just as capable of inspiring phobic horror, even though there is nothing "evil" or "sinister" associated with them. "What frightens me," says one patient, "is the quiet, sneaky way in which they move and they're so quick, they can dart out and crawl on you. If they made a noise, that would be a warning, but they move silently and don't give you any warning. I'm afraid to try to kill them because if I miss, they'll run toward me and crawl up my leg." Her husband says of her: "When she sees a roach, it isn't a roach. It's mighty Joe the Gorilla coming at her." She admits that "it takes a gorilla to frighten some people—all I need is a June bug."

Flying insects, too, even those that do not sting, are also quite capable of arousing phobic terror and dread. "It is their fuzziness, and the beating of their wings, and the way they come at you blindly and you feel they're going to light on your face or in your hair, and the thought of it makes my skin crawl." That is the way one young woman describes her sensations. Another says: "Have you ever looked at them close up, with the barbs on their legs and the wicked looking mouth and eyes, and their feelers vibrating in the air? When I hear or see one even outside on the screen, I am paralyzed and can't move. If I wake up in the middle of the night, and I think there is a moth in the room, I start screaming and run out."

Bees and wasps do sting, and the reports of severe reactions, though rare, may contribute to the general state of anxiety and aversion aroused by these insects. Those who have a phobia for these insects insist, however, that it is not any real feeling of danger that arouses the phobic reaction, but rather a generalized fright aroused by the buzzing, swooping, and darting.

Insect phobias can be quite limited, amounting to little more than a nuisance. They can, on the other hand, undermine a person's entire life. Millicent H. tells about her experience with a phobia for ants and bees.

> I have always had a fear about bees but it never stopped me from living a normal life. I just avoided places where I might come upon them. But the real phobia started about two years ago. I happened to notice carpenter ants in the kitchen, and it frightened the life out of me. I could see them darting around on the counter and under the sink and I felt that crawly feeling of them crawling up my leg or on my arm. So I ran out and wouldn't go into the kitchen again. Then I saw some of them in the hallway and in the bathroom, and it was as though the whole house was swarming with them—it was an exaggeration, but that was the way I felt. I told my husband he would have to get the exterminator, but he became angry and refused, so I called in the exterminator myself.

Then came the bees. The whole garden was full of them that spring. I became hysterical. I couldn't stand it, and I went into the house and locked myself in and started to cry, all day long. The next thing, there were bees in the garage, and so I couldn't even go into the garage to get into my car. (Mrs. H. conceded that "there weren't really that many bees there but it just felt like they were swarming all over the garage.") Why those bees decided to start a colony in my garden and garage, I don't know. But they were in there, buzzing, flying around and landing on the beams overhead and I knew they would fall down on me, so I wouldn't even go out of the house. Even in the house, one of them gets in sometimes and when I hear the buzzing, I almost faint. I get hot and cold and sweaty and my hands start shaking and I have to run. If I think it's in the kitchen, I won't go in and I have had whole meals burn because of that. I keep an insect spray in my hand practically every minute of the time, in case I see one.

If my husband is around, I am not so frightened; or even during the day, when the neighbor's little children are nearby. Those children couldn't help me, even if something did happen, but their just being there makes me feel safe.

I'm afraid to go outside because they might be there and so I have to park my car right outside the door, and then I make a dash for it and jump into my car and shut the door. I keep a spray in the car, too, in case one got in. When I come home from work, I sit in the car for fifteen minutes to make sure there are no bees out there and then I make a dash for it.

My husband is so sick of the whole thing, he just won't go through the whole routine with me, and so we don't go anywhere anymore, not movies, not friends, and except for my work, I don't leave the house.

Birds. That anyone can feel a horror for birds is difficult for most people to understand, especially those who take delight in songbirds and other small birds that come to nest and feed in the yards and gardens of suburban and rural dwellings. Yet, people who have a phobia for these creatures may see them as evil, insidious, and threatening, attributing to them the traits that are more generally associated with bats. No one has captured this sinister quality as dramatically and powerfully as did Daphne Du Maurier in her story entitled "The Birds" and by Alfred Hitchcock who directed the film with the same title, based on the Du Maurier story. Anyone who has read the story or seen the film will have a better understanding of what phobic persons feel in their reaction to birds. The sight, even of a robin or a sparrow, will send the phobic person fleeing from the area. The thought of being in the same room as a bird "fluttering and swooping about, with its wings beating and flapping" is enough to create wild terror in the afflicted person. The "beating wings" and the "wicked beak and claws" are the physical attributes most often mentioned.

One woman who lived in a large house out in the suburbs had the chimney in her fireplace bricked up and double screens installed in doors and windows to prevent any likelihood of a bird getting into the house. When the dread became too strong, even this stratagem was not enough, and she finally had to give up this home and move to the city.

Another had to change her way of life entirely after developing a phobia for birds.

> It started with my experience in the zoo. As a child I wouldn't go with my parents to the zoo because I didn't like the birds. But when I had children of my own, I didn't want to deprive them of the pleasure of going to the zoo. I tried to avoid the aviaries but they insisted on going. The second we walked in, it seemed as though a pall of darkness and evil had come over the place, and the birds looked evil, and brooding, with their beady eyes and sharp beaks. One of the large ones, lighting on a branch and fluttering its heavy, powerful wings, looked right at me. I found myself gasping for breath and my heart started pounding and I had to run out. Until then, I had paid no attention to birds in my surroundings, but after that I was aware of them, alert, every minute, that I might encounter one. I avoided parks and wouldn't even walk within blocks of a street where I knew there were trees. I used to go with friends for picnics and hikes in the country, and that was out. If I knew a friend had a songbird in a cage, I refused to visit. My big problem was with my job. The office building was in a part of town heavily infested with pigeons, and they would come roost on the window sills. If I saw one there, I would become hysterical and run out of the office. Even changing to an inside office without windows didn't lessen the fright and I had to quit my job. It got so bad I couldn't even watch a movie or a TV show that had birds in it.

Closely allied to bird phobia is phobia for feathers. Joy Melville reports the case of a woman in her sixties who had had a horror of feathers from childhood on. Just looking at them caused this woman's body to feel "as though it were on fire." It started, she believes, when she was about five and went out with her mother to feed the chickens. "I picked up one of the chicks and before I knew what had happened I was on my back and a very angry hen was sitting on my face pecking at me." Several years later she was set on by a gander who hissed and pecked at her legs. She was so terrified that she caught hold of the bird by its neck and flung it away from her. She lost her voice for several days, and from then on the mere sight, not only of a chicken, but of a feather all by itself, would throw her into a panic.

Another woman with a phobia for feathers found it necessary to rid her household of a dozen down pillows and two feather beds handed down to her by her grandmother. "The thought of putting my head down on a feather or down pillow or covering myself with a feather bed was worse than if you were to ask me to plunge into a sheet of flame."

Snakes. Few people like snakes. Most speak of them with dislike, loathing, and fear. Some of this dislike and fear may be accounted for by the fact that so many different types of snakes are poisonous. The snake is also associated in fable and myth with cunning and deceit, the prototype of this characterization being the serpent in the Garden of Eden. The metaphor "snake in the grass" alludes to the hidden enemy who strikes without warning.

Any or all of these factors may enter into the initiation of the phobic reaction to snakes. But what phobic patients comment upon most is the speed and stealth of their movement, the thought of the snake "slithering up on you" and "coiling itself around you," "the slimy feel of their skin." That this has to be the work of a very lively imagination is obvious since few people with snake phobias report ever having seen a live snake, except possibly in a zoo, or having encountered one in its natural habitat. Yet, the imagery can be so powerful that even the picture of a snake in an illustrated book is capable of producing a powerful phobic reaction. Some patients say they can actually "see" the snake in the picture moving toward them. In the following case, we see the power of the phobogenic process— how it can convert a harmless little garter snake into a terrifying monster.

Sophia S. had had a dislike of snakes as far back as she could remember—not extraordinary, nor to the point of phobia. "But," she says, "I have always loathed them. They're so slithery, and when I think of them, I see the ugly head and the beady eyes and the flicking tongue and I can see that head dart forward and sink its poisonous fangs into somebody's arm or leg." She recalls that, as a child and as an adult, she would always avoid the reptile houses on visits to the zoo. She could not even tolerate looking at them behind the thick plate glass windows of their cages.

When she and her husband came to the United States from Italy, they bought a house out in the country, with some animals, a barn, and several acres of land. One of the things Mrs. S. loved about this most was the vegetable garden she planted there. She would come out each morning to tend the garden and see how things were growing. One morning, early, as she was digging around the vegetables, a small green garter snake darted out. Dropping her garden implements, she ran into the house screaming. Her husband, startled out of his sleep, seized his shotgun and ran downstairs ready to kill the intruder. He laughed when his wife told him about what had happened, but for her it was no laughing matter.

From that day on, she would not go out into her garden, as much as she loved it. After that she stopped walking in the woods—another thing she loved to do—for fear she might encounter a snake. The barn was next, and after that she would not even walk across the lawn to where her automobile was parked. Her husband would have to drive the car right up to the brick steps, so she could step into it without setting foot on the grass. Once inside the car she felt safe, and on the city streets she felt safe. But she would not visit friends in the suburbs or country, unless she could get into the house through the garage, or drive right up to the entrance. So intense was her phobic anticipation and so limited had her life become that she threatened to move back to Italy, with or without her family.

Cats. Like snakes and spiders, cats are associated in myth and fable with evil. Seldom do you see a picture of a witch that does not include the image of a cat. Cats are portrayed as witches who have transformed themselves, temporarily, into an animal. Black cats are an omen of misfortune, disaster, and death. Yet it is not these attributes that phobic people find frightening. To the best of their knowledge these do not enter into the phobic reaction at all. Nor do they perceive any danger of being bitten or scratched by a cat. It is the eyes, the fur, the claws, the movement, the nearness of the animal which troubles them; the possibility that the cat might rub up against them or that they might touch the cat's fur with their hands or legs. The cat's tendency to jump unexpectedly is mentioned by numerous phobic patients, who add that they are horrified by the thought that a cat might jump on them.

Anita N., a married woman, about forty at the time she came for treatment, said she had disliked cats even as a child, and thought this dislike was intensified when her brother threw a cat at her. After that, she found herself disliking cats more than ever, but did not take extraordinary measures to avoid them. She would simply not go near one if she saw one in the street and would ask friends who had pet cats to keep them locked up when she visited. The aversion intensified gradually with the years, and she found herself deliberately avoiding places where a cat was likely to appear, even at a distance. She avoided entirely any home in which there was a cat, as well as small neighborhood stores where the owner had a pet cat. Then an incident occurred which produced an acute phobic reaction and intensified her avoidance of this animal.

As she was walking toward her car in the parking lot of a shopping center, she noticed that in one car which she had to pass, there was a large cat seated in the back, near the closed window. She experienced, suddenly, a terror that the cat would jump on her. There was not any way that she could get to her automobile without passing the cat. The reaction was so intense she had to telephone her husband to come for her. From that day on, she would not park her car in a parking lot, nor on a street where "there might be a car there with a cat in it." She realized how irrational it was to think that a cat in an automobile, with doors and windows locked, might jump out at her. Yet the idea was so powerful in its effects as to overwhelm reason.

Subsequently, she found that no matter where she went—whether shopping, or to a restaurant, or to the theater, or to visit friends—she was constantly on the lookout for a cat, to the point where she remained in an almost constant state of anxiety, spoiling whatever pleasure she had had in these situations. The only place she felt safe from cats was in her home.

It is noteworthy that in this instance, as in the case· of Sophia S. with the snake phobia and Millicent H. with the bee phobia, that the avoidance reaction resulted in the very same kind of isolation and sequestration in the home as might have been produced by agoraphobia.

Not as many dog phobias come to the attention of phobia treatment services as do cases of cat phobia. Whether this indicates that there is a lower incidence of dog phobia in the population, or that there is some special reason why people with this phobia do not come for treatment, we do not know. What seems to stand out in the cases of dog phobia is that, in a fairly large proportion of cases, the sufferer had had a traumatic experience with a dog in childhood—having been attacked or bitten or dragged by a dog. There are, however, many cases in which no such experience had occurred, or, at least, could not be remembered. Notwithstanding, the phobic reaction—even in cases where there had been a traumatic incident—is not that of fright because of possible real danger of being bitten or attacked again, but rather of being touched, approached, or "stared at" by a dog, of touching the dog's fur, or of having the dog brush up against an arm or leg. For those who love dogs, the thought of having a puppy jump up in your lap and curling up there is a delightful prospect. For those with a phobia for dogs, it is a source of horror.

CHAPTER THREE

The Social Phobias

THE SOCIAL PHOBIAS all have in common the dread and avoidance of doing something in the presence of other people or while being observed by others. In some respects, social phobias present an extremely exaggerated picture of ordinary shyness. In others, they bear no resemblance at all to this normal phenomenon. Here is a sampling of cases, representing a wide variety of phobic situations.

Edward K.: "I am terrified to sit down opposite anybody on the bus or subway, because they'll stare at me and I'll start shaking and blushing. I'm afraid that I might faint or do something strange and ridiculous."

Leola N.: "I won't go out on the beach in a bathing suit, because my body would be exposed and people would be able to see it and that is a very painful thought. It has nothing to do with my physical appearance. I've got a nice looking body. But it is just having people see it that terrifies me. So whenever my family insists that I go to the beach with them I keep on my dress and give some excuse about not getting sunburned, or else I refuse to go altogether. I won't undress in front of anybody either—not even my own sisters. The thought of anybody seeing any intimate part of my body is dreadful; I can't even stand to have them see my bare back or legs or stomach."

Fred McM.: "Whenever I'm introduced to anybody or have to

61

talk to someone, even relatives and friends of the family, I break out in a sweat and my throat chokes and no sound can come out. I can see them looking right at me and thinking 'what a weirdo.' I'm afraid I'll do something absurd and they'll start laughing at me."

Randolph W.: "If I am eating and I think somebody is looking at me, I can actually feel my foodpipe tightening up and I am afraid that while I'm swallowing I'll choke to death so I jump up. Sometimes, I will cut my food into tiny bits so that if I feel this tightness coming on, I won't have to stop eating so they won't ask me why I stopped. I can't eat in a restaurant because I get so nervous and I'm afraid this is going to happen. I can't go to a party where there's food."

Ethel W.: "If I have to sign my name at a bank, or in a department store when I buy something, my hand starts shaking and I have to put the pen down and leave. I don't know why, but I can't stand somebody seeing me when I am signing my name. I have to run out."

Violet B.: "I used to work in a gift shop but had to give up my job, because when a customer asked me to wrap up a gift package for them, I couldn't do it. I was afraid my hands would shake. It did happen several times, and I had to stop. When the customer was shopping around while I was doing it, it didn't bother me. But when they stood there and watched, it was impossible."

Esther S.: "I can't eat when anybody else is there because I'm afraid my hand will shake and I'll drop the fork, or I'll drop the food off my fork. Soup is out of the question. I know I'll spill it, and I won't pick up a cup, because I'm afraid I'll drop it and spill the coffee over everything. I can't go anywhere where there are people and food is served, because I just couldn't eat."

Donald V.: "I'm so frightened I'll vomit in public that I won't go on a bus where I can smell the traffic fumes and get nauseous, or on a rowboat or a canoe, because the motion might make me nauseous and I'd vomit. The smell of certain foods, like asparagus, does that to me, and I make sure that if I am invited anywhere, I tell them please not to serve any asparagus, which can get very embarrassing."

Enid C.: "Sometimes when I'm with people, I feel all of a sudden that I can't breathe, and I become so frightened I feel I'm going to faint. So I make myself breathe, I breathe consciously, to make sure I draw air into my lungs, or I'll pass out. I just force the air in by making myself take deep breaths. I won't go out on a date because I'm afraid it will happen, and now I'm afraid it will happen on the job, I'm staying away from people. It isn't just being around people, but having someone paying attention to me, or looking at me."

Lawrence S.: "I go into a panic when I'm doing something as simple and unimportant as buttoning my coat, and somebody looks at me, or while I'm putting a letter into an envelope, or taking a can or package from the shelf in a supermarket."

Eleanor V.: "If I am on a plane, and I think somebody is going to get sick and vomit, I have to move to another part of the plane; otherwise, I'm afraid I'd start screaming if I had to watch that person. If I'm at a party where there's a lot of drinking and if somebody just looks pale as though he might be getting sick, I have to leave. I can't take the chance that it might happen while I'm there. There doesn't even have to be anything as specific as that. If I just look at a person's face and see a funny look and I think he or she is going to be sick, I get faint and run away. I am terrified even to go to work because of that, and it's impossible for me to lead a normal life."

It had once been thought that social phobia was predominantly an ailment of women, but with the gradual liberalization of public attitudes, and the increased willingness of men to come forward with their phobic problems, the ratio has shifted and clinicians are now seeing almost as many men with this particular type of phobia as women.

Some patients report that the problem came on slowly and gradually over several years; others, that it started with a mild anxiety about the particular phobic situation and developed into a full-blown panic reaction within only a few months; others, that it came on as open panic with the very first incident.

Most cases of social phobia have their initial onset between the ages of fifteen and thirty, very few before or after those ages. Once initiated, they tend to persist in a rather unwavering course for many years after their onset.

A substantial proportion of social phobia patients report that they were unusually fearful, timid, or shy as children and that by the time they had reached adolescence, they had become quite isolated socially. Self-consciousness, as might be expected, is a dominant trait in the childhood personality configuration of these patients, reflected to an extraordinary degree by sensitivity to what others think of them, and by an almost paranoid concern about being observed.

Excessive resort to alcohol and to pills shows up with a noticeable frequency among these patients. It appears that, because these phobias center around interpersonal contact, they are more disturbing and pervasive than are other phobias related to specific objects or place situations, and that since avoidance is not often possible with respect to many of the social phobias, relief is sought through alcohol and drugs.

DEPRESSION

Depression is another condition frequently found to be associated with social phobias—and with agoraphobia as well. We think it will be useful, therefore, to elaborate on it somewhat here.

Depression, in a mild form, is experienced from time to time by nearly everyone in the normal course of life. When a person says he is dejected, "blue," "low," or "down," he is actually feeling a very mild, normal passing depression. These moods come on generally, when things have not been going well, when a venture has not worked out, when a friendship or love relationship is experiencing problems, when someone important has moved away, when an expected telephone call doesn't come, or an expected invitation to a party is not extended. The core feeling in this reaction is one of having lost something or of not temporarily being able to attain something that one wants, and, in addition, a feeling of helplessness to do anything about it. Most people who go through such normal, transient depressive reactions generally have enough else going on in their lives to make up for the loss or deprivation and to buoy them up.

However, when the disappointment, frustration, failure, or loss is more severe, the reaction is much more intense, deep, and persistent. Then it is no longer dejection, but depression. Depression can be expected to occur, with those who are vulnerable, when a deeply felt loss is experienced: A child, spouse, parent, brother, or sister dies. A marriage or other long-lasting relationship breaks up, in which there has been a deep emotional attachment. A person loses a job he has had for a long time and he cannot find another that will give him the same level of gratification for his ego and sense of importance. A person endures a wearing, debilitating chronic illness from which there is little hope of recovery. In all of these, the mood of helplessness and hopelessness is intense. The underlying feelings are: "It's just no use. There's nothing I can do about it. I can't go on," and these thoughts and feelings are translated into a state of physical immobilization. The afflicted person finds it impossible to summon up the energy to do something about his difficulty, to pull himself together and start out on a new course that will remedy his failure, disappointment, or loss. Instead, there is tiredness and weariness and there isn't enough energy even to carry on the simple, elementary functions of daily life such as getting out of bed, bathing and dressing oneself, or shopping and preparing food. Appetite is lost and there is no interest whatever in sex. The hours drag on, and the days drag on in an endless, grey succession. There is an underlying feeling of uselessness and worthlessness expressed in such thoughts as "I have wasted my whole life." "I have never done anything worthwhile." "I have been a miserable mother (father, wife, husband, daughter, son)." "I have caused everybody so much trouble." "Nobody would really care whether I live or die, and I don't care either."

The feeling of despair and the overall painfulness of the mood can be so intense as to inspire such thoughts as: "I wish I were dead. I pray to God that he does not let me wake in the morning." "I am going to swallow those sleeping pills (or tranquilizers) and end it all."

Not everyone reacts to disappointment, loss, and failure with the depressive reaction. There are some who are blessed—either through heredity or upbringing or a combination of both—with a realistic, positive attitude about themselves and about life. When they endure a loss or a failure, they suffer, but they do not go to pieces. They are able to say to themselves: "That's rough and it hurts, but I can't let it get me. I have got to find a way to overcome this, to do something else which will work, to find new things or make new relationships, to rebuild and go on from here." They do not have unrealistic expectations. They don't set themselves impossible goals and punish themselves if they do not achieve these goals. They are not perfectionists, expecting one hundred percent performance in everything they do, and "eating themselves up alive" if they achieve only seventy or eighty percent. Since they do not set themselves impossible, unrealistic goals and expectations, a disappointment, loss, or failure doesn't crush them.

The realistic attitude about themselves is tied up with a realistic attitude about life. They don't expect life to be "a bed of roses." They know to expect pain, suffering, and loss as part of living. They feel they have the capability to change things, to manipulate their environment, but only up to a point. They know that certain things, like illness, accidents, losses, and death are inevitable, beyond their control. Then when something bad happens, they do not blame themselves, and they do not feel hopeless and helpless. They go through their suffering or grieving and then pull themselves together and start out all over again. They do not become depressed, or if they do, it is only a mild transitory depression.

Since phobic people characteristically set themselves unrealistic goals and expectations, and demand so much of themselves, disappointment, frustration, and self-blame are part of the ongoing picture. Hence we can expect depression of varying degrees of intensity to be an integral part of the pattern. The resultant depressive state may be mild and consist only of unhappiness and fatigue, or it may be intense, resulting in near-total immobilization with suicidal thoughts and inclinations. While depression interferes with motivation and effort to deal with the phobic condition, it is possible to counteract it with psychotherapy, and sometimes with antidepressant medication. With this deterrent removed—at least temporarily—progress can be made in dealing with the phobia. The ensuing successes in controlling the phobia then work to bring about a lifting of the depression.

CLUSTERS OF SOCIAL PHOBIAS

In some cases, the social phobia is restricted to one particular type of situation, such as eating while being observed or writing in the presence of others. In most cases, however, the individual is sensitive to several different types of situations. Typical is the case of Cindy B.

Cindy's phobia have to do with speaking, writing and eating in public.

She is now thirty-two, married, and the mother of three children. Speaking about her children and the shyness of her oldest child, who is ten, she recalls her own problems as a child. She, too, she says, was bashful and would shrink from the demonstrative, affectionate gestures of her aunts and uncles. Much of her time while growing up was spent by herself, reading and playing imaginary roles in her mind—being a mother, a princess, a champion swimmer. She had few friends and, unlike other children in her school and neighborhood, did very little visiting around her neighborhood. She had little confidence in herself and thought she could not do anything at all on her own initiative; yet she did, and quite capably. She was concerned with her health to an unusual degree and became quite concerned about dying even when she had nothing more than a cold or stomachache. She recalls also the fright and trauma she lived through when, at the time she was eleven, her mother had become seriously ill and the children were told their mother was going to die.

This anxiety persisted on a moderate, but fairly constant, level, throughout adolescence and into early adult life. Then, when Cindy was twenty-one, she gave birth to her first child, an event which was followed by an outbreak of acute anxiety. She began to experience physical symptoms and pains which she interpreted as being evidence of a serious illness. Sometimes it was a heart attack; at other times cancer; at others paralysis of the limbs or multiple sclerosis. She ran from one doctor to another, each one of whom reassured her that she had nothing wrong with her, but this did nothing to ease her anxiety. As soon as one "disease" faded, another took its place. A course of supportive psychotherapy at a mental health clinic relieved the problem considerably, and the anxiety receded to its moderate, chronic state, until about two years ago.

I was doing some shopping for clothing for the children and I was standing on line, waiting to have the cashier lay them away for a later date. Suddenly, I got this panicky feeling—I don't know where it came from—but I got panicky and very nervous and I just couldn't stand being on line. The feeling frightened me since nothing like this had ever happened to me before. I was about ready to drop all the packages right then and there and run out of the store. But it was my turn and I had to stay. When I put the bundles down on the counter and tried to tell the saleslady what I wanted, I couldn't get out a sound. My throat was choked up tight and I couldn't say a word. Finally I was able to get out a few words to tell her what I wanted. She took out some forms, and after filling in the items, she asked me to sign. She handed me the pen and when I picked it up I could barely hold it and my hand began to shake something terrible. I just couldn't control it. The saleslady looked at me like I was crazy. Finally I made my fingers get a tight hold on the pen and forced them to write, but instead of writing on the line, they scrawled out my name across the whole page. I could see the cashier's eyes opening wide with amazement, not being able to believe what was going on before her eyes. From then on, I haven't been able to sign anything in front of anybody, except where I absolutely have to do so or else give up my sales business, where I do have to sign some forms. Each time, I make some excuse about having to go where the light is brighter, or I try to delay until the other party is looking away, or walks off, and even then, I have palpitations and I feel like I am going to pass out. Afterwards, I'm exhausted.

Her problem with eating started within a month or two after the onset of the writing phobia.

We were all visiting my mother for dinner. My brothers and their wives were there, and we were all seated around the table talking and then my mother started serving and when I picked up my fork to eat, my hand started to shake and I couldn't pick up anything with my fork and bring it to my mouth. I was frightened and thought I was having some kind of a fit, but I realized that this had something to do with my hand shaking when I write. I waited a little and my mother asked why I wasn't eating. So I tried again but couldn't. I told my mother I wasn't feeling too well and couldn't eat anything. Everybody was looking at me. Inside I was in a panic, but I didn't let it show. They took me at my word and just let me alone, while they went on talking and eating, for which I was so thankful. The upset inside of me was still there, but I made myself sound natural and calm. After a while, I calmed down but I didn't eat. Then it happened again when I was out to dinner in a restaurant with my girlfriend. Now I just don't eat anywhere except at home in front of my family.

Cindy's work requires that she give sales talks to small groups. During the same period when the eating and writing difficulties started, she also experienced a panic attack while waiting her turn to be called to the podium to speak.

I had this sudden panic that I would forget everything I was planning to say and that I would just get up there with a blank mind. I tried to make myself remember, right then, what my speech was going to be, and all that came into my head were a bunch of jumbled scraps of thoughts. I got dizzy and my hand started to shake and I almost dropped the paper with my notes. There was a brief break and I had a chance to tell the chairman I would have to be excused; I wasn't feeling well. I haven't been able to tell anybody about this problem, so I have made myself go up a few times and choke out a few words, but it's like going to an execution. Before I go on, and when I'm speaking, it's as though it was somebody else up there, not me. My heart is beating, I am perspiring, I am dizzy, and my legs are rubbery. I don't know how I make myself stick it out, and I don't know how long I'm going to be able to keep this up without getting a stroke or something terrible happening to me.

Cindy thinks her phobic condition may have to do with some severe anxieties she was experiencing at the time it started. Her husband had just concluded arrangements to go into a new business, one that would require the investment of all the money they had saved, and considerable indebtedness besides. She was also afraid that, with her husband's total involvement in the business, she would be left to shoulder all of the burdens and responsibilities of the household and the children. She resented being left in this position and was angry at her husband but could not complain because there was no justification. At the same time, Cindy's younger sister was preparing to be married, and Cindy's mother, who had been quite attentive to Cindy and her children, was now being totally absorbed in the preparations for the wedding. Cindy said she now felt deserted and abandoned on two fronts. "I felt so helpless, so tired and weak. I felt I wasn't going to be able to do anything at all, with my business or in the house or with the children." She realizes now, she says, that she was quite depressed at the time and that in some way this made her prone to the phobia.

AN UNUSUAL SOCIAL PHOBIA

Most social phobias follow a fairly uniform pattern: a certain act, such as writing, or eating, or speaking while being observed produces a reaction of distress, including a variety of physical symptoms, such as involuntary shaking of the hands, faintness, perspiration, blushing, dizziness, weakness in the limbs, palpitations, hyperventilation, and others. The person so affected then flees from the situation and avoids it henceforward, in order to escape the unendurable reactions associated with the phobogenic process.

There is one social phobia—phobia for urination—that follows the general formula of distress and avoidance, but differs with respect to the physical reaction. The case of Ernest G., twenty-eight years old, will illustrate this.

Ernest has a phobia about urinating when anyone is nearby. If he is out of view and out of earshot of the other person, there is no problem. But if he thinks the other person is aware of his presence, he finds it impossible to urinate. "My apparatus closes down," he says, "and will not function." Before using a urinal in a public toilet, he will make sure there is no one else there. If there is, he will not go in. If there isn't, he will proceed, but should he hear someone open the door and enter after he has initiated the effort to relieve himself, he will flush the urinal, pretend he is finished, leave the public toilet, and contain himself until he can get to another toilet where he will be alone. This has caused him, on many occasions, to retain his urine for hours and suffer both mortification and pain.

Ernest has the same problem at home. He is single and lives with his parents. If his parents are in the house and he thinks they might hear him, he cannot function. To prevent their hearing him he will run the shower, or turn on the radio, or create other distractions. If none of these stratagems work, he will wait for his parents to leave the house. Otherwise, he will go to the home of a friend where the bathroom is well removed from the living quarters and where no one can possibly hear him.

This has been going on for more than fifteen years. The phobia is restricted to this one specific function and does not create too great a problem for him nor interfere too much with his living routine or his work. He simply avoids situations in which there is someone present while he is urinating.

What is lacking in the picture is the extreme distress reaction if someone comes into the public toilet while he is relieving himself, or if he hears someone outside his bathroom at home.

> I feel embarrassed and get tense and nervous. I can also feel my heart going a little faster. But I do not feel any terrifying, overwhelming dread. All that happens is that my machinery shuts down. It just does not operate. There are times when I get frightened that something might be wrong with me physically, but I have had that checked out. I have had several examinations by urologists and they assure me that, physically, everything is in order.

A COMPLICATED CASE

This is the case of Diana G., a divorcee of about fifty-eight, who has for more than thirty years been the victim of an extraordinary combination of several social phobias, some of them quite unique, as well as a number of specific phobias found commonly in the agoraphobic syndrome.

Because of its unusual interest, and because of the remarkable changes that took place in a matter of eight weeks in the course of Mrs. G.'s participation in the White Plains Hospital Phobia Clinic, we will relate the case in some detail.

For thirty years, Mrs. G. has been unable to give anyone a gift —nobody—not her children, not any other relative, not anyone where she works.

> When I think about having to give someone a gift, it throws me into a panic. I am in agony all night and I can't sleep. It's torture. I try to push the thought away, but it keeps on coming back. If I know the gift is due a week from now, I suffer day and night every minute of the time, and then I end up by not giving it. I know what people must think, but I can't help it. It would be easier for me to cut off my hand than to give that gift.

In the course of her therapy, Mrs. G. thought she would make an attempt at breaking this pattern.

> I bought this little money tree that I was going to give to the little granddaughter of my good friend Rose. Rose is like a sister to me. I spend more time at her home than I do at mine. I go there in the evening, and we play cards, sometimes all night long—it's like my second home. So I bought this little money tree, but once I got it in my house, I couldn't look at it. It was like a horror lying there on the floor. I had to cover it up so I wouldn't be able to see it. . . .

The phobia for giving gifts is complicated by another phobia—that for signing anything. "For more than thirty years," Mrs. G. said at another session, "I wouldn't sign anything or pay for anything by check. I would get paid in cash and pay for everything in cash. A few times when I did have to sign, I was in torture for a week before I actually had to do it."

As the clinic progressed, Mrs. G. brought up her concern about two gifts she was going to have to give within the next few weeks—one, a gift to her employer's daughter, and one to her grandson who was graduating from college.

> I could give it in cash—but that would still be a gift, and I just can't make myself do it. But if I do make myself give the gift,

how can I give cash to my boss's daughter? It would be an insult.
And my grandson would think I'm crazy. So the only way is to
write checks, but the thought of that just throws me into a terror
—a panic. I get hot and cold flashes just thinking about it. If you
told me I was going to be executed tomorrow, it wouldn't be as
terrible.

Part of her aversion for giving gifts was a strange dread about
not being able to get them back. After the fifth clinic session,
Mrs. G., with the encouragement of the group, decided that she
was going to give the money tree to her friend Rose's grand-
daughter "no matter what." Here is what happened, as she
related it.

I got up in the morning with the feeling that today I am going to
give that gift, even if it is so terrible that I throw myself out of
the window. I can't go through this torture any longer; I won't go
through it any longer. So I went to Rose's house and I gave her
the gift for the child. She hugged me and kissed me and I cried.
Then the friends came over and we started to play cards. We
played for hours, and not once did the thought of the gift bother
me. But after I got home and went to sleep, I woke up in the
middle of the night in a panic, in terror. I wanted to get that gift
back, but I knew I wouldn't be able to do it. The thought was
terrifying. I had to get out of bed and distract myself, so I started
cooking. Then the panic went away and I said to myself, "That's
it; that gift is gone forever. You'll never be able to do anything
about it so forget it." And then I started to feel a little better.

A week later, Mrs. G. came in with this report.

I finally made myself do it. I wrote a check and sent it off to my
grandson. Then I wrote out a check for my boss's daughter and
put it in my pocketbook. I had it there all day and all day I was
saying to myself, "Now, do it now," but I couldn't make myself
do it. But finally, at the end of the day, when he was leaving, I
pulled out the check and shoved it in his hand and said, "Here,
give this to Ginny; wish her my best." But it was terrible. The
aftereffects were awful. All week long, I was shaky and panicky.
I wanted to do it and it made me very happy that I did it, but I
also kept thinking, "Why did you do it? Why did you do it?" I
went to bed thinking, "They have my checks and I can't get
them back." It was a torture all day and all night, for days, but
then it started to get a little easier.

Associated with Mrs. G.'s phobia about giving things away was an obsession about saving things, about not being able to throw anything away. Over a period of three decades, she has been unable to throw away a single card, letter, receipt, advertisement, or anything else she has received in the mail. As a result, her dresser drawers and closets were literally stuffed with thousands upon thousands of these items, as were a dozen or more cartons. "I don't know why, but I just couldn't throw anything away. I had a compulsion that I had to keep it. It isn't that I thought those papers were valuable or that I could do anything with them. I just had to keep them; I couldn't throw them away." In the seventh session, Mrs. G. reported to the group that something else "unbelievable" had happened, something she thought would never happen.

It was Saturday morning, and I was looking for something and I didn't know what it was. Then I got this terrible feeling, a feeling that I was going to die—that this was going to be the last day of my life. But I thought that before I die, I am going to get rid of all those papers. I don't want anybody to come into this house after I'm dead and find all this junk. So I went down to the store and got some of those big plastic bags for trash, and I started emptying those drawers, and I just threw in that junk in big bunches, old junk that had been there for as long as thirty years. And I kept on emptying and emptying, one drawer after another, one closet after another, and all the time I'm crying and I don't know why I'm crying. And then I went to the bathroom and threw up. Then, that night, I felt I had to get out of the house or I would go crazy. I ran over to Rose's house and stayed there until five in the morning, playing cards, and then I went home and, without going to bed, I started emptying again, one drawer after another, all the time crying, and I didn't stop crying for three days.

Mrs. G.'s eating phobias follow patterns commonly found in others with these social phobias. She is unable to eat in anyone's presence. If someone is nearby and observing her, her hand will shake and she will be unable to hold a knife, fork or cup. She has still another problem. At times when she is able to hold a cup or fork without shaking, she is unable to bring it up to her mouth. "It is as though my arm is paralyzed. I can't will it to move no matter how hard I try. It just won't move and I

have to put down the cup or the fork." Also, she is constantly in
fear of choking when she eats, even when nobody else is looking. She has had the very frequent experience of taking a bite of
food into her mouth and not being able to swallow it, even after
she had chewed it into a pulp. "My throat just closes down and
I can't get anything down." She has, to the extent possible,
shifted to liquid and soft food which can be taken in small
amounts and swallowed. Occasionally, she is able to manage
small bites of solid food. She has lost considerable weight and is
worried about her health.

Among Mrs. G.'s more common phobias are those having to
do with trains, elevators, and planes, all of which give her a
feeling of being locked in, of "not being able to get out if
something should happen."

She had never had a panic attack while in an elevator, but
developed the phobia just the same. For decades before coming
to the clinic, Mrs. G. has been avoiding situations involving the
use of elevators, and where it was compulsory that she get to an
upper floor in an apartment or office building, "I would just go
to the staircase and walk."

The last airplane ride she took was some fifteen years ago. "I
took a boxful of Valium and fell asleep. But when I awoke and
we were still up in the air, I went out of my mind. They
practically had to tie me down."

She did have a phobic attack on a train, some thirty years
ago, when she was riding on the subway, and thought she had
left one of her children on the platform. "When the train started,
I started screaming—'my child—my child—he's out there on
the platform.' I was hysterical. But a man came over and
grabbed my arm and said—'both your kids are here'—and they
were. But that was the end of trains for me."

Before the eight-week clinic was over, Mrs. G. had taken
several rides on an elevator, first with her phobia aide, and then
by herself. She had also taken a ride on a train, with the aide,
for several stations. "I was numb every minute of the trip, but
then we took the same ride back, and on the return trip it
wasn't so bad. Then when I got home, I sat down and cried that
I had wasted more than thirty years of my life with this stupid
fear and all those other stupid fears. I made up my mind that I
was going to get rid of them now, that I still had many good
years left in my life, and that I was going to live them and enjoy
them, from now on."

CHAPTER FOUR

Agoraphobia

THE TERM AGORAPHOBIA was coined in 1871 by a German psychologist, Dr. G. Westphal, to describe a peculiar syndrome he had discovered in three of his patients. These patients came to him because they had developed sudden, inexplicable terror in various places in which they found themselves during the day—the places where they worked, the street, the town square, the market place. Each experienced this reaction in a variety of different settings, but in all cases the end result was the same: The man had to flee from the situation to a place in which he felt safe, generally his home.

Westphal described the phenomenon as "the impossibility of walking through certain streets or places or the possibility of doing so only with resultant dread or anxiety." Following the prevailing custom, Westphal gave this syndrome a Greek name —*agoraphobia*—"agora" meaning market, marketplace, place of assembly, and "phobia" meaning dread.

In the effort to make this meaningful in the English language, writers who came after Westphal fell into the error of over-simplification and translated it to mean "fear of open places." This definition is in error on two scores. First, it is not fear, but dread. Second, the dread is experienced not only in open and unprotected places, but in closed and confined spaces; in high and in low places; in empty as well as crowded places; on, in, and over the water; on the surface of the earth, above it in the air, and beneath it in the depths. It may, in fact, be experienced in any kind of a situation into which the individual ventures.

An inventory of the places in which agoraphobic persons say they have this reaction would include streets, stores, traffic, shopping centers, bridges, expressways, automobiles, trains, elevators, buses, tall buildings, heights of any kind, classrooms, churches, theaters, parties, meeting halls, hairdressing chairs, dentists' chairs, waiting lines and waiting rooms, rivers and lakes, bridges, parking lots, mountains, sports stadiums, banks, laundromats, crowded areas, deserted areas, and many others.

Some who have this condition are phobic to a large number of these places and situations; others to a smaller number, the combination varying from individual to individual. But regardless of the specific items included in these combinations, and regardless of the differences from one combination to the next, the end result is almost invariably the same: flight from and avoidance of so many different situations that the individual ends up being confined to the only place in which he or she feels safe—the home or a very small area around the home, and occasionally only a bed in the house.

We would define agoraphobia as habitual avoidance of a variety of situations in which the subject experiences inexplicable dread and the urgent need to flee from them to safety—as he sees it—which may mean a safe person or a safe place or both. In simple phobias, the retreat is from only one specific situation, enabling the subject to operate in all other areas of life. In agoraphobia, the pattern is different. Typically, once the dread starts in one place, it spreads from that situation to others. Ultimately, so many situations are involved as to make it impossible for the individual to operate outside the home or the presence of a trusted person, generally a close relative.

A number of cases of agoraphobia have already been described in this book, and we would recommend that the reader turn back to these cases and reread them, to note how similar they are in some respects, how different they are in others, and how, regardless of these differences, they culminate in the same way. In the first chapter, the cases of agoraphobia are those of the flutist who is a hermit in her own home, unable to tolerate the presence of any other person (page 2); the young woman who broke off her engagement because she felt her phobia made her "just half a person" (page 2); the young woman who persuaded the airplane pilot to turn his plane around and take it back to the terminal (page 11); and Maureen, who tells about the warm, supportive reaction from her friends when she informed them about her phobia (page 22).

DEVELOPMENT DIFFERS FROM CASE TO CASE

By the time a person with agoraphobia has come for treatment, the condition has sometimes reached an advanced stage of near-total immobilization. But the course which this disorder has travelled, and the time it has taken to reach this stage, may vary greatly from individual to individual.

Some patients report that the progression from the initial attack to the stage of retreat into the home was quick, culminating in a matter of months. Others report that the spread from the first attack—in a bus, or store, or street—to other situations was gradual and slow, and that at times, during the progression, total avoidance was not always necessary. They had been able to move into these situations, suffering intense distress, yet not having to flee. They were able to cope and to carry on whatever activities were involved.

In the stages when the condition was relatively mild, they were able to find relief from the phobic anxiety in the presence of a trusted companion. This might be a family member, a friend, or another adult. It might even be a child, a dog or cat, or even an inanimate object such as an umbrella or shopping basket.

Agoraphobia does not always follow a straight-line course. In many cases, it follows a fluctuating course—waxing and waning, becoming intense, then moderate, then intense again.

The first attack may take place at the time of a stressful experience, when emotional resources are low, when the emotional state is one of anxiety and insecurity. As conditions improve and a feeling of security is restored, the agoraphobic reaction tends to become less and less intense, and may even disappear for some time. Then some other upsetting event occurs, the state of equanimity is shattered, and the phobic reaction returns in force. This fluctuation in intensity may continue over a stretch of years, during which the afflicted person can still carry on most functions of daily life, the condition remaining at a long-term plateau, without ever deteriorating into total or near-total immobilization.

There are cases, even severe ones, which may last only for a

short time, and then go into remission, recurring only infre-
quently over a period of many years, or perhaps not even recurring at all. Clinicians have found, however, that where a case
has persisted at a high level of intensity for more than a year, a
spontaneous remission is unlikely and the condition will continue to get worse over the next several years and, unless it is
treated, may even reach a state of total immobilization.

PREPONDERANCE OF FEMALE PATIENTS

It may have struck the reader that the subject in every one of
the agoraphobia cases we have discussed is a woman. The fact
is that the large majority of people coming for help because of
agoraphobia *are* women. But this does not mean that there are
no men with this disorder. In fact, there are many, even though
they are in the minority at present count. We say "at present
count" because we do not know if the low representation of
men among agoraphobia patients actually reflects a low percentage in the general population. It is possible that men are actually
underrepresented in the patient population. Men are reluctant to
admit having this disorder. They see it as a "weakness," and it
hurts their masculine pride. It is also probable that many men
may have more opportunity to "bury" their phobic problem by
immersing themselves in work, or escaping by means of alcohol,
than do housewives who are at home. Since these men do not,
for these various reasons, come forward to seek help, they cannot be counted. It is possible that with increased publicity about
successful treatment of phobias, the pattern will change, with
more men seeking help. If so, their cases should be represented
in greater number in the future.

Regardless, we can say that, except for specific differences in
the life-styles of men and women, the pattern and course of
agoraphobia are indistinguishable for the two sexes. The following case is related by Mrs. Fern Overlock, a phobia aide at the
White Plains Hospital Phobia Clinic. (Phobia aides, or "helpers," are men or women who usually have themselves been
through a phobia and who, after training, are working with
patients, helping them to overcome their phobias.)

One day I got a telephone call from a friend to ask if I could help
someone with a severe case of agoraphobia. This person, a car-

penter and mechanic, had not been out of his house at all for eleven years. He wanted help but was afraid to ask for it. My friend asked if I would go out to visit him. I found him sitting in his living room, pasty-faced, hesitant in speech, slow in his movement. He presented a picture of pained resignation to a life of dullness and imprisonment. He wouldn't even look up while he was talking to me.

John's first phobic attack had come "out of the blue," the way it does with most phobic people. He was driving to work when it happened, and it frightened him so badly that he turned right around, drove back home, and wouldn't venture out again for several days. He then went to see a doctor who told him it was probably "overwork and nerves" and suggested he take a few days off. John returned to his home after this visit to the doctor, and just didn't venture out again. He and his wife, who also was working, had put aside enough money to buy a delicatessen store about four blocks from where they lived. He managed to make the trip up and back each day and to keep the store going. But every minute was filled with anxiety: He couldn't even say what he was afraid of; he was just frightened all the time. Finally his wife had to quit her job and take over the store. He retired to his home and didn't leave the house for eleven years, except for a few futile tries. He just took over the household while the wife took over the task of making a living. He cooked, cleaned, and did the laundry and other household chores. He panelled several rooms, painted, and repaired, but never stepped out the door.

After about the fifth year, his wife had a baby. John couldn't go to the hospital to be with her. When the baby was christened, he couldn't attend. When he wasn't puttering around, he just sat and watched TV—hour after hour—until it became almost his entire life. Friends visited occasionally, but not many. His wife managed to keep up friendships with a few women, and she managed to get out now and then to be with them. Many times he got panic attacks in the middle of the night and stayed up watching TV. That was the only thing that would calm him. He couldn't get up in the morning and stayed in bed until eleven or twelve o'clock. He would spend the rest of the day frittering away the time, waiting for his wife to get home, just eating, watching TV, and sleeping.

After I started working with him, I was able to get him to walk with me for several blocks. We would stop in front of his church and he would look at it sadly and say, "Someday I'm going to be able to go in there again." But even as he was saying that, he would be urging me to walk back with him to the house. He has a fear that something will happen to him while he's out and he wants to rush back home. He keeps on saying, "I'm scared, I'm scared. But I don't know of what or why." There are four other men in the same town who have the same problem. They are terrified, from the time they get up, that they're going to have an attack, and they call each other when they're frightened and need some friendly reassurance.

There's a camper in John's driveway. He says he bought it with the thought that it might give him the courage to get out and take his family on a trip. The camper has been sitting there for five years. It hasn't moved out yet. "Maybe someday," John says, looking at it sadly.

Mrs. Overlock tells of another case in which the man involved hasn't been out of his house for twenty years, except for brief sorties by automobile, but never by himself.

He will not move out of his house unless his wife or one of his children is with him. He is afraid he is going to get a heart attack or that something else terrible will happen to him—he is unable to tell me exactly what that "something else" might be.

Rudolph came to this country from Germany when he was a boy, and when he was twenty-three, he took over his father's share of a family importing business. The other end of the business in Germany is run by an uncle and cousin. Rudolph's first phobic attack came while he was at a social gathering with a large number of compatriots. He suddenly felt himself gasping for breath, choking, and suffocating, and he was afraid he was dying. He got up and ran out and his wife followed him. The following day at the office, he got another attack and left quickly. He stayed home a couple of days, and then his wife took him to a doctor who prescribed pills for his "nerves" which just didn't do anything at all for him. For several weeks, he had his wife drive him to the office, but he was so full of anxiety during the day that he couldn't take care of his business. He finally decided, and his wife agreed, that if the only place he felt safe was at home, then the business should be moved there. Without revealing to anyone except his wife the reason for doing so, he converted a small guest cottage into an office and removed his business to that site. But the move did not allay the phobic anxiety. He was constantly fearful he might have another attack during the course of a business meeting. Each morning when he arose, the anxiety was there that he might have another attack that day.

And that has been going on for twenty years. How he survives it—this constant state of anxiety, waiting for a panic attack to strike—I don't know. You can see it in his face—the tension, the pain, the suffering, the unhappiness. He can't walk down the street alone. He can't drive anywhere alone. He will go out with his wife to a store, but they have to come back quickly. They'll stop for a bite at a fast food place, but he will not go into a restaurant. They will go together to a party, but the minute he gets there he starts drinking and stays intoxicated. His wife is virtually a prisoner in the home. When she goes out, he gets very uncomfortable. They have teenage children who resent his not going to see them play soccer or come to school to meet with their teachers. It's so sad. He has a beautiful house, a great deal of money, and they could be enjoying life if it weren't for his phobia. He knows it and that's what's eating him up, that and the children's resentment. He keeps on saying, "Why me? Why did it happen to me? I'll just never get over it and I'll probably die soon—that will be a blessing because life isn't worth living this way."

SOME TRAITS OF PEOPLE WITH AGORAPHOBIA

Although it is incorrect to speak of an agoraphobic personality, certain personality traits show up quite consistently among the people who have this disorder. They are highly imaginative and recall having been so as children. They tend to underrate their value and their capabilities. They set high and unrealistic goals for themselves and worry a great deal about failing. They allow others to set high goals for them and strive to live up to these expectations, lest they be criticized or rejected. They are over-conscientious in performance of duties and obligations, making greater demands on themselves than would be called for. In short, they are "perfectionists."

Their great sensitivity to what others think about them makes them what Dr. Arthur Hardy calls "people pleasers." Much of what they do, they do to accommodate, to avoid conflict, to gain approval. In another aspect of their sensitivity to what others think about them, these people are terribly afraid of "being embarrassed," "making a fool of myself," "doing something that would give other people the idea that there's something wrong with me." This is intensified during the course of the phobia, when they think that "if other people really knew the things I am thinking and feeling and doing, they'd really think that I'm crazy, that I'm some kind of a nut." This urgent need for concealment works directly to intensify the phobia. Unable to discuss their fears with others, they keep them bottled up in their own minds. A good opportunity for reality-testing (to see that there is little validity to their fears) is lost, and the fears persist and become magnified.

Many people who have agoraphobia report that they were anxious and tense as children, and that they were almost constantly plagued by a sense of insecurity, a vague feeling of not being safe. They tell of childhood fright, nightmares and night terrors, fear of the dark, fear of becoming ill, and fear of dying.

Why do some children become overfearful? A number of factors enter into the formation of this personality trait.

Research studies indicate that children who are unusually fearful are highly sensitive, have very active imaginations, and are more acutely reactive to sensations—sounds, smell, visual stimuli, touch, and taste.

In addition, they are likely to be the children of parents who are themselves fearful people. Listening to parents tell about the things that frighten them and watching them react with anxiety and fright to situations others might ignore or take lightly, the children "model" themselves after the parents, accepting their evaluations of threat and danger without ever checking these out for themselves.

At the other extreme, parents may conceal their fears entirely, manifesting only unusual behavior which the child cannot understand. This may inspire the child to imagine hidden dangers and to embellish them. Both extremes—excessive demonstration of fear and concealment of fear—on the part of the parents are apt to produce the same effect on the child—a predisposition to be excessively anxious and fearful.

The alternative to both of these types of parental behavior— and the most constructive one, we believe—is an open, honest, straightforward approach. This prepares a child best to deal with his own fears.

The parents of overfearful children are also likely to be overanxious and overprotective of the child. The child is constantly being warned to "be careful," to "watch out," not to get too close to other children for fear of "catching something," not to get overheated or chilled, not to eat "unhealthy" food, not to get hurt. When the child gets a cold, the parent is likely to react as though the child has pneumonia. If he cuts himself, the parent might react as though he is going to bleed to death. The child quickly picks up this anxiety and reacts to minor illnesses, hurts, difficulties, and other problems as though they were major catastrophes.

The parent may overreact in the very opposite direction, yet produce the same result. These are parents who, instead of shielding and overprotecting the child, try to push their children into being little heroes. "Don't be afraid" they tell the child in situations where there is good, realistic reason for the child to be hesitant and fearful. "Don't be a baby." "Don't be a sissy." Fearful of being rejected or scolded by the parent, the child is not only afraid to show fear, but even to feel it, when he rightfully should. The end result is that the child becomes more frightened—not less—and his fearfulness spreads to other areas, becoming part of his personality pattern.

Often a patient will say, when asked about fearfulness as a child, "Not I! I was a regular daredevil. I'd get into everything and be absolutely fearless." And in the case of women, "I was a regular tomboy. There's nothing the boys would do that I was afraid to do."

In cases such as these we think of the possibility of counterphobic reaction, meaning that the child acts fearlessly in the face of real danger, which is his way of masking a fear he is unable to confront and handle. But then, in a crisis situation, this protective layer is broken down and the underlying vulnerability is exposed, with the possibility of a phobic eruption.

The case of Mrs. Anita M., thirty-eight years old and the mother of three children, provides a remarakble illustration how a mother's abnormal anxiety can transmit itself to the child and how this can shape the child's personality right on into adult life.

Anita came for help because she was in "a terrible state."

I'm afraid. I'm afraid to go out and I'm afraid to stay home. When I go to drive anywhere, even with somebody else in the car, I get a panic attack. I get a rapid pulse. I hyperventilate. I begin to choke and I get dizzy. My palms get sweaty. I feel like something terrible is going to happen. I want to jump out of the car to get away. I have to run. I have to escape. I'm not safe. I don't feel safe in the house and I don't feel safe outside. I don't even feel safe in my doctor's office. If I'm away from my house, I'm afraid that I might get an attack and no one is going to be there to get me to a hospital. Hospitals are scary, but I know that if something happens to me, that would be the only safe place where they would take care of me—the only place where I would feel safe.

The last six months have been a living hell. I can't even go a couple of miles away from my house without getting the physical symptoms—the fast heartbeat, the hyperventilation, the sweaty palms, the shaking all over. I feel like I'm going to pass out. I don't feel normal, like my body is detached. I feel like my insides are running away from my body—like another person was inside of me, running, escaping, to keep up with my rapid pulse. I won't get on an elevator because I'm afraid it'll get stuck and I'll have a heart attack and I won't be able to get out. I get up early in the morning so as to avoid crowds, because I can't breathe in crowds.

I'm constantly worried about my husband cheating on me, and this has been going on for eighteen years—every year since we've been married. He says he can't take it any longer. He has to go to San Francisco for a week on business and he wants me to go with him. I want to go, but I don't want to. If I stay home, I'm afraid he'll cheat on me. If I go, I can't stand being in a hotel room by myself. I just don't feel safe anywhere.

This recitation, which opened Mrs. M.'s first therapy interview, was made in just the very same jerky frenetic way in which it is recorded here, reflecting Mrs. M.'s frantic state of mind. A little later in the interview, she spoke about her childhood and her early youth.

I was always a scared child. I had bad dreams, night after night. Many of them had to do with death. I was terribly afraid of dying. My mother was very neurotic. When I was sick, she would run out into the streets screaming that I was dying. When any one of us was sick, she used to run out of the house saying she couldn't take care of us, that we were too sick. That's where I got the idea I was going to die. As a child and teenager, I was a very nervous person. If I had a bloody nose or cut myself, I knew I was going to bleed to death; if I had the flu, I'd think I was dying. It never was the way it was with other kids: "So I've got a bloody nose; so what." For me it was the end.

My phobia started when I was fourteen. I was on a bus, all the way in the back and it was packed. All of a sudden I panicked. I had to get to the front where I could breathe. But no one moved. I felt like I was lost. I feel lost a lot of the time, even in places where I've been a hundred times.

After the bus incident, I didn't want to be in any crowded place because I couldn't breathe. . . . I was afraid I wouldn't get enough oxygen, and die. I used to miss a lot of time from school so I wouldn't have to go through the halls with all the kids; I was afraid I wouldn't be able to breathe. When I was sixteen, I stopped taking ballet because I couldn't catch my breath. I went to all sorts of doctors and got all sorts of hospitals tests and they all told me there was nothing wrong with me, but that didn't make me any the less afraid.

EXCESSIVE DEPENDENCY ON PARENTS

Excessive fearfulness in children is generally associated with excessive dependency on parents—a condition psychiatrists refer to as "separation anxiety." The child is terribly frightened when he is separated from the mother, even when she is out of sight for only a few minutes. Being lost can be, for these children, a terrifying experience. Absence of the mother when she goes on a visit or to the hospital can be greatly upsetting. Separation from the mother when the child has to go off to school can be traumatic, and in the more extreme cases, we see the development of school phobia.

Elisa, twenty-four years old, gives this account of some of her experiences in childhood.

As a child I was afraid of being separated from my mother. When I went to school, she had to stand by the school window where I could see her. When I went away to camp as a child, I would put up every kind of resistance to going, and when I got there, I would get sick and cry and they had to send me home. I remember when I was watching a TV movie about Heidi—I was about seven years old—and when it came to the part where her parents died, I got an anxiety attack, and I even started to hyperventilate then, the way I do today. Even when I grew up, even after I was dating, when I went away on vacation and I was away from my mother, I would get very nervous.

Elisa lives with her mother now (her parents are divorced). She worked in the same office as her mother, before the onset of her phobia. Her mother drives her to and from the phobia clinic. Elisa dreads being by herself during the day when her mother goes to work (now that Elisa is no longer going to work with her). She stays in bed as long as she can, sleeping and dreaming and making the hours go away until her mother comes home from work. It is uncanny how so many young agoraphobic patients tell you that this is what they do when their mother is off to work, even using almost exactly the same words.

Another patient, Henry M., recalls how he and his mother were inseparable. He was the youngest and when the other children were off to school, his mother would take him with her everywhere, since there was no one with whom she could leave him. He remembers something that happened when he was about five years of age.

My mother had to leave me alone for about a half hour. There was something she needed to do, where she just couldn't take me along. She gave me some candy, and told me to play with my toys and she would be back in just a few minutes. I started to cry and clung to her, but she had to go and just pushed me away and left, locking the door behind her. I was able to wait a little while, without crying, thinking she'd be right back, but when she didn't I started to cry and scream and beat the door—it reminds me a little of the way I feel now when I get a phobic attack. It also reminds me of the way I felt, when I was already phobic and my wife and I were up on the Cape for a few weeks. I would stay inside the cottage we rented, except when we both drove to get groceries. When we went into the supermarket, I would cling to my wife—almost physically—and I trailed her every step like a puppy dog. One instant my attention was attracted to something else and when I turned to look for her she wasn't there. If I wasn't a grown man I would have started crying. At first I was petrified, but then I started running up and down the aisles, becoming more and more agitated when I didn't see her. I was ready to run to the courtesy booth and have her paged. But then I saw her and I felt the kind of relief I must have felt when my mother came back after leaving me in the house alone that time.

We see, from these examples, that the "separation anxiety" is not just a fear of being separated from the mother, but rather a fear of being separated from the safety which the mother has always provided in a situation where danger or injury is anticipated.

This pattern begins to manifest itself from early infancy on. As the infant begins to crawl and later to toddle around, exploring his surroundings and venturing into new activities, he is reassured by his mother's presence. If something frightens him or hurts him, he comes scooting back to the safety of his mother. If, as he is growing up, he has frightening dreams, is told a frightening story, is threatened by another child or an animal, he comes running to his mother for reassurance and protection. If he cuts himself, falls, or burns himself, he comes to mother to be comforted.

Most children are able, little by little, to move away from this area of safety, developing a feeling of confidence about themselves and an ability to cope emotionally with their own injuries and frights. They continue to be more and more involved in the reality of their surroundings and their activities, and consequently are able to expand their area of safety. Places outside of the home become "safe places"—school, friends' homes, the street outside the home—and the circumference widens and expands continually. People other than the mother become "safe people"—teachers, older brothers and sisters, neighbors, aunts and uncles.

But this does not happen with equal ease and certainty for all children. Some children—because of inborn temperament, upbringing, or both—remain closely dependent on the mother and father as their basic "safe people" and to the home as the basic "safe place." They cling to the parents and the home as safe havens, not only in the case of real dangers but also for protection from imaginary dangers. When they are alone—when the mother is away—whatever fears these children have become worse. With the mother—their basic reality contact—absent, the imagination is given free play, without restraint. The child experiences this as spiralling terror culminating in an outbreak of panic. School phobia is a perfect example.

The child in whom the problem of school phobia develops is one who has remained closely attached to the mother and the home for safety, and feels frightened on being separated from the mother, even for brief periods. Up to the time when he has to go off to school, this child has hardly ever been out of the mother's (or father's) presence for more than a few minutes at a time. Then comes the day when mother will bring him to school and leave him there. Days before the actual event, the child begins to have all sorts of imaginary fears—fears that he will be left in school and never be able to come home again; fears that something might happen to his mother while he is away at school, and that she will not be there when he comes home; fears that the strange adults with whom his mother is going to leave him may hurt or punish him—whatever frightening ideas and images his overactive little imagination can manufacture. These frightening thoughts and images multiply and intensify, and by the time the first day of school arrives, they are out of control. The experience is so distressing that the child frequently develops some sort of physical ailment. If that doesn't save him, he will put up all sorts of resistances to going, and then, when he is finally deposited in school, his mother's departure evokes an explosion of frightened weeping and screaming. Every instinctive force in the child is mobilized to take him away from this "dangerous place" and get him back to the safety of his mother.

The reaction of the agoraphobic person is not unlike that of the child with school phobia; the underlying process is the same. For this child, school is the phobic situation. It sets the child's imagination to creating a host of frightening thoughts and images, impelling the child to flee to the safety of home and mother. For people with agoraphobia, there can be a whole range of phobic situations, each one having the same effect, culminating in flight to the safety of the home, and in many cases to mother—or if not mother, then some other safe and trusted adult who offers the same kind of protection as was once offered by the mother.

OCCURRENCE AT TIME OF IMPORTANT LIFE CHANGES

The first agoraphobic attack generally occurs between the ages of seventeen and thirty-five. This happens also to be the period in life when the young adult encounters and has to deal with many of the major tasks and responsibilities of life. This doesn't just happen to be coincidental. It is our belief that agoraphobia erupts when a person confronts a major life change and feels unable to handle it. The phobia is an acute expression of the feeling of fright, helplessness, and powerlessness in dealing with the new life problem or task. It happens, in our opinion, to those who have not learned, because of circumstances, to deal with fears, worries, problems, and difficulties at the time when they arose.

Let us trace this development, beginning with the time of adolescence. At this point in life, the emerging adult is breaking away from parental protection and striking out, more or less on his own, either going off to school or finding work. The first serious sexual encounters are made, involving deep and sometimes upsetting interpersonal relationships. A little later come the questions about "the future," engagement, marriage, setting up a home, having children, sickness, death, and in these days, separation and divorce.

Some young people, as they are growing up, are able to anticipate the important tasks and changes that are due to come their way, well in advance of the time they have to deal with them. They handle the anxiety and do realistic planning. Then, when the task or problem comes up and has to be dealt with, they are prepared, practically and emotionally. Other young people are not able to develop this kind of realistic and effective approach. Instead of tackling a task or problem, they push it aside or let others worry about it, repressing their fears and anxieties. But reality cannot be held off forever, and when it comes time for a major life move, they are unable to make it. The dangers and difficulties associated with leaving home, getting a job, entering into a serious relationship, becoming engaged, getting married, and having a child loom up too suddenly for them, and they are unable to handle them. Their worst fears, which they had buried, break through and multiply. The emotional disturbance which follows becomes invasive and pervasive, affecting most other areas of life. In this state the individual is sensitive and vulnerable to irrational frights and the outbreak of agoraphobia.

When asked about the initial occurrence of their agoraphobia, patients will generally report that they were not aware of anything special happening in their lives at the time of the occurrence. Most say—"It just came on, out of nowhere." But as the therapy continues and as they continue to talk about their life situation, it comes out, in a very large percentage of cases, that the attack came on at a point where an important life change was occurring, or was going to occur. The significant factor in the change seemed, in these cases, to be the confrontation of new fears for which old systems of security were no longer adequate.

In the case of one patient, the phobia erupted at a time when her fiance was pressing her to get married. The marriage would entail not only that she be separated from her mother, on whom she was intensely dependent, but also that she move from the United States to live with her husband in England, and that she travel with him, because of his business, to Japan, Australia, and other faraway places. Here is her account:

> Can you imagine me doing all that and I had never been further away from home than a vacation trip in North Carolina? Even on those short trips away from home, I would feel anxious and homesick, and I couldn't stand being away from my mother for that long. I had to call her every night and even that didn't help. I had to cut the trip short, every time, and come home. This happened, mind you, when I was nineteen and twenty years old. But don't get the idea that I'm a helpless baby. I have run my own travel agency; I have owned and operated a gourmet shop —and this while I was still in my early twenties. So, my being a capable person had nothing to do with it. It was just the separation from the home I had known all my life, and from mother. I was upset by the idea of settling in a new country, with a new mother—my mother-in-law to be—and then having to fly to all those distant parts of the earth.

In the case of another patient, several important life changes were occurring at about the same time, and it was in the course of these changes that her first agoraphobic attack occurred.

> I was three months pregnant at the time, and it wasn't anything I was looking forward to. I had been an anxious and overprotected child myself and was never able to take on any responsibilities without becoming fearful and upset. I didn't have much confidence in myself, and was afraid of difficulties and problems. The thought of going through childbirth was frightening, but the thought of having this helpless little infant that would be dependent on me for survival was terrifying. I didn't take the pregnancy very well physically, either. I would get morning sickness, weak spells, dizziness, and whatnot. At just about the same time, my father died, and while I was never attached to him too closely, I had felt secure with him around. When he died, it was as though I was left without anyone to lean on. My mother was too involved in her business enterprise, and I had the feeling she hardly ever knew that I was even around. Then, along came the war [World War II], and I was frightened to death that they were going to draft my husband and that I would be left by myself with the baby.

The attack came as this patient was on a train heading for New York to meet friends for lunch and a theater matinee.

I wasn't paying any attention to anything, just reading and relaxing, when I felt a stab of pain in my insides. The first thought that flashed into my mind was, "Oh my God, I am going to have a miscarriage right here on the train." Then I became terribly frightened. I had a vision of myself going into a convulsion, of the fetus being expelled and slipping down to the filthy floor, and this was more than I could bear. I became faint, and it became dark in the car, as though the lights had gone out. I got out at the next station and called my husband, who drove all that way to get me and take me home.

From that point on the phobia spread in rapid order to buses, bridges, highways, city traffic, country and mountain roads, stores, streets, and auto travel of any kind except when accompanied by someone else. For five years, this woman was unable to leave her house at all, but then, with the help of psychotherapy, she was able to open up a little "safe area," within a two-mile radius of her home, within which she could move—going to stores, meetings, and social visits—but only if accompanied by her husband or close friends. This situation continued, unimproved, until 1980—when she entered into contextual therapy.

Pregnancy and the birth of a child are reported with remarkable frequency in the reports of patients as they tell about significant life changes in process at the time of the first phobic attack, as do commitments to be married and marriages. Also mentioned with some frequency are taking on new and responsible jobs, moving out of the parents' household and setting up one's own, the breakup of a love relationship, or the serious illness or death of someone to whom the patient has been closely attached.

In all of these situations, the individual is either threatened with the loss or breakup of a setting or relationship in which he or she feels safe and secure, or else is actually going through or has already gone through such a disruption.

Childbirth can be threatening for a number of reasons. Some women are terribly frightened of the pain they may have to endure. They may also be anxious about the possibility of having to go through a complicated pregnancy with its attendant risk to life, and since phobic people are notoriously imaginative in anticipating dangers, their minds may be filled with frightening thoughts of dying in childbirth.

Childbirth may also be threatening on a purely psychological level. Giving birth to a child means giving up one's own status as a dependent person and becoming a mother. One patient expressed this concern very succinctly, in these words:

> I had to come to terms with the fact that I could no longer be the baby, where I could continue to look to my mother to worry about me and comfort me, to make me feel safe and reassure me that nothing bad was going to happen to me. The birth of my baby would mean that I would have to give up the role of the protected child and become the protector of a new little soul. That was hard to take. It was frightening. It felt like I was leaving the womb and would have to take on life and all its problems by myself, standing on my own two feet.

This patient was also terrified about taking on the physical responsibility of caring for a helpless infant, of not being competent to take care of it, of not knowing what to do if the infant became sick, of being responsible for the infant's life.

Engagement to be married and marriage mean taking on adult responsibilities in permanent relationships. Most people can handle this more or less routinely. They just swing into it, naturally. For others, this can be very frightening, testing their confidence and self-reliance. Engagement and marriage also mean moving out of the safe and protected haven of the parental home and working to build a new haven with another person, and that is why so many young people insist on staying in the same household. They are frightened to move away and be separated from the safety they have known all their lives.

Young men and women who have been overly dependent on a parent or parents are likely to transfer this dependence to a wife or husband upon marriage. They look to the spouse for the protection and safety which they had formerly received from the parents. When the marital relationship is threatened or broken up, this newly found safety is lost, which for most people—and especially for an overdependent person—can be a very frightening experience, resulting frequently in a prolonged period of heightened anxiety and depression. The death or prolonged illness of a spouse or parent, with whom there has been a close dependency relationship, is capable of producing the same effect.

Marital quarrels can be as potent as an actual marital breakup in producing the state of intense, chronic anxiety out of which a phobic reaction is likely to erupt. People who are overly fearful and insecure carry this insecurity into their marriage, never really sure of themselves, never really confident that the relationship—one on which they are greatly dependent for their sense of safety—is going to last. When a quarrel occurs, it brings to the surface, in a forceful and frightening way, long-standing and often repressed fears that this person is going to be abandoned and left to live out his life alone.

There are some cases where exploration fails to reveal that any observable life change was taking place at the time of the phobia's onset. This does not necessarily mean that nothing of importance was happening at the time; only that it may not have been observable, meaning that the change may have been going on inside the person's mind, and that he or she might not even have been aware of it.

There was, for example, a case that was reported by a psychiatrist in a professional journal. It had to do with a young man who was still living with his parents at the age of thirty, never having had a serious love affair, and still dating only occasionally on a casual basis. He had had his first phobic attack when he was twenty years old, and from then on he had been housebound except for an occasional venture away from his home, accompanied by a brother or one of his parents. His work was that of carpenter and cabinetmaker, and he operated a little woodworking shop just a block away from his home. He came for psychiatric help because of depression and intense anxiety attacks. His problem with agoraphobia had not come up until after several sessions. He had accommodated so well to its restrictions that he didn't even regard it as an important problem. Therapeutic exploration disclosed that at the time his phobia came on, he was dating a young woman who was pressuring him to get married. His parents, anxious for him to become independent and start his own family, were also pressuring him. He, however, was frightened to leave his parents' home; further, he was not strongly motivated by sexual needs, nor by a desire to have a family. When his phobia came on, he had no idea it had anything to do with this problem, and even after months of therapy, he would not acknowledge any association. Yet, from other evidence that he provided, it seemed possible to the psychiatrist that not only did his phobia reflect his intense emotional upset at the time, but also that it served the purpose of keeping him where he wanted to be—at home with his parents.

DEPRESSION

Many of those who suffer from agoraphobia report that throughout the course of their disorder, they have also been experiencing intermittent spells of depression of varying degrees of intensity, ranging from mild dejection to near-total immobilization. The nature of and explanation for depression has already been discussed in detail in Chapter Three, and we refer the interested reader to that discussion. In some cases, patients say they were troubled by depression before the onset of their phobia; others, that it became apparent only during the course of the phobia and appeared to be a reaction to the helplessness and hopelessness imposed by their sharply curtailed life-style and by their being deprived of the friendships and pleasures which they had formerly enjoyed.

The case of Annette V. is typical. Here is how she tells it.

I don't know whether my sister's problems had any bearing on mine, but they always affected me very deeply and so I will tell you about them. She was ten years older than I, and she was not only my "big sister," but in many ways I felt about her as though she was my mother. So, when about eleven years ago she developed diabetes, then thyroid illness, then cancer, I was in a state of constant worry and upset about her, and I must have been depressed, too. I didn't know it by that name and I wasn't even aware that there was anything wrong with me, but now that I know about depression I'm sure that's what I had. I couldn't concentrate on my work. I was moody lots of the time and just couldn't enjoy anything. I would get up in the morning feeling very tired and could barely get up the energy to get out of bed, and when I did finally get up, I had this feeling: "What's the point. Life is so difficult and it's such a drag. I wish I would just die during the night and not get up in the morning." Sometimes I would wake up at four or five in the morning and not be able to get back to sleep, and all the time I would be feeling very anxious about something terrible going to happen, like losing my job and all my savings and having to go on relief, which of course was nonsense, but that was the way I felt.

About seven years ago, I had my first attack—my first panic attack. I was driving on the expressway when it happened. It was a route I had to travel daily, and then it happened again several times during that week; then it happened a number of times, driving in town the following week. I went to the doctor and he diagnosed it as "vertigo virus." The medicine he gave me didn't help, so I went to several more doctors—you know the routine, I'm sure. I stayed home for three months and didn't go anywhere. Then I got really depressed, and I knew I had to do something. I couldn't just abandon my children, and I didn't want to give up my work—I'm a teacher. So I made myself get out a little at a time, and I resumed local chores in my town and surrounding towns. You could say I hacked out a safe area within which I could operate. I did have anxiety, but no real panic attacks, and I was able to function fairly well within those limits. But I was terrified to venture further alone, and even with somebody along, I would not travel too far. I also have phobia for heights, open spaces, open parkways, and being off the ground in a chair lift. Planes, escalators, and elevators don't bother me.

The worst depression came when I was at home, three months after my first attacks. Every day when I got up, I would think of myself being imprisoned in my home, unable to do the things I loved to do—driving, skiing, concerts, the theater. I had anxieties about my children being out there in the world, without me, and I imagined all sorts of things happening to them. My husband became impatient with me, and that depressed me even more, because I felt so alone, suffering all by myself. But, fortunately, I must have had strong internal fortitude, because I was able to drag myself out a little at a time, and make myself operative again, even if only to a limited degree.

Even today, I continue to be depressed about still being subject to my phobias, about not being able to go where I want to, and do what I want to. All of life has such a gray, colorless, tasteless feeling. Just dragging on from one day to the next, without any enjoyment or hope or anticipation.

DEPERSONALIZATION

Depersonalization is not actually a trait, but rather a symptom that occurs, in many cases, as part of the agoraphobic syndrome.

The patient may feel unreal, disembodied, or cut off from his surroundings.

Here is how one patient described this experience:

> It happened while I was having lunch in the department store restaurant. I was feeling tired and a little worried about a pain in my chest. Then, for no reason at all, I was seized with an attack of anxiety, a feeling that something terrible was going to happen. I could feel my heart pumping and miss a beat, and that frightened me worse. My hands were shaking. I stood up but my legs wouldn't carry me. *The lights seemed to get dark and the people looked unreal. I had a funny feeling that I was outside my body observing myself as though I were somebody else, a stranger.*

And another patient described it this way:

> My mother had gone out and I was alone in the house. I knew I was going to become anxious, so I deliberately went about doing things to keep myself busy. I did the dishes, dusted, moved around some furniture, but that just helped a little. *I started to feel a dullness in my head as though it was filling with cotton. Then I went into the bathroom to wash my hands and looked at myself in the mirror. It was a stranger's face looking out at me. There were two people there: one in the mirror looking out at me, and me looking in at that other person in the mirror.*

And still another description:

> This sort of thing used to happen to me when I was growing up and still keeps on happening to me these days, as an adult. *I'll be sitting in a room with people and all of a sudden I have a feeling that I am not really there; that my mind is outside my body. When this happens, I get up and walk out and it stops, and when I get back it's alright—normal again.*

Depersonalization occurs not only in phobia but in other psychological disturbances. At times when one is strongly preoccupied by an imaginary danger—a condition existing in most psychological disturbances—contact with reality stimuli fades and both the world and the body (which is part of the objective, real world) can feel unreal.

Another related experience phobic people report is the intensification of their imagery to the point where they can actually "see and hear" the object or person that is being imagined. This may be explained by the fact that during an extraordinarily frightening experience, the mind is lifted out of reality because the organism must pay attention to and devote itself exclusively to the danger, even if it is an imaginary danger. When this happens, reality stimuli are excluded and the imagination has free play.

A case which illustrates this quite aptly is reported in a psychological periodical by Dr. Morton Schatzman, a psychiatrist. One of Dr. Schatzman's patients was a young woman who could imagine, when she was alone, her father's presence as though he were actually there. She could see "the grey hairs on his bushy eyebrows, the teeth in his mouth, the plaid pattern in his shirt; when he walked, she heard the footsteps and the rustling of his trousers; and she smelled his odor even after he'd left the room."

To get a physiological understanding of what was going on, this patient was hooked up to an electroencephalogram, and was asked to look at a square of neon lights. As she did this, the mechanism registered the electrical impulses which were generated by the visual stimuli in the occipital lobe, that part of the brain in which the center of vision is located. But when she looked at the lights and at the same time imagined her father's presence, the visual impulses from the neon lights did not register. They had been blocked or diverted and so did not arrive in the brain.

This would indicate that when a phobic person focuses intently upon some private, imagined danger, stimuli from the realistic environment do not reach the brain. Consequently, the imagery, having nothing to oppose it, is experienced as being real—similar to what occurs in a nightmare.

OBSESSIVE PHOBIAS

Agoraphobia is sometimes complicated by an obsessive dread of harming oneself or others, including fears of stabbing, strangling, shooting, or maiming. This produces a phobic reaction in which the individual assiduously avoids coming in contact with the implement he fears he might use to commit the assault. Actually the risk of translating this obsessive idea into an actual stabbing or shooting is minute indeed, and we know of no such occurrence. While the ideas themselves are very frightening, it needs to be remembered that anyone can have them. While it may not be possible for us to determine what thoughts and feelings will come into our minds, we can decide what actions we will or will not take. A person does not all of a sudden lose the inhibitions and controls which have kept him, all of his life, from committing acts of violence or aggression. It is also true that people who do have phobic-obsessive fears about maiming and killing are generally very mild, unaggressive people who would not, ordinarily, "harm a fly." In such people, restraint against violence is built deeply into the character and is hardly likely to be overcome by an obsessive idea no matter how insistent it may appear to be. Yet it can be deeply distressing, as Miriam W. relates.

> Dan and I [Dan is her husband] had been on vacation in Ver-
> mont, and we were coming home along the Massachusetts Turn-
> pike, going about sixty miles an hour. Dan was driving. I had
> nothing of any importance on my mind. Suddenly, I felt that I
> was going to reach for the door handle, open the door, and jump
> out. I became very frightened, grabbed my husband's arm, and
> told him we had to get off. I told him about this crazy thought
> and that I knew it was ridiculous. He was very sympathetic and
> understanding and he drove off the turnpike. We stopped for a
> while then agreed to take a two-lane country road and continue.
> We drove slowly, and it was alright. We were able to talk about
> it and tried to figure out what had caused it. I thought maybe it
> was the Midol I had taken. Talking about it helped, too. We
> thought that was going to be the end of that, but it wasn't. The
> next day I was frightened to get into the car. But I finally made
> myself do it, and my husband drove very slowly, and kept on
> talking to me and reassuring me. We finally made it home over
> the distance of about one hundred and fifty miles.
>   I thought that it would be different with myself driving; my
> hands would be on the steering wheel and I couldn't grab the
> door handle. But it was worse. Now I was afraid I would turn the
> wheel and deliberately crash into another car, so I stopped driv-
> ing altogether. About two weeks later, I read a book about a
> woman who imagined that she was going to kill her two little
> children. My husband was away at a friend's house. My little
> boy—he's four—was playing near where I was sitting, reading.
> My two older children were upstairs doing their homework. Sud-
> denly I got this terrible thought that I was going to harm my little

boy, that I was going to go to the hallway where my husband keeps his tools and take a hammer—it's just too horrible to say it, but I have to—that I was going to take a hammer and crush in my little boy's skull, or go to the kitchen and take a knife and stab him. I jumped up and called my two older children to come down and stay with us. I gave them some kind of excuse. Next day, when they left for school, I was in a panic. My stomach was in a knot. I couldn't eat. I got nauseous and threw up. I wondered whether I was going crazy. I didn't let myself stay alone in the house with my little boy and went out shopping and visiting, anything to not be in there alone with him, for fear I would do that horrible thing. I tried to stay out until school was over and the other children came home. With them there, or with my husband there, I felt safe, that I wouldn't do anything.

Then, something new started. I started to be afraid to go out because I might do something crazy. I was afraid I might jump in front of a car and get killed. I had no desire to kill myself. I was just afraid I would get this terrible compulsion to do it. Then, when I did go outside, especially when the children were with me, or when I was visiting or at the store, it was better. Sometimes, when we were walking and I felt this thought coming on, I moved away from the edge of the sidewalk and walked very close to the buildings and grabbed hold of my child's hand or arm, to keep myself from doing something terrible.

A STEEL WORKER WITH OBSESSIVE PHOBIA

Another case of obsessive phobia concerns the steel worker mentioned very briefly in an earlier chapter—the one who had his first phobic attack while walking out on a girder of a building under construction. It occurred, as you may recall, when a gust of wind caught him and almost upset his balance. Until that time, he had never been sensitive to the heights at which he had been working. Suddenly he became aware of the height and was afraid not only that he would fall, but also that he might jump. After that, he would not venture onto any exposed elevation, and in short order his phobia spread to other heights, automobiles, trains, expressways, bridges, city streets, and other situations.

As his perimeter of operation narrowed and as he had to spend more and more time in his home, a new anxiety erupted, a fear that he might harm himself or his wife or children with some lethal weapon or implement.

I have had a shotgun ever since I was a teenager, and I have used it to go hunting every fall. Now, all of a sudden, it became a frightening weapon. I was afraid I might take it and shoot one of my two boys or my wife. I can't be in a room alone with a sharp knife. I'm afraid I might take it and stab somebody. I'm becoming more and more depressed and now I'm afraid I might lose control and kill my whole family, then commit suicide. A few nights ago I was watching TV with the boys, and my wife was doing some sewing. I had to make some excuse about getting her to stop sewing. I wanted her to take her sharp scissors out of the den, because I was afraid I might go nutty and stab her. I was passing a place where they had dug a deep excavation for a building—about forty feet down—and I had to move away because I was afraid I might jump in. This thing has become so frightening and upsetting, I think I'm going to go crazy; I've even thought about putting the muzzle of the shotgun in my mouth and blowing my brains out.

Thoughts and impulses of the kind experienced by the woman and man whose cases we have just reviewed are part of the human repertory. Where they come from and why they arise we do not fully understand. But we know that it is entirely natural in our culture for a person to have these frightening impulses, and that having them certainly does not mean that they will be carried into action. People become frightened of the thought as though it were the act. It needs to be remembered that normally and routinely we have unpleasant and undesirable thoughts, but that we do not carry them out into action. How often do we say and really feel, "I could kill that man," and then, of course, do nothing of the kind. It is true that the unbidden thought about killing one's child or mate with a knife, gun, or hammer is much more painful to deal with, and much more irrational. But it, too, is no more than a thought and should not be regarded with abhorrence and terror as though it were an act.

We need to be aware that we are constantly being bombarded, on television and radio, with violent images and ideas, and that we are subject to their arousal, from within, by chance associations. The fact that they do come into our minds should not be given any special significance.

Is it ever possible at all that such thoughts might be converted into action? Yes, it is theoretically within the realm of possibility, but it is most improbable and is not dependent on some turn of fate. It is dependent on the control each of us has, and uses constantly, to keep harmful thoughts from becoming harmful deeds.

Some people who have these thoughts are not only frightened of the thought itself, but also of the fact that they could have such thoughts. They think, "What kind of horrible person am I to have such thoughts?" They flagellate themselves for even having them, thinking that this is a blemish on their character or that it makes them out to be an undesirable person. This is an extremely high and rigid standard to impose on oneself—not only *not to do bad things* but *not even to have bad thoughts*. When these thoughts come, these people attempt to banish them, to push them out of mind, to deny them. Aside from the fact that this imposes an unbearable burden, it is also impossible to achieve. Once these thoughts and feelings are generated, once they come into the mind, it is impossible to push them out. They are beyond voluntary control. What is more, the harder one tries to squelch these thoughts, the more intense and powerful they become.

These thoughts about harming a child or spouse are handled, in contextual therapy, in the same way as are other phobic thoughts and images—by lifting the patient out of his preoccupation with his imagination, and putting him back into contact again with the realm of familiar and comforting reality. The actual procedures will be discussed later.

CHAPTER FIVE

Causes and Treatment of Phobias

MANY PATIENTS, in the course of their treatment, ask about the causes of their phobia. They want to know: "Why did it happen to me? Does it have something to do with my personality, my upbringing? Is it hereditary?" We believe that our readers, too, want to know.

There are no certain answers to these questions, but there are several theories, including the one on which contextual therapy is based. But before we proceed to set forth these different explanations, we need to make it clear that in our opinion, knowledge about the past, though helpful, is not essential for the effective control of a phobia. It is more important that people know the *immediate cause* of their phobic behavior. This cause—the same for everyone—is to be found in the nature of the process by which the human organism reacts to the imagined dangers in the phobic situation, namely, the phobogenic process.

Because of their basic personality and because of the special experiences they have had, some people will come to a point where they perceive a particular situation or object or animal as being highly threatening or dangerous, and will react to it automatically with fright or dread, although no real danger is present or perceived.

The reaction to the imagined danger generates a host of

thoughts, images, and bodily changes, which themselves are frightening, and which in turn trigger a new series of reactions. This escalating and spiralling sequence culminates in a state of chaos or panic.

In the process, the individual loses contact with those elements in the phobic setting which are familiar and reassuring, and which he can otherwise manage and handle. The frightening thoughts and feelings are so powerful, they blot out everything else.

Treatment is therefore directed toward helping the person to learn how to stay involved, deliberately and systematically, with familiar, reassuring, and manageable aspects of the phobic situation, and to understand what is happening. This halts the disorganizing, fear-generating (phobogenic) process, controls the level of fear, and overcomes the phobic reaction.

WHAT CAUSES PHOBIAS?

Having made these points about the immediate cause of phobias, we will discuss the various theories concerning the causes in the past—the paths by which people arrive at the point where they are susceptible to the eruption of a phobia.

The Contextual Therapy View

The central idea in the contextual therapy view is this: People reach the point where they can become phobic because they have never learned to deal with and handle the real and imaginary fears which are a normal part of the human experience.

Some fear reactions become evident very early in infancy: fear of any intense, unexpected stimulus, such as a loud sound or a sudden movement; also, strangers, heights, loss of support, and animals. Later there is an expansion in this catalogue to include the dark, illness, doctors, storms, and supernatural phenomena (the "boogeyman," witches, monsters, ghosts, demons, and the like). The inventory will also include all those situations in which the child—or someone he knows—has been injured. He will become afraid of sharp knives and razors, hot stoves, uncontrolled fire, unprotected heights, speeding automobiles, and so forth. He will also react with fearful anticipation to scolding, punishment, rejection, disapproval, embarrassment, and failure.

When a fear besets a child—whether it be fear of a stranger, a dog, a monster, or any of the other hundreds of things of which a child might be frightened—he reacts with instinctive responses. He may scream or weep, or hide under a bed, or run to mommy or daddy. He has nothing to fall back on, by way of knowledge, understanding, or experience, that will enable him to put these feared objects in their proper, realistic perspective, and thus come to the conclusion, on his own, that they are not dangerous. The way he eventually learns that the stranger will not harm him, that the dog will not bite him, and that the "boogeyman" is not really there, is mainly through actual experiences, guided by communication with his parents. The parents feed into his perceptions accurate information about the things of which he is frightened. He then uses this information to do his own reality testing, to prove to himself—by not running away and hiding—that some of the things he fears are not as dangerous as he thought them to be or not dangerous at all. He is now able to interpret his own experiences more realistically, and to learn gradually to differentiate between what is real and what is a creation of his imagination.

This is a long process for most children, and for some a very difficult one. The exaggerated, unrealistic fears can be so powerful that it takes endless relearning, with the consistent and patient help of the parents, to overcome them. If the parents do not communicate with the child about his fears, if they ignore or ridicule him and he is left to grapple with the phantoms of his imagination, he may never be able to develop sufficiently his capability to distinguish between the imaginary and the real, and may remain subject, all his life, to emotional arousal by situations and objects which in reality present no danger. Failure to communicate with the child about his fears is but one way in which this unfortunate result may be produced.

Some parents will not only ignore the child when he comes to them weeping in fright, they will scold him and punish him for bothering them, or for being a "fraidy cat." He is thus left with imaginary fears and phantoms inside his head, to cope with as best he can. The kind of devices children contrive when put in that kind of a situation is illustrated by the case of the little boy who was able to dominate the "monster" of which he was frightened by imagining himself to be "Superman." This strategy worked only as long as he was able to continue to believe himself to be this omnipotent being. But as he grew up, his reason told him that he was not and could not be Superman, stripping him of his only protection from the monster. His fear reemerged, stronger than before.

Some parents do the opposite of "pooh-poohing" a child's fears or scolding him. They exaggerate the child's danger and feed his fright with elaborations of all the things that might happen to him. Or they may themselves react with unrealistic anxiety and fright when the child comes to them after he has been hurt or has had a frightening experience. This excessive anxiety is communicated to the child, who becomes even more upset when he sees the frightened reaction of his parent. His level of sensitivity to fear is heightened, making him susceptible to arousal of fear in situations which present only the slightest danger. There are families in which fearfulness is pervasive. Children growing up in such a family are likely to become fearful by imitation, anticipating danger at every turn as they emerge from the shelter of their homes and make contact with people and problems in the world outside. Not having ever developed the capacity to distinguish between real and imaginary dangers, these children (and later, these adults) are likely to create imaginary dangers in almost any kind of a situation, and experience them as real.

Parents may have their own irrational fears which they fail to discuss with the child, leaving the child mystified and apprehensive. A mother who had brought her little six-year-old girl to be treated for school phobia disclosed that she herself was phobic about rain. This meant that on rainy days she could not accompany the little girl on the five-block walk to school, and would have to call on a neighbor to do this or keep the child at home. The child was never given a reasonable explanation, only vague excuses. All she was able to get out of this was that it had something to do with school, something frightening she could not understand. With nothing else to go on, she filled in the vacuum with her own frightening thoughts about school, which then became the basis for her school phobia.

There is still another way in which some parents thwart the communication that would enable the child to learn how to distinguish between true and imaginary dangers. There are families in which the child is taught not to discuss or admit feelings of any kind, to keep his feelings to himself, and, most of all, not to discuss feelings, thoughts, or imaginings which might make him out to be strange, unusual, or in any way different from an idealized image of what "proper behavior and appearance" should be. Thus, when a child has a frightening thought which the family might consider to be abnormal—for example, that there is a witch in his bedroom, or that he will vomit in class or "freeze" when called upon to recite—he will keep these fears to himself, and be constantly susceptible to their rearousal. Further, he will think himself strange, different, and inferior for having them. Consequently, he is likely to try to avoid these frightening thoughts and feelings, to try to push them out of consciousness when they arise. This will cause him to be even more sensitive and worried about anything that might trigger them.

The net result of any of these misguided approaches to dealing with a child's fears is likely to make the child vulnerable to the arousal of uncontrollable, imaginary fears in any situation. In this way, one condition is established which makes that particular individual a candidate for the initiation of a phobia.

Another condition is created by the faulty methods parents employ in helping the child to adapt to and handle the real and inevitable problems and tragedies of life.

In their earnest desire to do the best for their children, and to help their children to excel, parents often make the error of hiding from the child his own limitations instead of helping the child to deal with them and put up with them. In many families, parents never talk about sickness or death. Children are kept from hospitals and funerals. Financial problems are never discussed with the children present, and family discord is kept a secret. In this kind of setting the child is likely to grow up with a rosy and unrealistic view of life, and truly expect that nothing "bad" is ever going to happen to him. Consequently, he will not get to know about the real problems and dangers of life in time to develop responses which will enable him to deal with them when they arise. Then when he is on his own—out of the reach of parental protection and buffering—he will panic when confronted with any new or difficult problem.

This, we believe, is a major reason why the onset of phobia occurs in young adults as they confront new and frightening situations: graduation from school and separation from the parents, engagements and marriage, the birth of a child, an operation or severe illness, the death of a loved one, or abandonment by a lover or spouse. The phobia is an acute expression of the hopelessness, helplessness, and abysmal, bewildering fright the individual experiences when confronted by any of these changes in his life.

As the phobia develops, this individual will be overwhelmed by the imaginary fears which beset him in the phobic situation and fall back into the understandable childhood pattern of confusing imaginary fears with real ones. Instead of reacting to them as products of his imagination, he will do as he did in childhood: react to them as though they were real.

The task of contextual therapy is to reorient the individual to the handling of imaginary fears for what they are so they do not dominate and control him. The methods by which this is done have been referred to briefly in an earlier chapter and will be discussed and elaborated in great detail in the chapters which follow.

Psychoanalytic Theory

Current psychoanalytic explanation of the phobias does not differ very much, basically, from the explanation put forward by Sigmund Freud in 1905, in his first extensive paper on the subject: "Analysis of a Phobia in a Five-Year-Old Boy." This case had to do with an Austrian child, "Hans," the son of one of Freud's colleagues, a physician. The psychoanalytic treatment was conducted by the father, guided by Freud through correspondence.

During his fifth year, the child developed a phobia for horses after seeing a horse fall down in the street. From that day on, the boy refused to venture out of his house. He was afraid that "a white horse would bite him." He even became afraid, later, that the horse would come into his room.

Before going on to Freud's explanation of this phobia, it is necessary to discuss, very briefly, Freud's idea concerning the cause of neuroses. It was Freud's original idea that when people have a distressing thought or feeling which they cannot endure because it is so painful, they get rid of it by "repressing it," by pushing it out of the conscious mind. This would apply (among others) to forbidden thoughts and wishes, those that the individual considers to be unacceptable to society. They might include incestuous sexual desires, homosexual desires, or a wish that a parent or spouse or child would be hurt or die. They might even include normal sexual feelings on the part of a child or adult who had been brought up to feel that sex is "wicked" or "dirty."

But repressed wishes and feelings do not just go away, the theory holds. They are stored in the "unconscious mind," where they continue to agitate for expression. Since they are not permitted to break through into consciousness in their original recognizable form, they emerge in disguised form. The disguised expression of the repressed wish or emotion is the symptom of the neurosis. Thus, the phobia for a horse, or elevator, or bridge, or automobile would be, in Freud's explanation, the disguised expression of a repressed wish or emotion.

Specifically, in the case of little Hans, the wishes and emotions the child repressed had to do with the mother and father. Hans was very closely attached to his mother and was very fond of being petted and caressed by her. He would miss her when she was away, even for a short while, saying that what he missed was being caressed by her. Freud interpreted this as an instinctual sexual wish for the mother. During the summer vacation that year, the mother and the child went to a resort and the father would come up for a while and then return to Vienna. When the father was away, the mother would take the child into bed with her at night. As a result, said Freud, the boy wished that his father would not come back, and later he even wished that his father were dead. These thoughts frightened the child. He was afraid that his father would find out about them and punish him. He also loved his father, and even though he saw him as a rival he could not tolerate the idea of his father being dead.

Little Hans handled these distressing feelings, says Freud, by repressing them. They then emerged, in disguised form, as fear and hatred of a horse. An unmanageable, internal fear had been externalized. The child could do nothing about his fears and other emotions pertaining to his father as they presented themselves to him consciously. But he could do something about them when they were attached to a horse, instead of to the father. (This process Freud called displacement.) Little Hans could avoid the horse. And this, said Freud, was the basis of the child's phobia. The same process, Freud asserted, is the basic explanation for all phobias—the repression of a distressing wish, fear, hate, or other emotion; its displacement from the original object to another, innocuous object; and avoidance of the object on which the emotion has been displaced.

When a phobia occurs in an adult, psychoanalysts say, it may result from the emergence of an emotion repressed in childhood, and never adequately dealt with since then, or it may be related to a problem faced by the person at the time. For example, they say, a young woman with a strong attachment to her father might develop a phobia when she is pressured by a boyfriend to get married (to leave her father). This might be because of an underlying but unrecognized sexual wish for the father. Or it may have no sexual connotations at all. The young woman might be frightened of leaving her parents' home and having to face all the new responsibilities of marriage. These feelings are repressed and may emerge as agoraphobia—a fear of being anywhere outside the parental home and safety. A man who finds marriage and its problems too difficult to deal with might wish he had never gotten married, or he might have fantasies of infidelity. While feelings such as these are not too upsetting to most people, they can be very frightening to timid, insecure people who have lived sheltered lives. Unable to deal with these feelings on a conscious level, they repress them. Then, the explanation continues, the feelings emerge as a phobia. It is no longer necessary to deal with the frightening feelings; they are "gone." They can be dealt with in their disguised form by avoiding the object or situation on which they have been displaced. Phobia offers another benefit to the person with a conflict about his marriage. Immobilized by the phobia, he does not have to make a decision about leaving the marriage. The conflict is solved for him; he cannot leave because of his phobia. This kind of additional benefit psychoanalysts call "secondary gain."

Another Psychoanalytic View

The late Dr. Silvano Arieti, a distinguished authority in the fields of psychiatry and psychoanalysis, had another view concerning the underlying psychodynamics of the phobias.

He believed that people who become phobic are especially sensitive human beings who cannot cope with their views of the world as a dangerous, treacherous place. Since they cannot escape from a world they cannot tolerate, they find a way to get rid of these feelings—they convert them into a phobia. The process would go somewhat as follows:

1. These patients have had a childhood in which they felt safe and secure. This was a state of innocence in which, protected by mother, they felt no harm could come to them.

2. From this first "stage of innocence," they pass brusquely into a second stage in which "they consider themselves exposed to the mysterious unpredictability of life, the sneak attack of a

danger, or to the errors or malevolence of others." This av̶
ing to insecurity may be brought on by the death of a re̶l̶a̶t̶i̶v̶e̶,
the discovery of a previously unsuspected dishonorable aspect
of life, or the realization that people who were once trusted
might in fact be untrustworthy or even dangerous. The future
patient has now to confront a dangerous universe. "In a way in
which he cannot verbalize, he experiences this danger as being
of vast proportions. . . . The life of everybody is always in a
precarious state, threatened by diseases, earthquakes, accidents,
fires, hurricanes, and so forth. . . ." But he feels himself to be
even more vulnerable than all the others, especially with respect
to what other people might do to him. "They may scold him,
neglect him, ignore him, ridicule him, belittle him, disregard his
rights, cheat him, rob him, enslave him, kill him."

3. With these feelings, he could become severely detached
from reality. But he doesn't. He holds on to life and reality and
becomes phobic instead. By doing so, he "reduces a diffuse and
global anxiety to a definite concrete fear; for instance, he is now
afraid only of crossing bridges. He handles this fear by avoiding
the phobic object; once he does he no longer feels the fear. He
has been able to change the source of fear from human beings
to nonhuman phobogenic objects." (In this last respect, Arieti
maintains that hardly ever, if ever at all—in the entire range of
phobias—is the phobic object or situation a human being. Almost always it is an inanimate object, or if animate, it is an
animal or insect.)

This interpretation, while somewhat elaborate, is in accordance with the views of many other clinicians that the phobic
person is one who has characteristically used avoidance as a
method of coping with emotionally difficult situations. The
avoidance technique carries over into the way he handles the
problem.

"Conditioning" or "Learning" Theory

The "behavioral" school of psychology holds that phobias
develop through a process of "conditioning" or "learning," and
that they can be "reconditioned" or "unconditioned" through
the processes of behavioral therapy. Following is an account of
the conditioning theory.

In the 1920s, John B. Watson, the founder of the "Behavior-
ism" school of psychology in this country, conducted a series of
experiments to prove that instinctive fear reactions can be trans-

ferred by "conditioning" to "innocent" stimuli, which in themselves have no fear-producing potential whatever. In one of
these experiments, a little boy ("little Albert") was given a white
rat to play with and became quite fond of it. Then, something
new was tried—the experiment. Each time the child reached for
the rat, a metal bar was struck with a hammer, producing a loud
noise. The child reacted to the frightening noise with a startle,
jumping, and tears. This was repeated several times. Then the
rat was presented to the child, without the striking of the metal
bar. The child reacted with fright—startle and crying—even in
the absence of the frightening stimulus. Just the sight of the rat
was enough to produce the reaction which had been produced
by the striking of the metal bar. An instinctive, fear-arousing
potential had been transferred to an "innocent" object which
had not produced it before.

Later, the researchers found that the fear of the rat began to
"generalize"—to spread out to a variety of other furry objects,
including a fur neckpiece, a Santa Claus mask, cotton wool, and
a toy rabbit.

The "conditioning" theory of phobias, exemplified by the
classic case of "little Albert," might be elaborated in the following contrived illustration. Each evening, for several evenings, a
mother leaves her little child alone in the house while she goes
out. The child responds automatically with fright—crying and
screaming—to the absence of his mother; eventually he becomes tired and falls asleep. The room in which the mother has
left the child happens to be across the street from a bar which
has a blinking neon light in the window. The light is reflected
into the room and is associated, in the child's mind, with the
frightening experience of being left alone. Weeks later the
mother takes the child shopping and they come to a store with a
blinking blue and red neon light very similar to the one in the
window of the bar. The child sees the light, starts screaming and
crying, and wants to run home. The mother hasn't the faintest
idea why the child is crying, thinks he is being a "bad boy," and
slaps him, reinforcing his fear reaction. The child continues to
be frightened by blinking neon lights, but manages to control
his reaction, for fear of being punished. Eventually, this specific
fright for blinking neon lights fades into the background.

The child grows up and all this is forgotten. Then comes a
stressful period, when his emotional resistance is low, and he is
susceptible to being upset by the slightest thing. Let us say he

and his wife have been quarrelling. All emotional and upset, he goes out for a walk. He happens to pass a store with a blinking red and blue neon light. Instantaneously, the old "conditioned" fear reaction is aroused. He feels a surge of terror and dread and bolts for home. He has had a phobic reaction to a specific stimulus: blinking red and blue neon lights. He hasn't the faintest notion why they arouse dread in him, but they do and so he avoids them. Later on this reaction "generalizes"—spreads to other stimuli which resemble the flashing blue and red neon lights—blinking lights of any color, neon or not; bar windows, with lights of any kind; restaurant windows that look like the original bar window. Each of these new stimuli—by "conditioning"—is able to provoke in this man the reaction produced originally, and a long time ago, when he was left alone by his mother. The dread and terror provoked in each of these phobic situations is inexplicable because the original incident has been long forgotten. But these feelings are also unendurable, and in order to avoid having them he avoids each of the situations which is capable of provoking them.

From that point on, it is possible for a new chain of conditioning to become operative. In each instance where he experienced the phobic reaction, this man found himself on a busy street. His fear reaction becomes attached not only to stores and restaurants, but also to streets and, from that point on, to any situation outside the home.

This—the conditioning theory—could conceivably account for the utter irrationality and "senselessness" of the phobic reaction. The chain connecting the phobic stimulus to the original frightening incident might be a very long one indeed, with so many links that one could not possibly relate the phobic object or situation—the phobic stimulus—at the end of the chain to the stimulus which produced the original fright at the beginning.

Dr. Isaac Marks illustrates this principle in his book *Fears and Phobias* with a case from the psychological literature. This case had to do with a woman, thirty-eight years old, who went to church very early one Sunday so she would have time to visit her husband, during visiting hours, in the hospital where he was recovering from an operation. Coming into her husband's hospital room unexpectedly, she found him holding hands with a girl she had never met before. From this encounter, she learned that her husband and this girl had been having an affair for several years. Shortly after this incident, this woman (the phobic patient) developed an intense phobic reaction for church, the section of the city where her husband's mistress worked, and several places where she had learned her husband had been with this girl—motels, restaurants, and certain streets and highways. She was entirely unaware of the connection between these phobic situations and the girl in question. They were just situations, which for reasons she did not understand, happened to arouse phobic dread. It was only after she had gone into treatment for her phobias that the connection became apparent.

Two other incidents are related here, to illustrate the dramatic turn that "phobia by conditioning" can take.

A patient with a phobia for the sound of bells was able to recall, after considerable probing in psychotherapy, that when he was a child living in Italy, he had been stricken with typhoid fever and had lain delirious and semiconscious for several days. The incident was terrifying, not only because he was afraid he was going to die, but also because he had overheard his parents quarrelling and his father threatening to leave. All this took place during a week-long celebration honoring the patron saint of the village. The church bells tolled incessantly—as he recalled it—day and evening. After his convalescence he forgot completely about the incident, and it never came to mind again until it was evoked in the therapeutic process. It came out, furthermore, that the phobia for bells came on suddenly, mysteriously, and "out of the blue" shortly after his wife had left him to go off with another man.

The other case involved a female college student. She and a group of friends had gone for an automobile ride after a party. It was wintertime, the road was iced over, and the driver lost control. The car plunged down an embankment, rolling over several times. Four passengers were killed. One, the subject of this story, remained alive. As she regained consciousness, she became aware that her friends were dead and that she herself seemed hopelessly pinned inside the wreckage. She lay that way for hours, regaining and losing consciousness. All this while, the automobile radio, which had somehow remained intact in the disaster, kept on playing rock music. Weeks after the episode, this girl developed a dislike for rock music—something she could not understand since she had always liked this type of music so much. Soon the dislike reached phobic proportions. But it did not stop there. The phobia spread—"generalized"—to situations associated with the playing of rock music—parties, dances, and concert halls.

Origin of Phobia in Trauma

The "phobia by conditioning" process we have been discussing, and which we have illustrated with several cases, has basically to do with "innocent" and essentially harmless stimuli that provoke a phobic fright reaction, having acquired the power to do so by their previous circumstantial association with a truly frightening stimulus or situation.

Somewhat different are the cases of phobia attributed to an earlier trauma involving the phobic object or situation itself, or one very similar to it. This view, too, belongs within the realm of conditioning and behavioral theory, although it is adhered to by many psychologists and psychiatrists who do not belong to this school of thought. Those who support the trauma theory cite cases of persons with dog phobia who can recall having been bitten by a dog; patients with height phobia who can recall having fallen from a height, or having seen one of their friends or relatives fall from a height; people with claustrophobia who have actually been trapped in a train, elevator, cave, tunnel, or the like; persons with an automobile phobia who have been in or witnessed a bad automobile accident; persons with a plane phobia who had been on a plane during a terrifying storm with lightning and thunder, or on a plane that had had engine problems in flight. Originating in such incidents, the phobias then spread to other situations.

Those who put forward the theory of trauma as a cause of phobia readily admit that, in a majority of cases, the individual cannot recall any traumatic incident involving the specific phobic object or situation. They are likely to add, however, that the trauma may have been so painful and frightening that it had been mercifully repressed and forgotten. The following case, which has by this time become something of a classic, is given to support and illustrate that view.

A psychiatrist was treating a young woman who had developed a phobia for running water. She could not hear a bathtub being filled or a shower running without fleeing in phobic terror. She became very frightened when she saw or heard anyone using a drinking fountain. When she rode on a train, she had to pull down the window curtain at places where the train was crossing a stream. She would resort to every kind of subterfuge to avoid running the water in the course of daily living.

Then, during a therapy session, she mentioned that an aunt she had not seen in twenty years had come to the city for a brief visit, and that during the visit the aunt said, "I haven't told anybody, have you?" The young woman had no idea what the aunt was talking about and was too flustered to ask for an explanation. The psychiatrist then suggested to the patient that she dig into her memory for any secret that she and the aunt had agreed to keep to themselves, but the patient could not produce a thing. Thereupon, the psychiatrist, who used hypnosis in therapy, put his patient into a hypnotic trance and asked her to recall what it was that she and her aunt had been keeping secret.

What came out was the story of a picnic on which the aunt had taken the patient when she was a child of seven. While the aunt was dozing, the child, disobeying orders to stay close, wandered off and was lost in the woods. When the aunt woke, she searched for the child and found her with her foot wedged between some rocks in a stream and a waterfall pounding down on her head. The child was hysterical. On the way home, the child pleaded with her aunt not to tell her mother about the incident, fearful that her mother would punish her for disobeying. The aunt, also concerned about her sister's anger, promised the child "I will never tell if you won't." With recall of the incident, the psychiatrist relates, the phobia disappeared.

Two other trauma cases are cited by Marks, in his *Fears and Phobias*, one involving dogs, the other a social phobia.

A little girl of four was playing with a pet dog, and while this was going on, the dog knocked over the child's baby sister, causing a splinter wound in her cheek. The wound became infected and the child died. Unaware of the dog's role in the accident, the mother accused the girl of knocking down her little sister and causing her death. The day of the funeral, the dog did some more damage, and again the mother blamed the child. Several days later, the little girl began to dislike dogs and soon developed a dog phobia which persisted for forty years.

The second case involves a young boy who would often pass an outdoor grocery stand on his way to school, and when passing would steal a handful of peanuts. One day the owner saw him coming and hid behind a barrel. Just as the boy put his hand into the pile of peanuts, the owner jumped out and grabbed him from behind. The boy screamed and fell, unconscious, to the sidewalk. From that point on, the boy developed a phobia for being grabbed from behind. This persisted into adult life. In social gatherings, he would arrange to have his chair with its back against the wall, so no one could come behind him. He could not go into any crowded place, such as a church, theater, or large store because it was impossible to avoid having someone behind him. When he was walking on the street, he would have to look back every few seconds, to make sure no one was walking close behind him. This phobia continued until he was fifty-five. At that time, he returned to the town of his childhood, and there he met the grocer. While they were reminiscing, the grocer told him about the incident. (The man with the phobia had forgotten it completely.) With the discussion and the recall, the phobia began to ebb, and then it disappeared entirely, after several months during which the man worked at learning to cope with his anxiety and to resist his impulses to avoid situations in which people could get behind him.

Among the case histories we have discussed earlier in this book, there are several that follow the pattern of phobia following a trauma: the man whose phobia for snow erupted after a frightening skid on an icy road to the edge of a precipice (page 45), the woman who developed a phobia for water after the boat in which she and her husband were sailing turned over in a storm (page 48), the man whose phobia for crowded places was traced to a frightening incident in a crowd in childhood (page 41), and the man whose phobia for blood had its origin in a frightening childhood injury (page 50).

It is important to repeat an observation which we have already made: In most cases, the patient is unable to recall any specific traumatic incident from which the phobia might have originated.

Instinctive Origin of Fears

An interesting hypothesis is put forward by Dr. Hans Eysenck, one of the most prolific research workers in the field of behavioral psychology. Dr. Eysenck proposes that many of the phobias are derived from instinctive fear reactions, which were useful to primitive man in dealing with life-threatening situations which he encountered in his natural environment. He would have had to fear heights because a fall from a height would kill him. Open spaces would also present a danger because they would afford him no protection in the event of a sudden attack by a human enemy or a wild animal. Confined, enclosed places would be threatening because they would prevent easy escape in the event of an attack. Snakes were natural enemies as were other animals, such as members of the cat family (lions, tigers, leopards). Darkness would be threatening because of the danger of an attack in the dark. Dr. Eysenck suggests that, although they are no longer of survival value today, since we no longer live in a wilderness, these instinctive reactions remain as part of our evolutionary, biological equipment.

All of us, Dr. Eysenck then adds, are likely to react fleetingly and faintly with an instinctive fear reaction when we find ourselves in a situation resembling the dangerous situations in which primitive man found himself—an unprotected height, a train stalled in a tunnel, a fierce dog, being lost in the woods in the dark, and so forth. But most of us do *not* develop phobic reactions to these situations. Some of us do. Why?

Reactions of this kind are quite common in childhood but fade as we grow older and as we become more confident about being able to control our environment and to deal with dangerous situations. But some children are more fearful than others. They may have been born more sensitive to such stimuli, or they may have been told frightening stories or may have had frightening experiences. They therefore remain more sensitive than other children to the arousal of the instinctive terror reactions. This sensitivity persists into late childhood, youth, and adult life, and the youth or young adult will thus be in a state of "preparedness" (a term used by Dr. Eysenck and Dr. M. E. Seligman, another psychologist) for the arousal of the instinctive fear reaction in the particular situation to which he has been sensitized. It will then take very little—only a weak stimulus resembling even faintly the primitive danger—to arouse the instinctive fear reaction in full force and bring on a phobic attack. For example, being caught in a stalled train in a tunnel, being locked briefly in a dark room, experiencing a brief surge of disorientation in unfamiliar surroundings, or experiencing a brief spell of dizziness or vertigo while standing near the edge of a roof or cliff.

The "Cognitive" View

The "cognitive" view pertains not only to phobias but to all emotional disorders. Adherents of the cognitive school believe that at the core of every emotional disorder (anxiety, depression, obsessive-compulsive behavior, phobias) is a system of erroneous ideas and beliefs the individual maintains with regard to himself and about the "threatening" world in which he lives.

The depressed person, for example, sees himself as a helpless, powerless person, one who cannot succeed, one for whom everything will go wrong. Because of this attitude, he is not motivated to set goals and avoids engaging in creative and constructive activities. His negative concepts contribute to the other symptoms of depression, such as sadness, melancholy, passivity, self-blame, loss of pleasure responses, and suicidal ideas.

The goal of cognitive therapy would be to get the patient to alter these erroneous beliefs; to see himself as a winner rather than a loser; to see himself as masterful and in control of his environment, rather than as a helpless, powerless creature controlled by forces outside himself.

In the phobias, the erroneous beliefs would have to do with what the phobic person thinks could happen to him in the phobic situation: he might fall or jump off the roof; he might drive his car off the bridge into the river; he might vomit in public or do something which will make him look ridiculous; he might be trapped in an elevator or train and suffocate; the snake might come at him and coil around his leg; the bugs might crawl up on him. Viewed from the perspective of the objective observer, none of these situations is probable or dangerous. Viewed from the perspective of the phobic person—according to his erroneous ideas and beliefs—these situations are in the realm of immediate possibility, and are fraught with danger.

How does a person arrive at these erroneous beliefs?

According to Dr. Aaron Beck, a leading exponent of the "cognitive" school of psychology, the phobias and the erroneous ideas on which they are based could develop in two ways: (1) through the persistence of childhood fears (fixation phobias) and (2) through traumatic experiences (traumatic phobias).

There are many fears which children commonly and normally experience: fear of dogs; the dark; storms; deep water; supernatural agents such as ghosts, witches, or monsters; being alone or being lost in a strange place; bodily injury; and sickness. As the child moves into social settings he also develops fears of being disliked, rejected, or ridiculed. Some children outgrow these fears; some do not. In the cases of children who do not outgrow their childhood fears, research psychologists have found the following: in many cases, the child learned these fears from a parent; in others, the parent, though free of fears, did little to help the child handle and master his fears; in still others, the child went through a painful or unpleasant experience at the time he already had a specific fear, reinforcing the potency of the fear.

When the childhood fear persisted into adult life, it served as the basis for a phobia based on the specific fear. In Beck's terminology, the adult developed a "fixated phobia" based on a childhood fear he had never outgrown.

The other route through which adult phobias may originate, says Dr. Beck, are specific traumatic events. He lists, for example, the following:

- A woman with a phobia for high places developed her phobia after she fell from a high diving board.
- A woman developed a phobia for thunder and lightning after seeing a little boy struck and killed by lightning.
- A girl developed a phobia for eating hot food, drinking hot drinks, or using a hot iron or hotplate after seeing the charred bodies of two victims being carried out of a burned house.
- A lawyer developed a phobia for appearing in court after enduring several days in court during which he feared he might lose control of his bowels because of an attack of intestinal flu and diarrhea.

The techniques which are used to correct the phobic patient's erroneous ideas and beliefs will be discussed later in this chapter.

FAMILY PATTERNS IN PHOBIAS

Several research studies have shown that "fear runs in families," meaning, first, that the general level of fearfulness is higher in some families than in others, and second, that members of the same family tend to be excessively fearful of the same things or eventualities, such as illness, contagion, electrical implements, dogs, holdups, auto accidents, darkness, strangers, travelling, and so forth.

Research also shows that phobias, too, tend to run in the family—that where one member of a family has a phobia, there is likely to be at least one other member in the immediate family or in the extended family with the same phobia or other phobias.

In the White Plains Hospital Phobia Clinic, patients report

with remarkable frequency that a mother, brother, aunt, or cousin suffers from a phobia, too. No statistical study has been made among the clinic patients about the extent of this correlation, but the impression comes through that it is high.

There is always the tendency, when a trait is found to run in a family, to see it as an inherited trait. However, it is possible to speak with equal credibility of "cultural transmission" of the trait, meaning that the young people in a family have this trait because they are imitating or being influenced by a parent, grandparent, uncle, or aunt who happens to have that same trait. There has not been enough research on the heredity-vs.-cultural transmission influences in phobias to warrant even a tentative conclusion.

How Phobias are Treated

Having gone through the various theories on the causes and the development of the phobias, we will now proceed to a discussion of the different treatment methods being used in accordance with the respective theories as to cause.

Treatment by Psychoanalysis

Psychoanalytic treatment of the phobias is by and large the same as it is for other neuroses. The therapist tries to help the patient to bring the repressed emotions into consciousness, to confront them, and to recognize that they are not "bad" or "immoral," and hence do not need to be repressed any longer. Once the patient understands these emotions, the symptoms should disappear.

Even though psychoanalysis is conducted in the office, away from the phobic situation, Freud himself stressed the importance of exposing the patient to the dreaded situation or object. Freud wrote the following:

> One can hardly master a phobia if one waits till the patient lets the analysis influence him to give it up. He will never in that case bring for the analysis the material indispensable for a convincing solution of the phobia. One must proceed differently. Take the example of agoraphobia. There are two classes of it, one slight and one severe. Patients suffering from the first indeed suffer when they go out alone; the others protect themselves

from anxiety by altogether giving up going out alone. With these last, one succeeds only when one can induce them through the influence of the analysis to behave like the first class, that is, to go out alone and to struggle with their anxiety while they make the attempt. One achieves, thereby, a considerable moderation of the phobia, and it is only when this has been attained by the physician's recommendations that the associations and memories come into the patient's mind, enabling the phobia to be solved.

Contextual therapy and other methods that bring the patient into the phobic situation do so, of course, for reasons other than those mentioned by Freud. Contextual therapy does not deal with hidden emotions and memories of the past. It deals with the current phobogenic process itself, providing the patient with techniques and understanding which serve him to reduce or block his preoccupation with imaginary threats and dangers provoked by the phobic situation.

Psychoanalytic theory is not indifferent to the relationship between phobias and patients' real life problems. It is noted, for example, in an article by Friedman and Goldstein in the authoritative *Handbook of Psychiatry* that "an adequate psychoanalytic approach to the interpretation and treatment of phobias must take cognizance of the fact that phobias are multiply determined and that an understanding of the origin of the phobic symptom often needs to be supplemented by a grasp (on the part of the therapist and the patient) of the role the phobia plays in the patient's current functioning. Thus, a phobia may become intensified—or reactivated—under conditions where realistic factors contribute to the general level of anxiety."

While psychoanalysis and psychoanalytically oriented psychotherapy continue to be used in the treatment of phobias, there is spreading recognition in the field that these methods are of limited value with this particular disorder. Friedman and Goldstein give recognition to this problem in their article in the *Handbook of Psychiatry*.

In some cases, the patient's acquisition of insight into the meaning of the phobia leads to the disappearance or substantial alleviation of the symptom, although further treatment may be needed to deal with the residual neurosis. In other cases, a good deal of working through may be needed before the insight brings about a substantial alleviation of the phobic symptoms. In still other cases, the phobias are extremely resistant to treatment.

Behavior Therapy

The behavior therapy approach to the treatment of phobias began with a classic animal experiment, in 1958, by Joseph Wolpe, a psychologist who is regarded as the founder of this school of psychological therapy.

Wolpe started the experiment by administering an electric shock to cats while they were inside a compartment of a certain color, shape, and size. The cats presumably associated the painful shock with the visual appearance of the compartment, and henceforward avoided going into that compartment or others resembling it in color and size. In the first step of the "conditioning" process, the pain-and-avoidance reaction caused by the electric shock had been transferred to the visual appearance of the compartment. Just the sight of the particular compartment was enough to cause the animal to turn away. Then this reaction "generalized"—it spread from that particular compartment to other compartments that looked like it.

This, Wolpe asserted, is what happens to people who have phobias. First, they react with dread and avoidance to one cat or one store or one bridge; then this reaction generalizes to all cats, stores, or bridges.

The next step was to devise some method by which this reaction could be reversed. Here is how Wolpe did it. He started with a compartment that was only slightly similar to the original "shock" compartment—enough to arouse some faint reaction but not similar enough to arouse total avoidance. At the same time, he fed the hungry cat some food. The drive to get the food and the pleasure experienced in eating it, Wolpe reasoned, should be powerful enough to counteract the slight anxiety and avoidance reaction stimulated by the sight of the somewhat familiar compartment. His presumption was correct. After some hesitation, the cat did enter this compartment. The next step was to repeat the process with a compartment which bore a somewhat closer resemblance to the original "shock" compartment. And again, it worked. He then proceeded with a succession of similar trials, but in each successive trial, the resemblance to the original box was greater, until finally, in the last trial, the animal would enter even the compartment in which he had originally been shocked.

This process Wolpe called "systematic desensitization." The first basic element was graded incremental exposure to the fear-and-avoidance provoking situation, paired with a pleasurable stimulus which worked to counteract the anxiety provoked by the encounter. The next step was to apply this technique to human phobias, and this, Wolpe and other researchers did do. But instead of bringing their human subjects into *real* phobic situations, as had been done with the cats, they worked with students in experimental situations in university laboratories, and asked them to *imagine* themselves going into a phobic situation, one step at a time. Here's how that would work. Let us say the student had a phobia for snakes. The research scientist would first draw up a series of situations, the first intended to induce just a little anxiety, the next a little more, the next even more, and so on up the scale. The first situation might be thinking about the word "snake," the second might be looking at a picture of a snake, the third might be looking at a snake skin, the fourth looking at a stuffed snake, the fifth looking at a tiny snake in a glass enclosure, the sixth looking at a large snake in an enclosure—right on up to the final step, which would be touching or holding a snake. All these steps, it must be remembered, were steps the subject was going to take in his *imagination*—not in reality. He was to *imagine* the word snake, then *imagine* looking at a picture of a snake, then *imagine* looking at a snake skin, etc. This succession of trials might take a week or several weeks or longer, depending on the student. Between steps, the student did deep-relaxation exercises which, like the food in the case of the cats, were intended to counteract the anxiety aroused by that step in the desensitization process. As soon as the student was able to handle the first step without experiencing anxiety, he moved on to the next, on up the scale.

This worked so well in experimental situations that it was applied next to patients in treatment, with considerable success. The results were most striking in the case of patients who had been getting traditional psychotherapy for their phobias for months or even years without much success. The new method —systematic desensitization—was enabling many patients to bring their phobias under control, some after only a few months of treatment. Furthermore, the gains were found to persist long after the completion of treatment.

Why the researchers and clinicians did not move immediately from in-the-office imaginal desensitization into actual exposure to the phobic situation is not clear. The fact is that several years elapsed before this was done. The move from the "imaginal" to the real—*"exposure"* or *"in vivo"*—approach was made on a theoretical basis. The theory behind desensitization was that it was first necessary to whittle away at the patient's reaction of dread to the phobic situation in the therapist's office, reducing it practically to zero before the patient could move into the phobic situation. Exposure or in vivo therapy was based on the theory that you did not need to "prepare" the phobic person by reducing his anxiety or dread in the therapist's office—that you could reduce the intensity of his reaction much more effectively, quickly, and permanently by introducing him into the phobic situation, letting him experience his distress, accommodate to it, and learn to cope with it.

Research and clinical experience demonstrated very quickly that real life (in vivo) exposure was superior to imaginal desensitization. Soon after this had been established, in vivo exposure became the method most commonly used in the treatment of the phobias.

At about the same time, a new procedure was being tested, called "flooding." This too was based on a prototypical experiment with laboratory animals. In this experiment, rats were placed in a cage one at a time, and the cage door was closed. A slight electric shock was then administered to their feet, through the metal floor of the cage. The rats could get away from the source of the shock—the floor—by jumping up on a shelf. This was repeated a number of times until the avoidance response was firmly established—the rats would jump up on the shelf the instant they were placed on the floor of the cage, even without being shocked. The rats' memory of the painful experience was enough to initiate the avoidance reaction. The next step in the experiment was to put the rats in a cage from which the shelf had been removed. Avoidance was thus made impossible. The rats reacted with fright and attempted to scurry up the walls of the cage. After several minutes they were removed from the cage. This was repeated again, and once more the rats tried to get away by climbing up the walls, but not quite as frantically as the first time. The third time their efforts to escape were even weaker, and after a number of additional trials, the avoidance reaction was gone. In the language of the behavioral psychologists, the avoidance response had been "extinguished."

Taking their cue from this experiment, behavioral psychologists set up research experiments with human beings—people who had simple phobias, such as a phobia for a snake or a cat. Starting again with the "imaginal" approach, the patients were asked to imagine themselves in the worst possible phobic situation. The man with a snake phobia might, for example, be asked to imagine himself in a pit full of writhing snakes, or with a snake coiled around one of his legs. These "imaginal" procedures were embellished with films and recordings about snakes. In effect the patient was being shut in with his phobic situation, "flooded" with painful phobic stimuli, and given no means of escape or avoidance. He might try to shut the dreadful images of the snakes out of his mind, but the films would keep them in front of him. If he shut his eyes, the recording would get to him through his ears. Some patients dropped out; they found they could not stand it. Others continued, and found, much to their surprise, that after a few trials the intensity of their dread was diminishing little by little, and that after several additional trials, it had become almost negligible.

The next step was to attempt this "flooding" procedure, not in an imaginal setting, but in a real-life, in vivo setting. In practice it would work something like this. With the therapist at his side, the patient would be advised to walk right into the elevator and ride up to the thirty-fifth floor, or to get into his automobile and drive across a bridge, or to get into a room with two or three cats and to stay in that situation just as long as possible, and not to attempt to leave until he felt that there was a drop in the level of his horror or dread. After this approach was tried in research and found to be effective in many cases, it was introduced by some therapists into clinical practice. At present, "in vivo flooding" is being used much less extensively than the step-at-a-time or graded exposure approach.

So much for flooding (or ungraded exposure, as it is sometimes called). In graded exposure, two different approaches are used. One is called "participant modeling"; the other is called "reinforced practice."

Participant modeling. The first step in this procedure is to set up a series of steps the patient is going to take, *in reality*, each one a little more fright-producing and difficult. (This is called a "hierarchy," which means an incremental succession, step by step, from the lowest to the highest.) In the next step, the *therapist* models each of these steps in turn; that is, he performs them one by one, in the presence of the patient. In the case of a snake phobia, for example, the therapist might first sit with the patient and look at snake pictures; then, with the patient present, he (the therapist) might handle a stuffed snake; then the therapist might approach a glass case with live snakes in it; then he might just open the lid and so forth. While he is doing this, the therapist is also doing two other things: First, he is talking to the patient reassuringly about each of the steps he is taking; second, he is observing the patient to make sure that the patient can tolerate the step he (the therapist) is taking. If the patient reacts with too much anxiety, the therapist desists, and then starts again. When the patient can tolerate seeing the therapist take that step without feeling distressed, the therapist moves on to the next step.

After the therapist has successfully mastered the most difficult step in the hierarchy—handling a snake—it is the patient's turn. This time, the process is repeated, with the therapist modeling, and the patient following him, in the step-by-step graded procedure, until the patient can master the final step, which would be handling the snake.

Reinforced practice. Here, too, a hierarchy is established, with a series of steps of increasing difficulty, the most difficult being actually staying in the phobic situation. The therapist does not model the mastery of each step. Instead, his role is to encourage and reassure the patient as he takes and manages each step, and to "reward" him at the successful management of each step by praise and congratulations. The words spoken by the therapist and his warmly expressed praise are a very important part of the process. In psychological terms, "reward"—whether it be in the form of a material object or prize, or in the form of recognition and praise—tends to "reinforce" or "stamp in" the particular piece of behavior which it follows. This is no different from giving a child a smile, a pat on the back, a "gold star," a crayon, or a cookie when he has done something that is correct. The patient may soon come to recognize that the praise he gets is part of the therapeutic procedure, but that won't make any difference. He responds to it, positively, just the same. It makes him feel good, and it serves to enable him to move on to the next, more difficult step.

A series of graded steps (hierarchy) might be, in the case of agoraphobia, the following: walking out on the stoop of the building; walking a half block accompanied by therapist; walking a half block alone, with the therapist waiting at the destination; walking two blocks with the therapist; walking two blocks with the therapist waiting at the destination; crossing a street with the therapist; crossing a street with the therapist walking on the other side; going into a store with the therapist, then going in alone with the therapist waiting outside; and so forth.

Where a therapist finds that even the simplest reality step is too threatening for the patient, he may resort to imaginal desensitization or imaginal flooding first, before moving into graded exposure (reality) techniques.

Cognitive Therapy

The cognitive conception of emotional disorders such as anxiety, compulsive behavior, depression, and phobias is that they are caused by distorted ideas and thoughts the person has about himself and about what other people and the world can do to him. The distorted thoughts lead to physiological and emotional changes which produce the symptoms of the disorder. To undo the disorder, it is necessary to undo the erroneous ideas—to help the patient to "straighten out his thinking."

The therapy is conducted in the therapist's office, and the procedure is an interpersonal one, as it is in other types of psychotherapy. The first step in the corrective process is to get the patient to sort through his thoughts and feelings related to his disorder so he can recognize and define the erroneous thoughts he is carrying around in his head. The cognitive therapists say that most phobic people do not have a clear, distinct idea about what it is that is frightening to them in the phobic situation and that they sense only an amorphous dread, an unbearable feeling that makes them want to flee. It is only when they come into therapy and are asked to try to pinpoint their frightening thoughts, feelings, sensations, and images that the erroneous thoughts begin to stand out clearly and distinctly. A man who has a dread of dogs, and has never figured out what it is about them that makes him want to run away, is able to see, after a session or two of therapy, that what he is really afraid of is that the dog will jump on him, bite him, wound him, and maybe cause him to die. He realizes that he is thinking such thoughts even about a tiny puppy, a caged dog, or a picture of a dog. Once he has teased out the basic erroneous thought, he is helped to "distance" himself from it, to see it objectively as a thought, not a fact; as an idea, not reality. Having done that, he is helped to bring into play his critical, reality-testing faculties and to see how far removed his thought is from reality, how remote is the possibility that his fear could be realized. He says to himself: "That picture, that puppy, that caged dog couldn't possibly harm me."

To take another example, a female patient had a phobia for elevators, tunnels, halls, dark rooms, riding in an open car, riding in an airplane, swimming, walking fast or running, strong winds, and hot muggy days. Each of these situations aroused various thoughts and images, but running through all of them was one idea—the idea that if she remained in the situation she would suffocate and die. It was first necessary to take her through every one of these different situations—in conversation—before she could recognize and identify this one central idea. Once she could do this, she was asked to see it as thought, not reality, and then to test it against the actual probability that she would suffocate in any of these situations.

An erroneous thought many phobic people have is that they will be disapproved of, rejected, ridiculed, embarrassed, humiliated, thought to be inferior or inadequate, or thought to be "odd" or "strange." Never, say the cognitive therapists, have these people really ever tested out for themselves what would happen to them if it did come to pass that somebody actually did dislike them, reject them, or thought them silly, foolish, strange, etc. To counteract this, the therapist takes the patient down this road to the ultimate and asks him to picture for himself what would happen. "Would you disintegrate and die? Would the world stop turning? Would all your friends and relatives desert you? Would you turn into a leper?" Patients come to realize that the consequences might be unpleasant, but not disastrous, that it would not be "the end."

In the case of the patient with a fear that she would suffocate, faint, and die if she went into a crowded place, the following strategy was tried: She was instructed to write on a pad her estimates of the probability that she would die, as she proceeded toward entering the store. During the following session, she came back with these estimates: "Leaving my house, chances of dying in store 1 in 1,000. Driving into town chances 1 in 100. Parking auto in lot, 1 in 50. Walking to store, 1 in 10. Entering store, 2 to 1. In middle of crowd in store, 10 to 1."

The therapist asked her whether she had actually died in the store. Then he asked her what she thought, right there and then, what were the probabilities she might die in the store. Her answer was: "One in a million." The erroneous thought had been corrected. It then had to be integrated into her rational thought processes, and the next time she approached the store, her anticipatory dread was considerably reduced.

Cognitive therapy uses many different techniques for the different neuroses and even for the different phobias, but essentially they all follow the same course: helping the patient to (1) get at and identify the erroneous idea about the phobic situation; (2) realize this is a thought, not a fact or reality; (3) test the erroneous thought against reality to see how improbable it is; and (4) revise and correct it.

In the "revise and correct" stage, many cognitive therapists use the "self statement" technique. The patient has, by this stage, realized that as he approaches or anticipates coming into the phobic situation, he is actually "saying" things to himself, mentally, such things as "It's going to be horrible"; "I'll be trapped and I won't be able to breathe"; "I'll pass out and nobody will be there to help me." The "self statement" technique requires that the patient say positive things to himself, mentally, which are the very opposite of his negative thoughts —such things, for example, as "I'm frightening myself without any good reason"; "I can't possibly be trapped in that elevator"; "I'm not going to faint, and even if I do, there are always people around and one of them will help me"; etc. Generally, the "self statements" which the patient is going to use are prepared in advance in a list, and the patient selects and practices the ones he wants to use. These are rehearsed in the session and the patient then uses them by himself away from the therapist's office. Many patients are reluctant, at first, to use this technique because they may find it awkward and contrived. But they are told that after a while the process will become smooth and automatic and will develop into a natural response.

Cognitive therapy techniques are not always used alone. More frequently, they are used together with behavioral therapy techniques. There are several other techniques that are used in cognitive therapy, but while they differ from each other in various respects, they all accept the assumption that the patient's cognitions—thoughts, ideas, and images—can cause psychological disturbances, producing emotional and behavioral symptoms, and they all attempt to modify these cognitions, from negative to positive, and from imagination to reality.

Pharmacological Treatment

Before beginning this very brief statement on the use of drugs in the treatment of phobias, we need to warn, emphatically, that this information is not intended as a guide to the reader on the use of medication. Only a psychiatrist working directly with a patient is able to give this kind of guidance. The information given here is intended only to report what has already been found to be the case concerning the effectiveness of various psychopharmacological agents in the treatment of the phobias.

Most of the patients at the White Plains Hospital Phobia Clinic have not required drugs to get better. However, various tranquilizers may be useful in reducing the level of fear and anxiety, and thus to help the person enter the phobic situation when he might otherwise have been too terrified to so do.

Drugs have been used not only to reduce the anxiety felt before going into the phobic situation, but also to control the actual dread and panic provoked while in the phobic situation. Xanax (a benzodiazepine drug related to Valium), the antidepressants Tofranil and Nardil, and several other medications have been reported in recent years to have a good record in this respect. How these drugs work to control panic, when they do, is not completely understood. Apparently, this capability is not related to their antidepressant properties. Some phobic patients have said that after taking these drugs, they still become afraid and upset in the phobic situation, expecting the panic to erupt, but that surprisingly it does not.

It must be kept in mind that although these drugs do work to reduce dread and panic in the phobic situation, they do so only on a temporary basis. The relapse rate is high when they are discontinued. However, by reducing blinding panic, these drugs, when their use is indicated, may enable the phobic person to confront the phobic situation—as in contextual therapy—and gain the experience and understanding which we believe are essential to more thorough and lasting control over the phobogenic reaction. Once this is accomplished, the drugs can be safely relinquished. Again, we want to make it clear that, while this is our view generally, only a qualified professional, such as a psychiatrist who is aware of your particular problems, can decide the use of drugs in your specific case.

Hypnosis

Psychiatrists and psychologists will sometimes use hypnosis in the treatment of a phobia, mainly as an adjunct to another therapeutic method. Since hypnosis is not used very often, only brief mention of these different uses will be made. Hypnosis may be used to induce relaxation in systematic desensitization or other behavioral therapy approaches. The therapist may also use hypnosis to give authoritative suggestions to the patient. The patient may, for example, be directed under hypnosis to feel calm and free of fear when he enters the phobic situation, or he may be instructed to observe a snake or dog as a harmless little creature, or he may be given similar instructions which are designed to counteract the frightening perceptions and imaginings which he has in the phobic situation. Hypnosis is sometimes used to bring back into memory a traumatic incident of childhood out of which the phobia is believed to have developed. Also, it may be used by psychoanalysts to help the patient recall a "forbidden wish" or socially unacceptable impulse which had been repressed earlier in life, and which is now manifesting itself in disguised form as a phobia.

It appears that in hypnosis, the process somehow alters the way a person thinks about future dangers in the phobic situation. There are as yet no statistics on this matter, but we would conjecture that the results obtained from hypnosis would not be firm and lasting since this procedure does not result in the phobic person's basic understanding of the phobogenic process, nor does it provide him with the conceptual tools he needs to use to bring this process under his voluntary control and under his own conscious direction.

Contextual Therapy

Contextual therapy is being mentioned briefly here to help the reader fit it into the framework of other exposure therapies. (Full discussion of contextual therapy techniques will be taken up starting with the next chapter.) Contextual therapy is a form of graded exposure (in vivo) therapy. It takes the patient into the phobic situation in graded steps, starting with those that are simple and easy to manage, and proceeding to those that are difficult. The steps are not chosen on an arbitrary basis, but rather are tailored to suit the individual's own requirements, style, and sensitivities. But contextual therapy does not rely on an automatic decrease in anxiety through passive exposure. It helps the patient (1) to enter the phobic situation; (2) to focus on and become responsive to and involved with the reality elements in the surroundings; (3) to perform some activities which he can manage and control; and (4) to observe, identify, study, and understand what happens in the phobogenic process—the automatic and uncontrolled spiralling of frightening thoughts, feelings, images, and bodily reactions. The system is thus forced to switch away from preoccupation with the frightening fantasies and imaginings produced in the phobogenic process and to reorganize around realistic functioning. This strategy undercuts the phobogenic process, weakens the phobia, and brings it under control.

A fuller explanation of how contextual therapy works can be found in Chapter Six. Chapters Seven through Ten explain the step-by-step techniques that you can use to understand and face your fear and to master your phobia.

CHAPTER SIX

The "Anatomy" of Your Phobic Reaction

FEW PEOPLE WHO COME FOR TREATMENT for a phobia have a true awareness of what happens to them in the phobic situation. Most are aware only of the sudden, unexplainable surge of fear, escalating quickly into panic, and of the uncontrollable impulse to flee.

Yet an awareness of what happens to a person in the context of the phobic situation—of the interplay between his thoughts, images and bodily reactions, on the one hand, and his behavior on the other—is a primary and essential step toward eventual control of the phobia.

That is the purpose of this chapter—to examine and study the phobic reaction in the context of the phobic situation. We start by taking a close look at what happened to one young woman, in the course of her first phobic experience.

The time is 8:25 at night, the place a skyscraper in the heart of New York City's business district. Except for a small number of occupants working late, the building is silent, dark, and deserted. In a law office on the twenty-second floor, Vicki G., an attorney, twenty-seven years old, is preparing a case for trial. Vicki glances at her watch, is startled to see how late it is, and prepares to leave. Down in the lobby of the building, Carl, the night superintendent, decides to leave his post for just a few

minutes to walk to a coffee shop a half block away. We will
now let the young attorney tell the rest of the story herself.

I was tired and hungry, but I had made good progress and so I
really didn't mind. In fact, I was feeling pretty good and looking
forward to having a late dinner at my favorite downtown bistro. I
put my papers away, turned off the lights, tried the door to make
sure it was locked, and started down the halls to the elevators.
The click-click-click of my heels echoing down the long corridor
gave me a lonely, frightened feeling, but I had worked late many
times before and I quickly shook off this feeling. I got to the
elevator, pushed the button, and waited. It took a few seconds
for the elevator to arrive. The doors opened, I stepped in, and
they closed behind me. I pressed the "lobby" button and the car
began its soundless, almost motionless descent. My mind was
three thousand miles away in London, working out the details of
a trip I was planning—the plays, restaurants, museums, fantasies
of romance. . . .

Suddenly I became aware that the elevator had stopped. I
knew the car couldn't have arrived at the lobby so soon. Well,
I thought some other workaholic must have rung for the car, and
I waited for the doors to open so I could see who it was. But the
doors didn't open. I looked up at the indicator to see where the
car had stopped, but not a single one of the little squares was
lighted up. This could mean that the indicator was not functioning, or it could mean that the machinery had broken down, the
elevator was stuck, and I was trapped! With that thought I felt
the first surge of fear in my stomach. In an instant, thoughts
flashed into my mind, which I had had many times before while
working late, but which I had brushed aside. What if the car was
stuck? What if I was trapped there and nobody knew about it,
and I had so stay there all night: What would happen to me?
Would I be able to stand it? Would I be frightened to death there,
all by myself? But then I grabbed hold of myself and started to
reassure myself, "Don't be an idiot. You're not stuck. The car will
start. Press the 'down' button." But even as I was saying that to
myself, I also knew that the "down" button wasn't supposed to
operate except when the car was being manually controlled. But
then I thought—maybe it was supposed to switch into action in
the case of an emergency. That gave me a flash of relief, and for
a split second I felt better. I searched for the "down" button
frantically, found it, and pressed it hard. Nothing happened. No
movement, no sound . . . nothing except the sound of my frightened breathing. I pressed it again because that was the only thing

I could think to do. Again, nothing. Now I knew I was trapped. Now this dreadful thing was actually happening to me. Then I had this dreadful mental picture of myself sealed up in a solid steel box without any opening. A cold sweat broke out over my body. My heart was racing madly. I became dizzy and thought I was going to faint. My legs began to buckle and I had to lean against the wall. I was terrified—in a panic. I knew I was going to have a heart attack. I would die right there, and nobody would know it. My mother would call me at home, and there would be no answer, and she would go out of her mind with worry.

Had I been in control of my wits, I would have realized that elevators do break down, and that building management people are prepared to deal with breakdowns when they occur. At the worst, I might have had to wait in the elevator a half hour, or an hour at the most, until somebody found out about it and got it operating again. But I was not in control of my wits. I was in a panic, with every wild thought imaginable racing through my head. I could see myself screaming and going berserk, and their finding me a raving maniac. I could see myself being carried out dead on a stretcher. Then the most ridiculous thing happened. I dropped my bag, and as it hit the floor, everything in it spilled out . . . wallet, keys, cosmetics, nail file, aspirins, Valiums, everything. The top of the Valium bottle must have been screwed on loose and the pills spilled out all over the floor. The next thing I knew, I was on my knees picking up the Valiums and gathering up all that junk off the floor. For those few seconds my panic had been pushed into the background while I was busy gathering up my "precious" belongings. But then when I had gotten everything back in order, the panic started to mount again, and again I could feel the dizziness and weakness coming back. But in the process, I had managed to keep hold of a slim thread of reason and I realized that I could press the alarm button. That's what it was there for. In my bewilderment and panic, I had completely forgotten about it.

I found the alarm button and pressed it, and the second I heard the clanging, my panic began to recede again. The sound was deafening and it jarred the inside of my skull, but I held my finger on the button and kept on ringing. I knew that Carl, the night superintendent, would hear it down in the lobby, or if not he, somebody else. That kept up my courage and kept me in control of my wits. Then I released the button and waited, all tensed up, waited for a click or voice on the intercom. Once more, there was nothing. Dead silence.

That was more than I could stand. I began to scream for help. I

banged on the walls with my fists. . . . I don't know how long
this went on; I must have slipped into a daze of some sort. Then,
in the midst of that, I heard a metallic tapping on the outside
door of the elevator. A woman's voice was telling me not to be
frightened, that she was going to get somebody from the building
to get me out. I was tremendously relieved to know someone had
actually found me, but at the same time, I knew she would have
to leave me by myself as she went to look for help. With this, a
new feeling of fright swept over me. I pictured myself alone, in
the inside of this huge building like Jonah in the belly of the
whale. It was as though I was lost in a strange place and I even
forgot where I was. I had the feeling of being somewhere on
Mars or another planet, far, far away from the earth. It was
unreal. The woman's voice got through to me in this daze, and
she was urging me to keep hold of myself, that she would get
help just as quickly as she could.

Then, it was as though I was outside my body and listening to
somebody else. I heard myself pleading and weeping and beg-
ging her to hurry, not to leave me there alone too long. She
assured me again she wouldn't.

The next ten minutes was an eternity. I tried to distract myself
by thinking about my court case, about my mother, about a
friend in my office, about what I was going to have for dinner
when I got out. But I was only partly successful in calming
myself. My legs gave way and I had to sit down. I huddled in the
corner, held my head in my hands, and fell back on a trick I had
used in childhood, when anything bad was happening and I
wanted time to pass. I started counting up to one hundred, and
when I reached a hundred, started counting backwards. Then I
would go to two hundred and do the same thing. This seemed to
have a lulling effect, because I felt myself getting less and less
frightened and tense, and it felt like my head was wrapped in
cotton . . . a dull feeling with no sensation. I lost all sense of time.
Then a sound penetrated through this vacuum. It was a click and
a voice on the intercom, Carl's German-accented voice telling me
he was down in the lobby and that he would be up in a few
seconds to get me out. This time I knew I was going to be
rescued and my panic receded. I was still tense and edgy and
frightened, but not as much. I was no longer in a nightmare. I
was back in reality, but holding on tight. A minute or two later, I
heard a sound of some metal object poking around inside the
elevator's mechanism, and then the doors parted. There stood the
two most beautiful people in the world—Carl and the woman

who had heard me and had gone to get Carl. I rushed out, threw my arms around each of them, and broke down and wept.

They grinned and patted me on the back and spoke to me with sympathy and understanding. This amazed me, because I thought they would be scornful and would ridicule me because of the way I had carried on. Anyhow, that was that. Carl and the helpful stranger started back to the elevator and beckoned me to follow. The minute they did that, my terror started to come back again, but I made myself get in, clenched my teeth, shut my eyes and waited for the doors to close and for the elevator to make its descent. We rode down in silence and when we got to the lobby, I thanked them again and told them good night.

Out on the sidewalk, I stopped and breathed in the beautiful, sweet, balmy air until I was dizzy. I forgot all about the bistro, hailed a taxi, and enjoyed a wonderful, peaceful ride home.

The following morning, as Vicki went through her customary routine of bathing, having breakfast, and getting dressed for work, she had faint glimmerings of the experience the night before, but the memories were without feeling and did not stay with her. The incident was completely gone from her mind as she sat reading in the bus on her way to her office. But the moment she got to her office building, stepped inside the lobby, and saw the banks of elevators, she felt the terror of the previous night surge up in her in full force.

I knew right then and there that I wasn't going to go up in an elevator and that nothing on earth could make me get inside one of those cars. I could feel, vividly, the horror of the previous night, and I turned and pushed my way through the people who were crowding in behind me and shoving me toward the elevators. When I had pulled myself free, I stood over to one side, frantic, not knowing what to do next. I was ashamed, embarrassed and terribly upset. What was this awful thing that was happening to me? I had heard about phobias before but had never dreamed it could happen to me. What was I going to do . . . now . . . right there? How was I going to get up to my office? There was only one course of action—for this moment, anyhow—and that was to walk up to my office without letting anybody know about it. The entrance to the stairway was around the corner and so I sidled around to it, sneaked inside, and started the twenty-two story climb. When I got to my floor, I was exhausted and my legs were trembling, but I steadied myself and, cracking the door, peered out. The coast was clear, so I sneaked out and made my way to my office. Nobody even noticed me, and that was a break. When lunchtime came, I ordered a sandwich in. That took care of my problem until quitting time. I worked until 6:30, when I knew most everybody would be gone, sneaked out to the stairway, and made the twenty-two story descent, by foot, down to the lobby.

I kept this up a few more days, but the strain of climbing, sneaking, and avoiding people was too great. I just couldn't keep it up. It was also affecting my work and my disposition. People were starting to wonder what was wrong with me. There was no continuing this way. I simply had to make a decision: Either tell my employer about my phobia—which would have been the mature, sensible way—or make up some excuse and get a leave of absence. My embarrassment, shame, and fright got the better of me and so I took the evasive way out. I asked for and got a three-month leave of absence for "personal reasons." I was well-liked and respected in that office, and so I had no difficulty doing this.

Ultimately, after seeing a number of physicians, and then going through a year of psychotherapy, Vicki came for treatment at the phobia clinic. After several months, she was able to return to work and resume a normal life.

The reason Vicki's case was presented in such great detail here is that her account provides us, admirably, with the material to make and illustrate two basic points about the phobic reaction.

Point One. People expect "the worst" to happen in the phobic situation, but we have never seen it happen. Take Vicki's case. Here was this young lady, trapped for a little more than fifteen minutes in a stalled elevator. Swept up in the spiralling swirl of frightening thoughts, imagery, and bodily reactions, she felt such intense, overwhelming distress that she thought she could not endure it for another second—that the only way she could get relief would be to faint, go berserk, go out of control, become insane, or die. But the most that actually did happen was that she screamed and beat on the elevator walls with her fists. Otherwise, she endured her distressful feelings quite well. The experience was painful, but it could be endured. She came out shaken, but all in one piece.

This is the nature of the phobic attack. The panic mounts to a level where it seems it simply cannot be tolerated. But it does not remain at that level for long. Then it begins to recede. It may rise again briefly, but then it will also fall once more.

In the vast majority of cases, people do not remain long enough in the phobic situation to find out that this is what happens. They flee when the panic attack is at its peak and, having gotten away, are convinced that they have barely escaped from a catastrophic experience from which there would have been "no return." It is possible, in Vicki's case, that had the night superintendent been there the morning following the incident, and had he offered to ride up with her that morning, and for several mornings thereafter, her dread on approaching the elevator might have worn off and she might then have been able to keep her phobia under control from then on.

But unfortunately for her it did not happen that way. No one was there to understand her problem and to help her. And, even though she had stayed in the phobic situation the previous night for more than fifteen minutes, without "something terrible" happening to her, her repeated avoidance strengthened her fear and magnified the danger to the point that she refused, absolutely, to go into an elevator again.

Point Two.   The distress a person feels in the phobic situation fluctuates up and down over a wide range of intensities. It gets worse as the person concentrates on and reacts automatically to the dangers he perceives in the phobic situation—all the frightening thoughts and images of what can happen to him. It gets better as he shifts his focus to elements and tasks of the phobic situation which are realistic, familiar, manageable, and reassuring, and becomes involved with them.

At any time, phobic behavior is a combined product of the individual's reaction to both the frightening and the reassuring elements. Phobic behavior changes as the focus of attention shifts from one aspect to the other, altering the relative strengths of these components.

This is clearly demonstrated in Vicki's account of what she thought, felt, and did during those fifteen to twenty minutes in which she was trapped in the elevator.

Let us pick her up where she realized that the machinery might have broken down, stalling the car midway in its descent down the elevator shaft.

"With that I felt the first surge of fear in my stomach. In an instant, frightening thoughts flashed through my mind. . . . What if I was trapped there? What if nobody knew I was there and I was stuck overnight? The thought was too terrible. . ."

As Vicki's attention concentrated on the frightening things that might happen to her, she experienced the first surge of intense fright. But quickly the focus of her attention was captured by comforting, reassuring thoughts, followed by practical, realistic action.

"I grabbed hold of myself and started talking to myself. 'Don't be an idiot. You're not stuck. The car will start. Press the "down" button.' "

And so, even though she had doubts about whether this would work, she did press the button. As her focus of attention shifted, the intensity of her distress diminished momentarily.

"That gave me a flash of relief, and for a split second I felt better."

She searched frantically for the "down" button, found it, and pressed it again and again, but nothing happened. This time she "knew" she was trapped—a terrifying prospect. Automatically her entire system responded with an escalating barrage of frightening mental and physical reactions which dominated most of her attention.

"Now I knew I was trapped. Now the dreadful thing was actually happening to me. I had an indescribably horrible feeling that I was sealed up in a solid metal box without any opening. A cold sweat broke out over my body. My heart was racing madly. I became dizzy and thought I was going to faint. My legs began to buckle and I had to lean against the wall. I was terrified—in a panic. I knew I was going to have a heart attack. I would die right then and there, and nobody would know it. My mother would call me at home, and there would be no answer and she would go out of her mind with worry."

Then a fortunate accident occurred, which seized her attention, pulling it from this spiral of terrifying thoughts, images, and bodily reactions—which by this time had reached the peak of intensity—to a realistic involvement with familiar and manageable tasks. Her pocketbook dropped, spilling all its contents on the floor, and she reacted, spontaneously, by getting down on her knees to pick up her belongings. With that the intensity of her distress decreased.

"For those few seconds, my panic had been pushed into the background while I was busy picking up my 'precious' belongings."

But once she had finished this task, her attention swung back to her frightening predicament, and her distress began to mount again.

"When I had gotten everything back in order, the panic started to mount again, and again I could feel the dizziness and weakness coming back."

Then, a "slender thread of reason" reasserted itself as she realized she had overlooked pressing the alarm button, and as she found it and pressed it—a realistic, practical, reassuring action—her panic "began to recede again."

She realized that the night superintendent or somebody else was bound to hear the alarm and come to get her out—reassuring thoughts—and this "kept up my courage and kept me in control of my wits." But this move, too, proved futile. She rang and rang and rang and waited for a reassuring voice on the intercom, but nobody had heard her. "There was nothing—only dead silence."

That was more than she could stand. Again the focus of her attention swung back to "the worst" and her control began to give way. She banged her fists on the wall and screamed. Then she "slipped into sort of a dazed state and lost track of time." The panic had peaked and then receded as she gave vent to her fright by screaming and banging on the elevator walls. Her phobic dread receded even further, when a tapping on the door and a woman's voice pulled her attention away from her frightening thoughts and focused it on reassuring reality. But, quickly, it shifted back again to her fearful fantasies as she imagined herself being left all by herself, separated from human contact, when the woman went down to the lobby or basement to get help. "With this, a new feeling of fright swept over me as I pictured myself alone in the insides of this huge building, like Jonah in the belly of the whale." During the next few seconds, she lapsed into a state of what we have already described as "depersonalization." She felt as though she were lost, on some strange planet, and, as she pleaded with the woman not to leave her there by herself, "it was as though I was outside my body listening to somebody else."

But the woman did have to leave her to look for help, and in the ensuing minutes, which seemed to her like an eternity, Vicki fell back automatically on a device she had used many times in the past in episodes of great distress. "I tried to distract myself by thinking about my court case, about my mother, about a friend in my office, about what I was going to have for dinner after I got out." And then she dredged up a trick she had used in childhood when "anything bad" was happening to her. She started to count backwards.

This strategy, which pulled her back to involvement with reassuring realities, seemed to have a lulling effect because she could feel herself getting less and less frightened and tense. Once more she lapsed into a semi-dazed state and remained there for a few minutes until the night superintendent's voice on the intercom jolted her back into welcome reality and the knowledge that help was on the way. Even with that, her fright did not vanish entirely. "I was still tense and edgy, but not as much. I was no longer in a nightmare." She became more deeply involved with reassuring reality when she heard her rescuer working on the mechanism that would open the door. And then, when the door finally did open and she saw the two persons standing there, her fright went altogether. She was shaken, but immensely relieved. At that instant her involvement with reality was total, and her involvement with frightening fantasy was nil. The phobic process had been completely reversed.

What we get from this close observation and study of Vicki's experience is this: (1) The way a person behaves and feels in the phobic situation can change from moment to moment. (2) How a person behaves and feels at any particular moment will depend directly on what is in the center of his or her attention at that moment. If a person is concentrating mainly on the frightening things that could happen—the things he or she perceives as dangers—then dread and panic will soar. On the other hand, if a person's attention is focused on that which is realistic, familiar, and reassuring, dread and panic will recede.

These are things few phobic people know or understand. They are aware only of the totality and the uncontrollability of their phobic reaction. They know that every time they had an attack of phobic panic, it went all the way instantaneously—that this consuming, overwhelming, bewildering feeling erupted, "full blown" in a split second, blotting out everything else. They cannot conceive or believe that there are or could be up-and-down fluctuations in the strength of their phobic terror. It is even more difficult for them to believe that they themselves have the power and ability to reduce the intensity of their reaction by shifting the focus of their thoughts and attention from the frightening thoughts and imagery to the comforting and the real.

Take the case of Arthur, a thirty-six-year-old man who came for contextual therapy treatment because he was phobic about driving and walking over bridges and ramps. At the outset, it was explained to this patient that what he thought and did in a phobic situation determined whether his fear got better or worse. To find out what actually happened to this man in the phobic situation, the therapist accompanied him from time to time, to different places where he experienced a phobic reaction.

In one of the early sessions, the therapist and patient drove across a three-hundred-foot span that passed over an expressway, and parked. They then proceeded to walk back over the span—the project for that day. Albert stopped and refused to proceed. He said he saw himself going out of control and jumping over the rail into the speeding traffic below. As he spoke, he reported that he felt his muscles tighten, his legs felt rubbery, he had become nauseated, his heart was racing, and "something like electricity" was going through his veins. He refused to go any further, despite the therapist's urging. The therapist accepted Arthur's decision, pointing out to him, at the same time, how his body was reacting automatically to his thoughts and imagery of danger.

Arthur reacted to this bit of insight in a way that is typical of phobic people. "Then I've got to stop these dumb thoughts and images. I've got to try to hold them back, to control them. If I can keep them from coming into my mind, I can get over my reaction."

This, the therapist told him, was exactly the wrong way to go. The phobic response—the bodily changes and the frightening thoughts—are automatic, outside of conscious control. No matter how hard Arthur might try to repress this reaction, he would be unable to do so. On the contrary, efforts to repress it would only make it worse.

What Arthur could and should do, the therapist added, would be to change his thinking by staying involved with realities. He could bend over and touch the ground with his hands; he could take the change out of his pocket and count it; he could look at the license plates of automobiles that were passing by and see how many different states were represented; he could recite some poetry or advertising jingles—these and anything else he might choose, which would keep him oriented in the present, in the realities of his surroundings. He might not be able to do this right away. His fears might be too overwhelming at first to permit him this freedom of choice. But the change would come with time, and he would find that after a while he would be able to shift the focus of attention to the real and familiar elements in his surroundings and perform little manageable tasks, all of which would keep him oriented to present realities instead of future fears—fears of what might happen. Instead of concentrating on "what if," he could control his fear by concentrating on "what is." When he could do this, the therapist told him, he would find that his fear would stay controlled and that he would no longer panic.

Arthur listened, tried to comprehend, and nodded his head in assent. But it was clear from observing him that his mind was still consumed with frightening imaginings and thoughts.

Several times the therapist undertook to lead Arthur across the overpass. Each time Arthur became afraid and stopped. As they went through these approaches, the therapist asked him to relate what was going on in his mind at the point where he stopped and retreated. Once he reported that he felt the pavement giving way beneath him. Another time he visualized himself sliding through the open railing and being run over by a truck. He reported also thinking: "What if I go berserk? What if Dr. _____ can't control me? What if I have a heart attack?"

As he talked to the therapist about what he was experiencing, Arthur began gradually to see the connections between his preoccupation with frightening conjectures—feelings, thoughts, and imagery—and his inability to walk across the overpass. He also was willing to accept the assurance that when he was able to shift his focus, the dread would diminish and he would be able to walk at least part of the way across.

Several days later, this began to happen. He took the first tentative steps across the overpass, keeping himself involved in reality by engaging in continuous, nonstop oral reportage about what he was observing and feeling. Session after session his control continued to increase, and within a few weeks he was walking over the overpass, accompanied by the therapist. Soon, he was driving by himself over some small bridges; later over some large ones. Each advance in physical accomplishments was accompanied by or followed by an increased comprehension of the relationship between his gains and his increased ability to keep himself involved with realities in the present. His ability to shift the focus of his attention was coming under stronger voluntary control, and his confidence in his ability grew.

At this stage, he himself chose to try the long walk over the span he had been avoiding. This time he succeeded, taking the walk all by himself, with the therapist waiting for him on the other side. Immediately after this successful effort, he was asked to tell what had accounted for the change. Here are excerpts from his reply.

Two weeks ago, I finally understood that I had to concentrate on how my mind builds fright and gets stuck. It was like I was back in school. I knew then that I could keep the fear at a point where I could function on the bridge. . . . Today, every time the fear came into the pit of my stomach, I can shift gears by talking out loud. I observe the reality and tell myself where I really am and what I am really doing. I look at the concrete road and don't focus on the height of the bridge or on the traffic below. Now I know the trucks can't really harm me even though the sight of them causes my body to react with fear. That was the thing I could never put together before.

I used to think my fear could not be overcome. To me it was like a terminal fear, unstoppable, and it could only get worse until it did me in somehow. I tried to stop any feeling at all, expecting the thunderbolt to hit me. I tried to be totally unafraid and not to get any bodily or mental reactions. Before it was all black or white—fear or no fear. Today I was afraid, but I knew that I could be afraid and not have to jump over the bridge because of the fear. Once I knew that, it was possible for me to walk across, afraid or not. It's helpful for me to equate the frightening situation I'm in with something I know, something that's familiar, like, "This is just a road made of concrete and it is here for my convenience." Before, the bridge was just a pure invitation to disaster, something I absolutely could not handle.

I feel terrific because of what I just did. Next week I'll do it the same way as I did today and I'll drive across that Tappan Zee Bridge [a long span across the Hudson River]. I'll whistle, sing, wiggle my ears, beat time with my left foot—anything. As long as I keep my attention on the road, I'll be okay. I won't worry about seeing the other shore or underneath the bridge or picture my car being hauled up from the river by a crane, with me dead inside, and a newspaper headline reading "Man Drives Off Bridge." *By the way, I just pictured that whole scene as I was talking to you.* But now I know that I can hold my own and drive across that bridge.

The following week, Arthur did indeed drive across the bridge with the therapist at his side. Several weeks later, he drove across with his family. A month after that he drove with his family to Canada, following a five-hundred-mile route that took him over many long overpasses and bridges. Arthur's major objective having been achieved, it was agreed that his treatment should end.

It had taken six months before Arthur could convince himself that where he focused his attention when phobic fear arose could *control* how he would feel and what he would do. The turning point came when he was able to achieve one small success after another utilizing this new approach. It was then that he began to believe in his ability to affect his behavior in the phobic situation. Because people differ, this "turning point" comes earlier for some than for others.

It is a basic assumption of contextual therapy that in the case of a long-standing phobia, the person's fear reaction has been repeatedly reinforced in the phobic situation by his painful, distressing reactions to his innumerable frightening thoughts and images. What Arthur needed and what had been lacking in his life (and this is true of most other people with phobias) were carefully guided experiences, suited to his own, individual situation: experiences that reinforced the realities of the context and identified his dread-filled reactions as products, mainly, of unrealistic perception. He had to learn in his own way, from new experiences, that while his distressing feelings from imagined dangers were real and immediate, the dangers themselves were not. His new understanding, which had developed gradually, eventually changed his reactions when he was confronted by phobic fear. Thus, instead of running automatically, as he had before, or dwelling on other imagined dangers and becoming even more upset, he shifted his focus and became involved with the comforting realities in the context. To develop the phobic person's ability to respond to realistic factors in the phobic situation—to make *them* instead of imagined dangers the dominant content of that person's attention at the time—is the primary task and objective of contextual therapy.

The following chapter will tell how this objective is achieved.

CHAPTER SEVEN

Mastering Your Phobia

THERE ARE THREE SUCCESSIVE STAGES in contextual therapy: (1) confronting the phobic reaction, (2) controlling the phobic reaction, and (3) understanding the phobic reaction. We will develop each of these, one at a time.

In contextual therapy, as it has been practiced to date, the patient usually works with a professional therapist or with a trained paraprofessional helper operating under the direction of a therapist.

The method described in this book assumes that the reader—the phobic person—will probably be working with an untrained phobia helper, a good friend or a trusted and willing relative. We will tell you, in full detail, how to go about enlisting the aid of your helper. We will also tell you precisely what you and your helper are expected to do.

But first we are going to give you a basic picture of how this is going to work—the steps that need to be taken, the guidelines to be observed.

STAGE ONE: CONFRONTING THE PHOBIC REACTION

The first practical step in contextual therapy is to enter the phobic situation and confront the phobic experience. This is the

basic in vivo approach. Experience has shown, in thousands of
cases, that little can be achieved in the control of phobias merely
by discussing the situation in an office. There is no way a
phobic person can gain control over his phobia merely by discussing it. Discussion may be a necessary prelude, a useful
preparatory step. But in order to achieve actual control of the
phobia the patient has to move into the phobic situation, confront the phobic reaction, and deal with it one step at a time
according to a planned strategy. We believe there is no effective
substitute for this approach. It is understandable how, on first
hearing or first reading, this proposal might elicit a negative
reaction. We know it is not easy for a phobic person to accept
the idea that the only way he is going to be able to get over his
phobia is to move into a situation which he has been avoiding
with horror and dread for years, even at the price of giving up
normal living and making a hermit of himself. It is conceivable
that the established avoidance habit may be so strongly entrenched that it might carry over even to an urge to turn away
from contextual therapy.

In the event any of our readers are experiencing that kind of a
reaction right now, let us offer these reassurances.

First, do not think that your reaction is unique. This is the
way most phobic people feel when they are told about the in
vivo approach, and no one can really blame them. The idea of
having to move into a situation about which they have built up
so much dread cannot be very attractive. However, when they
learn that the distress is much less intense than they expected
and that they will only have to endure it for a while, they are
quite willing to cope with it in exchange for all the years of
suffering they have had to endure as a result of their phobic
avoidance.

Second, we can assure those readers who have some concern
about going into the phobic situation that what they will actually experience will not be nearly as bad as they may anticipate
it to be. We have it on the testimony of hundreds of patients
that, almost invariably, the anticipation is much worse than the
reality.

Third, you will not be expected to go into the phobic situation
alone. Your phobia helper will be there, by your side. You will
find that with the helper there, your fright will not be as great;
you will feel much more safe and secure. His very presence will
be an important factor in keeping you connected to reassuring
realities. But he will be helping you in many more ways than

that; we will tell you about those, in just a little while.

Fourth, no one is going to be asked to jump into the phobic situation all at once. It is going to be a step-at-a-time approach. The arrangement will be to break down each task into small, manageable steps, steps that the particular individual thinks he or she is going to be able to achieve without too much distress. What one person may think is not much of a step may loom as huge as a mountain for another. That is why contextual therapy stresses "individually graded steps," steps arranged according to what the individual thinks he can handle at that particular time.

For example, one person who has not been out of his or her house for years may find it possible, on the very first try, to walk a whole block accompanied by the phobia helper. Another may only be able to manage opening the apartment door and walking the length of the hall to the elevator.

Or take an example of what might happen in the case of a phobia for cats. One person might be able to tolerate only looking at a picture of a cat the very first time; another might be able to look at or even handle a toy kitten; and still a third might be able to look at some live kittens in the window of a pet shop.

The choice is left to the person with the phobia as to how much of a step he wants to take and when he wants to take it. The only exception to this would be if the same steps were repeated over and over again because they were easy and did not arouse much of a phobic reaction. Under those circumstances, the phobic helper would try to encourage moving ahead to a more difficult step—but only encourage, never coerce or force. It is a basic rule in contextual therapy that the phobic person sets the pace. If he feels, despite encouragement, that he can handle only a small step that day, then only a small step is taken. If he feels he can handle a more difficult step, then that is what is arranged. Also—and this is also a basic rule—the phobic person is free, whenever he wants, to retreat or escape from a situation if he should find it more than he can endure at that time. Everybody understands this at the outset, so that there is no fear that a retreat or escape will be greeted with scolding or derision.

STAGE TWO: CONTROLLING THE PHOBIC REACTION

Avoidance reinforces the phobic reaction. Confrontation enables you to experience your phobic dread, deal with it, and learn that you can control it. That is why the phobic person has to move into the phobic situation—to confront and learn to deal with the dread and avoidance produced by the phobogenic process.

But that does not mean moving in passively and waiting for improvement to take place by itself. It means moving into the phobic situation and performing a planned set of activities.

The basic six points of contextual therapy that follow summarize how you can handle your fear and panic in the phobic situation, and what tools and techniques you should use to bring them under control.

Point One. *Expect, allow, and accept that fear will arise.* When you enter the phobic situation, your first, automatic reaction may be to try to steel yourself against the fear you expect to experience. You may grit your teeth, set your jaws, close your eyes, clench your fists, and determine that "by Heavens" you are not going to be afraid. You are going to show yourself how tough you can be and how you are not going to let this ridiculous thing get the better of you. We will tell you in advance that if this is how you expect it to work out, you will be badly disappointed; not only that, the fear is likely to become more intense than if you did not "set yourself" at all and let the fear come on as it just naturally has to, because of your previous experience.

We have to remember here the point that has been made over and over again: that the reaction in phobia is automatic, just the way it is in any fear reaction. The fact that the phobic dangers are imaginary and unreal does not make any difference. The bodily systems—glandular, circulatory, respiratory, digestive, excretory, and the rest—spring into action automatically, just as though the dangers were real. Have you ever found it possible to quiet your fear and anxiety when a child is seriously ill or when you were caught in some life-threatening situation? You may have tried to tell yourself—"Don't be frightened"—but not with very much success, we would guess. The systems involved in the reaction to danger—real or imaginary—are outside of conscious control. They operate automatically.

Suppose that while you are reading this book, you hear a noise and imagine an intruder is breaking into your home. Do you think you would be able to control your reaction of fright? No more should you expect to be able to control or hold back your reaction in a phobic situation.

Take the case of a veteran of the Vietnam war. After two years of shattering experiences, he comes home in a state of what we used to call battle fatigue. At night he wakes up with nightmares. During the day, any jarring experience can upset him. He hears a loud bang—the backfire of a truck—and reacts to it with panic, as though it is a gunshot. That part of his brain which keeps him in touch with the present reality tells him he's at home and no longer in Vietnam. Another part of his brain, where his wartime experiences are stored, reacts to the shot as though he still were in Vietnam. He tries to control his reaction, but like all other fear reactions, it is automatic and minimally subject to conscious control. It is going to take a good deal of relearning based on new experiences at home before he will be able to feel, with certainty, that he is not in Vietnam but at home. When that happens he will no longer respond as he does today—but it will take time and it will take repeated confrontation with his fear reaction before this can be achieved.

A person with a phobia is like that Vietnam veteran. The phobic person, too, reacts automatically with body, mind, and emotions to the imagined dangers in the phobic situation as though they were present and real. The reaction is outside of conscious control. It is impossible to stop it or to banish it from consciousness. There is only one basic difference between the Vietnam vet and the phobic person. In a way, the veteran has it easier, so far as his relearning task is concerned. He knows why he is sensitized to loud noises and other stimuli reminiscent of Vietnam. The phobic person may not know why he is sensitized to the particular phobic situation. He cannot—in most cases— remember the different experiences he had which make him react with panic to that particular situation. Nevertheless, the reaction does occur, and there is just no way for him to stop it or prevent it. Further, there is really no need for him to do so. He, like the veteran, can go through a relearning process which will enable him to deal with his phobic thoughts and feelings as products of his imagination, no longer triggering a reaction of overwhelming dread or panic. It may take some time before this change takes place, but when it does, he will *know it and believe it*, not just think it or wish it. His cognition will have changed.

But until that happens with you, and it certainly will not happen on your first reentry into the phobic situation, you will expect the fear to come, allow it to come, and accept the fact that this is the way it has to be.

Point Two. *When fear comes, wait. Let it be.* The chances are very good that, for two or three days before you reenter the phobic situation, your anxiety and tension will build, in anticipation of "how bad it is going to be," and that you will consider a hundred times cancelling the appointment with your helper. This resistance is likely to intensify, and when you do enter the phobic situation and the automatic fear reaction sets in, you may very likely be seized by a strong impulse to flee. Since you know that this is likely to happen, there is something you *can* do to deal with it. First, and this is repeating what we said a few minutes ago, don't try to fight it. Don't try to hold the feeling back. Expect it and let it come. You will find that it is not as bad as you anticipated. Second, set yourself a goal—a deliberate goal—to stay in there and wait and see what is going to happen. Instead of expecting that it will get worse, expect that it can get better—expect that your fear reaction will become less intense, and that you will be able to stay there and endure it. Think of it as a wave that builds up quickly and crests, then subsides and rolls right by. Remember, too, that if it should happen to remain at a level that you cannot stand, you are free to move out. That is your option. But try to decide, in advance, that you are going to refuse that option when it thrusts itself into your mind. Set yourself the goal of saying: "No, I'm going to stay, and I'm going to stay until it feels a little better. Then, if I still feel I want to withdraw, I can." If you withdraw before it gets better, you will have gained something: You will at least be able to say to yourself that you did try. But if you stay until the level of your fears comes under control or goes down, then you will have made a very large gain. It is the first positive step in the direction in which you want to go. Continued success will be dependent on your learning to remain in the phobic situation, at each successive step, until the level of fear goes down.

Point Three. *Focus on and do manageable things in the present.* The key to control of the phobic situation is staying connected to and involved with the realistic and reassuring elements in the phobic situation. This is achieved by performing little tasks, engaging in little routines, conducting any kind of activity that will compel your thoughts to concentrate and focus on present realities (the "what is") instead of permitting them to stay consumed by all the imaginary, frightening things that could happen (the "what if's").

There is no set list of things to do, but there are some examples of what other phobic persons have done and found to be effective:

Reading signs out loud to yourself; counting automobiles or people; reciting jingles, poetry, or nursery rhymes; talking to whoever is around; reading addresses and telephone numbers in your little memo book; sorting out your credit cards; working out a crossword puzzle; counting the change in your pocket or pocketbook; chewing candy or a mint; rereading letters from your pocket or purse; observing the design of women's dresses or feeling the texture of nearby objects; counting forwards and backwards; listening to a portable radio; snapping a rubber band against your skin or pinching yourself; or doing muscle relaxation exercises.

There is no end to the list of things you can do, and you and your helper can be as creative as you wish in thinking up some others. The principle is simple: involvement with familiar, concrete things and achievable objectives reduces involvement with imaginary dangers and controls or reduces the fear.

When you first start out, your helper will be right there with you, at your side, all the time as you are moving into, and remaining in, the phobic situation. If you should become confused and not be able to remember some of the things you were planning to do to keep you connected to present realities, your helper will be able to remind you and help you with some others. Later on, however, building on what you have learned with your helper, you will be moving around in the phobic situation by yourself. Your helper may be waiting for you around the corner, or outside the store or elevator. This means you will not be able to get any help from him should you forget. Therefore, it will be a good idea for you to write down on a little card the different activities in which you are planning to engage, the different things you are planning to do. Then, should you become confused, you can pull out the card and get your cue from that. You don't need to make a note of this right now. We will remind you about it later, when you come to that part of the book in which you and your helper are actually planning out your move into the phobic situation.

We can also let you in on something else that is going to happen later on. You are going to find that once you are engaged in these "reality" activities and have learned how effective they can be in giving you control over your phobic feelings of dread and panic, you will lose your feelings of helplessness and develop a sense of confidence and hope. This, in turn, will reduce your fear overall, and make the next step much easier to take.

Point Four. *Label your fear from 0 to 10 and watch it go up and down.* In addition to performing various "manageable" tasks in the phobic situation, you are going to be asked to do one thing more—to monitor your fear, observe how it goes up and down, and assign a numerical value from 0 to 10 to the level of fear at some particular moment. Zero means "I don't feel any fear at all." Ten means, "It is so bad, it couldn't be worse. I don't think I'm going to be able to stand it." The numbers 1 to 9 represent varying degrees of fear in between.

Do you remember the cases of Vicki and Arthur in Chapter Six? Do you remember that they were able to observe that their fear did not remain at a steady level while they were in the phobic situation? That it moved up and down, depending on where their attention was focused, moving up when it was focused on their imaginary dangers, moving down when it was focused on the familiar and comforting elements of reality?

As you monitor your fear in the phobic situation, you, too, will find that it moves up and down, depending on where your attention is focused. As this happens—and as you are observing the changes—assign a numerical value, from 0 to 10—to your level of fear, just after the change has taken place. You won't have to do this all by yourself. Your helper will say to you, at significant times, "What is the level? Label it," and you will answer by telling him the numerical level.

There are two reasons for this activity. First, you will be able to see for yourself how dramatically your fear levels change from moment to moment—that they do not necessarily reach a peak and stay there or get even worse. Once you are able to observe this, you will no longer feel so strongly the impulse to flee in order to get relief. You will see that it is *you*—what you are doing and thinking—and not the phobic situation that determines your level of fear, and that you can control it by shifting your focus of attention and involvements. Second, in the process of monitoring and labeling your level of fear, you "objectify" the experience. You put yourself—your thinking, cognitive mind —in the position of observing your phobic fear as you might observe a toothache or a stomachache. You have had toothaches and stomachaches many times. You have learned to adjust to them, and so they no longer frighten you. They may hurt you, but not frighten you. Now, when you monitor your fear, watch it go up and down, and label it, you are learning to adjust realistically to your phobic fear, and not to let it frighten you. You learn to regard it as just a different kind of a pain which comes and goes, one that you can handle and endure, one that is no longer as frightening as it used to be.

Since this is going to be an important part of your activity when you go into your phobic situation, we are going to run through a couple of exercises so you can see exactly what we have in mind and be prepared to label the level of your fear as it goes up and down.

David, twenty-eight, has a phobia for the dark and for closed-in places. He has already been through several graded steps, with the help of his brother, Alan, in confronting his phobic situation. They have worked out for David's next step that both of them will go into a windowless pantry in David's apartment (measuring about six feet by nine feet), turn off the overhead lights, close the door behind them, and remain there several minutes. They are now in David's living room.

Alan says, "Okay, Dave, let's go." They arise and start toward the pantry which opens off the hallway.

David is speaking: "Hey, I wish we didn't have to do this. I'm feeling pretty scared, but not bad yet. It's about a number 4; now it's getting worse, about a number 7. I'm going to sing 'Home, Home on the Range.'" (Sings a few bars.) "That helps a little; it's a little better."

They have just come to the pantry door. David freezes. "I'm sorry. I'm not going to go in there. I don't think I can stand it. I can feel my heart going a million miles a minute."

Alan takes him gently by the arm and leads him: "Here's some of your candy. Chew on it. What's your level, Dave?"

David answers: "It's about an 8."

With Alan still holding him by the arm, they enter the pantry. Alan shuts the door and turns off the lights. They are in total darkness.

David, screaming in panic: "Alan, where are you? I can't stand this. I'm going to faint."

Alan: "Here I am, Dave. Right next to you. Take it easy. It's going to be alright. Now tell me what you are feeling. What level?"

David: "What level? What are you talking about. I'm scared to death. I feel like I'm going to suffocate. Okay, I remember, it's a number 100. I mean 10. Alan, say something to me. Let me know you are there. Let's get out of here."

Alan: "Take it easy, Dave. Nothing is going to happen to you. Here, take one of these mints." (David feels around for this brother's hand and takes a mint and puts it in his mouth.) "There, isn't that better?"

"Yeah, a little."

"Alright, label it."

"It's about a 7 now."

"That's good. Now just feel around you. You can't see a thing but you can feel things. Feel around the shelves and tell me what you are touching."

"Here are some paper boxes. That's got to be cereal. Then there are a couple of tall cans. That's got to be tomato juice or something."

"Okay, Dave. Tell me how you feel. What level?"

"Hey, I feel a little better now. I think it's gone down to about a 5. How's that?"

"Terrific. Tell me what else you feel on the shelf."

"I don't know what that is. It feels funny. Feels like a shoe box. What's a shoe box doing on the pantry shelf?" They both laugh.

"Okay, Dave. Are you getting used to it? Can you stand the dark a little better?"

"Just a little. Not much. I feel it going up again. I feel lousy. I feel like this thing is closing in around me. It's terrible."

"Okay. How about singing 'Mary Had a Little Lamb'?" David does. They laugh.

"What level, Dave?"

"Still about a 7. How much longer do we have to do this? I'm starting to get nervous all over again. I'm starting to get that terrible feeling like I'm locked in here and can't get out. I'm choking. It's hard to breathe. I want to get into the light. I want to see things. I can't stand this."

"Okay, what's the level?"

"I can't tell you what level. I'm too scared. Alright, it's a million. Let's get out of here. Let's get out, Alan, right now." (Starts to pull away from Alan, who tries to hold him gently by the arm.)

"David, you're doing great. Don't quit. Here, I want you to

put your hand on the doorknob." (Guides David's hand to the doorknob.) "Now, I want you to turn it; not open it; just twist it. Tell me what it feels like."

"It's cool and smooth; never even noticed it before."

"What's it made of?"

"Feels like brass; maybe steel. I dunno."

"What's it like now? What level?"

"Feels better. About a 5."

"Okay, I think this is enough for this try. What do you say?"

"Are you kidding? It's enough!!"

David pulls open the door, steps out and heaves a big sigh of relief.

Alan: "Okay, Dave. What level?"

David: "A big, beautiful 0."

About fifteen minutes later, while they are having some coffee in the kitchen, Alan played back the tape recording of their experience in the pantry and pointed out to his brother what a direct connection there was between what David was thinking and doing, and the level of his fear. Whenever he was caught up in his imaginary dangers, the level would go up. Whenever he pulled himself back into contact with reality by performing some simple, manageable task, his fear level would go down.

Let us move on to the next illustration. This is the case of Sally, thirty-two, a housewife with a phobia for dogs. Sally's case was complicated by a fear that dogs—any dog—would give her a case of rabies if one of them would just touch her with its paws or if the dog's fur brushed up against her skin. The fact that she knew these fears were baseless made no difference. They were obsessive and she could not shake them, no matter how hard she tried to reason herself out of them. Because her phobia was so intense, she and her helper decided on a very slow and gradual approach.

Down the street from where Sally lived, there was a family with several children and their pet beagle puppy, a friendly little dog. The dog was allowed to run free inside a fenced enclosure, and in order to avoid even looking at it, Sally would have to make a detour of several blocks on her way to work, or to the store. Sally and her helper, her friend Anne, decided to have Sally try to walk past the yard where the dog played, but across the street from it. The distance gave Sally a feeling of safety. We pick up Sally and Anne as they are walking along the opposite sidewalk, approaching a position opposite the neighbor's yard.

Sally: "I can hear the dog barking, but I can't see him. He must be behind those bushes. I'm scared."

Anne: "Oh, don't be scared, Sally. He's closed in by that fence and he can't possibly come out. Are you frightened even to look at him?"

Sally: "Yes, Anne. Let me hold your arm."

Anne: "Okay, Sally. Hold on. How frightened are you? How bad is it? What level?"

Sally: "It must be a number 4." Then, stopping dead in her tracks: "I see him. He's coming from behind the bushes. I don't know what he's going to do next. Are you sure he can't jump over the fence?"

Anne: "Positive. He's just a little puppy. How bad is it?"

Sally: "It's a 7. Anne, have you got that apple? Please give it to me quick."

Anne: "Here it is. And after you've taken a couple of bites, try telling me about those little children who live there. They're nice children, aren't they?"

Sally: "There's the little boy, Timmy. He's about five. He doesn't go to school yet. I see him and his mother in the store occasionally and they're very friendly and pleasant. I think the older boy, John, is about ten. I see him and his friends playing ball on the street sometimes."

Anne: "What's your level now?"

Sally: "About six."

Their walk has slowed and they are now directly opposite the neighbor's house and yard.

Anne: "Alright, Sally. We'll stay here a few seconds and see what happens. Do you want to?"

Sally: "I don't know. I feel jittery. I don't like it. I have some pretty high levels, maybe about a 7. Oh my God. There he is, by the fence. He's going to jump."

The little dog has come out from behind the bushes and, seeing Sally and Anne across the street, has run up to the fence and is greeting them with a friendly barking, his tail wagging, his front paws up on the fence. Sally turns and starts to run back to the house. Anne tries to slow her retreat.

Anne: "Sally, don't run away. Remember, we knew this was going to happen and we agreed that you were going to stand here and cope with it and not run away. Remember what we said? We rehearsed it. . . . When fear comes, stop and wait. Let it come. Let it be. Don't try to fight it back. Let it come. No matter how bad you feel, stand there and let it happen."

Sally: (Now clutching her friend's arm) "Alright, I'm standing still. I'm letting fear come. Hail Mary full of grace, the Lord is with Thee . . . It's all the way up to a 9, Anne, but I'm doing what you told me. Hail Mary full of grace, the Lord is with Thee, blessed art Thou amongst women and blessed. . . . It's a little better now, about a 7. But I still don't feel so good. I feel dizzy."

Anne: "Alright, Sally, I want you to open your pocketbook and show me what you have in it. Take out that letter from your brother, the one you got this morning, and read it to me." (Sally follows these suggestions.)

Anne: (When Sally finishes) "Alright, how do you feel now? What level?"

Sally: "Phew. It's better. It's about a 5."

Anne: "Good. Now try describing that little dog to me. I can see him but I want you to tell me about him."

Sally: (Forces herself to look at the dog.) "He's brown and he's got some white spots. He's got long, floppy ears. He's little. He must be a very young puppy. That's a hound dog, isn't it? All hound dogs have big ears, don't they? I wonder why."

Anne: "See, I can tell you're not frightened now. That's great! What level?"

Sally: "About a number 5, I think. Yeah, I do feel a lot better. I did let the fear come, and it did get so I can stand it, just like you said. I guess it's even down to about a 3 now."

Anne: "You are doing real great. Would you like to stay here a little longer?"

Sally: "If we have to, okay. If you say it will help, okay. He's gone away from the fence now and he's running around the other side of the house. Let's stay a little longer. I think I can manage it."

Notice how, in both these illustrations, the helpers were very sensitive to the feelings of the patient, encouraging them, but never forcing them, permitting them to set their own pace. The helpers were also helpful in suggesting things the patient could do to stay connected to reality. Touching is also something the helpers did which was very comforting to the patient. Alan held his brother David's arm. Anne let Sally hold her arm. The touch is not only comforting; it is another way of keeping the phobic person connected to reality. So is the helper's voice.

Point Five. *Function with a level of fear. Appreciate the achievement.* The one thing phobic people yearn for most intensely is to be rid of the dread, the panic, the distress that they experience in the phobic situation. Hence, when they come into contextual therapy (or any other kind of therapy), they are expecting that one of the first things that is going to happen is that there is going to be a quick and sharp decline in their fear reaction when they enter into the phobic situation, and that this will be gone in not too long a time after that. They tend to measure success by the speed with which the fear reaction disappears. They think that any fear at all still means the onset of total panic. When they find that it does not vanish right away, or after several weeks of therapy, they may think that the treatment is not working, or that it is their fault that they are not responding as quickly and completely as they had expected.

But that is not the way it works, and you should know not to expect it.

When patients enter contextual therapy, they are told that the goal for several weeks at least, and perhaps for a number of weeks thereafter, is to learn to function in the phobic situation, at moderately high levels of fear. This is part of the process by which the phobic reaction is diminished, little by little, until, sometime thereafter—the length of time depending on the individual—it is possible to enter into the phobic situation without experiencing any fear at all, or a very faint twinge of fear, at most.

You will find that as you move along in contextual therapy, you will be able to remain longer and longer in the phobic situation. Fear will continue to come, but the levels will diminish as you gain greater confidence in the techniques for controlling it. After a while you will be able to continue functioning in the phobic situation, remaining in it for considerable stretches of time, even while you are experiencing fear. This is an essential part of the process by which fear levels are kept from going out of control. Keeping the fear from going out of control by performing some constructive tasks is the goal of contextual therapy during the first stages. The continued reduction and eventual "phasing out" of the fear reaction will come with continued practice and confidence in your methods of control.

Hence, when you find, in the first several sessions of your contextual therapy, that you are able to stay in the phobic situation for fifteen minutes, a half hour, or longer while experiencing fluctuating levels of fear, you should recognize this as a very definite sign of progress and know that you are moving along very well.

Point Six. *Expect, allow, and accept that fear will reappear.* There is another thing for which you should be prepared, so that you will not be disappointed when it happens. You may find that after a month or two of contextual therapy practice, your levels of fear in the phobic situation have been reduced considerably. Then, without warning, you may experience another sharp surge of fear in the phobic situation, and become terribly upset because you think that everything you have gained is lost, and that you are back right where you started. Not so. The recurrence of fear in the phobic situation, after it has been at a low for days and weeks, *does not mean* that you are suffering a relapse, or that your contextual therapy has failed. You are going through a protracted relearning process, and learning (or relearning) never proceeds in a straight, uninterrupted line. You need to think back to your early learning experiences in school, and recall that once you had achieved a fairly high level in a particular school subject, in dramatics, or in sports, you did not remain at that level constantly and without any fluctuation. You may have remained at a certain level on the average but that average was made up of ups and downs. There were times when you just zipped along and you thought it was just going to be that way forever. Then came a spell of illness, or a disappointment, or some troubling problem in the family, or just a period of consolidation. During that time your performance would slip a little, or even a good deal. During those "down" periods, you may have felt that all your learning and practicing had been for naught, that you had forgotten everything you had learned. Then when the problem had resolved itself or when you had gotten over the disappointment or family problem, or for no known reason at all, your performance would move back up again to where it was before, or even higher.

You must remember, too, that your predisposition to react in a phobic manner was acquired over many, many years of reacting to imagined dangers in many areas of life in general, and in the phobic situation in particular. The old ideas, assumptions, and beliefs developed in the course of those years do not disappear by any magic process. They go little by little as they yield to realistic ideas derived from new experiences in the phobic situation.

When setbacks come, they should not be regarded as failures, but rather as opportunites to study *why* this is happening, what processes are at work, whether adequate effort and practice are being put into reorienting yourself to the new way of thinking about and dealing with the imaginary dangers and fears in the phobic situation. This is no different from what happens when a good baseball player is in the slump. His coach does not let him go off and sulk. He asks him to see what has changed in his stance, or in his swing, or in the position of his hands on the bat, or in his timing. Then, when they have identified the problem, they work together on correcting it. The same model may be applied to ballet dancing, figure skating, dramatics, or contextual therapy—anything in which the learning process is at work.

Some Traits That May Get in the Way

Earlier in the book, we spoke about some personality traits which are associated with agoraphobia and which are believed to play a role in causing that condition to develop and persist. We now need to point out that these very same traits may get in the way of recovery not only from agoraphobia but from other phobias as well.

It is important that you take note and see if any of these traits apply to you so you can work on modifying them, simultaneously, in the course of your contextual therapy. You can do this during the weeks and months in which you are learning how to stay in the phobic situation while experiencing some distress. You will find that, as these traits are weakened, added progress in contextual therapy will occur. Doing this will also improve your life in other areas. You will probably observe that the effect is reciprocal: Whatever you do to modify your attitudes will speed up recovery from your phobia, and whatever you do to speed up recovery from your phobia will help modify your personality traits. Here are the traits in question:

The drive to be perfect (perfectionism). This will· manifest itself in a failure to be pleased with small gains or with gradual progress. Anything except very quick and large-scale success will be interpreted as failure. Obviously, this kind of a reaction is self-defeating. There is the old saying that "nothing succeeds like success." Applied to contextual therapy, this would mean that a person who is pleased with little bits of progress will be very happy about being able to stay in the phobic situation a few minutes at a time while experiencing some levels of distress. His satisfaction and appreciation will spur him on to stay a little longer, even at higher levels of distress. It is a process of self-encouragement and self-motivation. On the other hand, a person who gets no satisfaction out of small gains, only a sense of failure, will be discouraged from trying harder and moving further. If you happen to be a perfectionist, it is futile for us to tell you not to be that way. A lifelong habit cannot be altered by counseling or advice. What we can suggest is that you set small gains in contextual therapy as your goal, regarding them as significant steps on the way to success and appreciating and enjoying them as they occur. If you can manage this, you will be surprised to see how much your progress improves. You may also find that you will, as a result, become easier on yourself about other things in life, not demanding so much of yourself, allowing yourself to be less than perfect and even to make mistakes.

The need to please others. This characteristic may operate as a deterrent to progress in several ways. If this happens to be a problem of yours, you will find yourself worrying about what your mother or father (brother, sister, uncles, friends, neighbors) think when you tell them you have a phobia and are planning to go into contextual therapy. Will they accept it or will they resist it? Will they think there's something abnormal about you and think the less of you for it? Is it going to cause them a problem? Will they be as concerned about you as they were before? If you are beset by doubts such as these, you will, in all likelihood, remain secretive and reticent about disclosing your problem and your plans. This would make it difficult for you to enlist a helper, cut you off from cooperation and emotional support, and block an important source of objective information which you need most urgently to counteract your false beliefs about the imaginary dangers of the phobic situation.

You may also be worrying that when you do go into the phobic situation, you are going to do something that is "embarrassing" or that will make you "look foolish," or make others think "there's something wrong" with you. If you continue to be preoccupied about such possibilities—which are not likely to come to pass—you will resist taking this essential step. The point may come where you simply have to ask yourself—and decide—"Which matters most—what other people think, or what happens to me and my phobia?"

The need to show no emotion. Professionals working with phobic people have observed that so many of them have in common the need and the ability to present a relatively placid, untroubled appearance to others, while suffering extreme distress on the inside. People with other kinds of emotional difficulties usually express their distress openly. It is possible to see by their dejection or agitation that they are enduring extreme psychological pain. But this is something few phobic people do. It is only when they are questioned and encouraged to talk that they open up, and then not always readily and fully. Many remain quiet and composed throughout the entire course of therapy. Almost invariably it is those who have the hardest time in treatment. Conversely, those who are willing to let others see them as they are, to let others know when they are hurting, seem to move ahead more quickly. Emotional release and exchange of information are essential if there is going to be change.

It is human and natural to feel and to show your feelings. It is unfortunate that in some cultures and in some families children are taught that it is wrong, a sign of weakness or of poor upbringing, to show what you are feeling, or even to feel at all. This can't help but contribute to and perpetuate such emotional difficulties as those that occur in phobic disorder.

If you happen to be one of these people, we suggest that you try to follow the example of others who find it possible and helpful to be open and expressive. It may be difficult for you to shed your reticence at first. But once you start, you will be surprised to see how quickly you can change. This is going to be important as you work with your helper in contextual therapy. Don't try to prove to your helper how brave you are. If entering the phobic situation upsets you very much, say so. Learn to "get in touch with" what you are really feeling and to communicate it to your helper—and to others. Don't try to repress your feelings of fright and upset. Above all, *don't try not to have them.* If you do this, you will find it more difficult to progress in contextual therapy. The whole point in contextual therapy is to experience fear in the phobic situation and, by learning ways to deal with it, to eliminate the perception of danger.

The need to avoid uncertainty. If it were possible for human beings to control everything that might happen to them, then all of life could be made safe and secure, and we would have no problem to worry about except dying of old age. But, of course, it is not possible for us to achieve this. Some things are within our control; many things are outside our control. In some families, children are taught that this is the case, that it is impossible to guard against all mishaps and tragedies, that we do the best we can to make our lives as secure as we can, but then make allowances for those things we can't control. We learn to increase the probabilities of safety, rather than seek certainty in vain. With this kind of an attitude, children are prepared for shocks and losses when they occur. They hurt, suffer, and then bounce back, resuming an active, constructive pursuit of life. In other families, parents who cannot tolerate uncertainty transmit to their children the attitude that nothing in life is safe, that unless they watch their every step and take absolutely no chances at all, they are likely to suffer some serious and irremediable harm. This sets these children on a course of trying to insure that everything that affects them is safe, that nothing should be done that might possibly harm them. This extends itself into trying to exercise strict and strong control over everything they do and everything that everybody else does. Everything has to follow a definite pattern or a definite formula; any deviation is threatening. Control means certainty and certainty means absolute safety. Uncertainty—which abounds in life today—is threatening because it breaks up this unrealistic, tight network of safety.

This inexorable drive for total safety, this avoidance of any uncertainty whatsoever, is one of the things which cause many phobic people to flee from one "unsafe" place after another until they have retreated into a tiny area, the only area in which they feel secure. Doing this may have cost them their jobs, their independence, their freedom of movement, their social life. But they are unwilling to give up this safety.

It is easy to see how this sort of attitude can interfere with progress in contextual therapy. To start with, people insistent on safety and certainty first will be resistant to breaking away from the protection offered by phobic avoidance, however destructive this has been in their lives. Further, when they do undertake contextual therapy, they may hesitate to venture into a new and, for them, an untested experience. Giving up old ways and adopting new ones—exploring, trying, taking some risks—may be a frightening prospect. Yet these are the steps that must be taken, with help, if contextual therapy is to be effective.

Should you be one of these people with an overriding need for certainty, then you are informed in advance of the understandable difficulties you may encounter as you move into contextual therapy. It will undoubtedly mean that you will have to put out extra effort, exercise extra self-discipline, and be more patient with yourself so you can carry out those tasks which help you stay in the phobic situation and control your phobic fear. Even though it may take you longer than others, you will have the satisfaction of knowing that in the process you will also be modifying personality traits which have probably restricted you in other aspects of living. As this happens, we believe, you will gain greater freedom and increased enjoyment from living.

STAGE THREE: UNDERSTANDING THE PHOBIC EXPERIENCE

We are now going to describe to you what is going to be happening as you move through one step of contextual therapy after another, up to the point where you yourself are gaining control of what you think and feel in the phobic situation, and no longer respond automatically with distressing, spiralling fear and panic.

We are doing this so that you gain an understanding of your phobic reaction.

Why do you need this understanding?

In Stage One and Stage Two you take certain prescribed measures to undercut the powerful grip of the phobic reaction. In Stage Three, Understanding the Phobic Reaction, you consolidate these gains and establish long-term, automatic control.

Let us start at the point where you are just venturing into the phobic situation, not very certain about how it is going to turn out. At that point, and for several weeks thereafter, you are very likely going to find it difficult to spot, sort out, separate, identify, and describe the frightening thoughts, images, sensations, bodily reactions, and perceptions that trigger each other automatically, into the expanding and accelerating spiral we call the phobogenic process. For some time, you will probably be able to grasp and report only gross feelings of dread and panic, at different levels of intensity, without being able to break these down into their component parts.

Also, you will be concentrating so hard on doing the "little manageable tasks," that there will not be much free attention left over for introspection (monitoring your inner reactions).

Since we anticipate that this is going to happen, we have provided you with a Sample Fear Level Chart which will help you track and understand what goes on in the phobic reaction. The idea will be for you to adapt the chart to fit your phobic situation and your goals. After you have drawn up a "custom-tailored" Fear Level Chart, you should take a copy with you each time you go into the phobic situation in the course of your contextual therapy. You will be recording on this chart the ups and downs in your fear level as well as your thoughts, feelings, sensations, and actions corresponding to each up and each down.

After filling out each Fear Level Chart, you will be able to see how the internal and external events in the context correlate to produce the ups and downs in your levels of fear. You will see that the "downs" occur when you are staying involved with familiar and reassuring realities, and the "ups" occur when you are caught up in your frightening expectations, thoughts, and images. Filling out these charts will give you practice in observing these events and seeing their relationships to the changes in the intensity of your fear. After repeated practice sessions, you will notice that these observations are becoming more and more spontaneous.

Then, several weeks later, another important change should take place. Frightening thoughts, images, and bodily reactions will still be coming to you on your entry into the phobic situation, but this will not automatically set off the ascending spiral. You will find yourself observing these thoughts, sensations, and feelings *objectively*, and saying such things to yourself as "That's just a product of my imagination. There's nothing there that I really need to be afraid of. I'll just do what I've learned to keep connected to reality. I'll stay with 'what is' instead of 'what if.' I do not have to react with terror and panic. I'll just let those feelings run their course and then they'll go away."

What, in fact, will have been happening in this process is that you will be gaining an *understanding* of the changes and the process, and through this understanding, acquiring more and more stable *cognitive control*. In the first stages of your contextual therapy, you were able to control the phobogenic process by doing those manageable things which kept you connected to reality. In this later, advanced stage, your emerging, new, realistic perception and cognition *replace the "manageable tasks,"* and the control is *now inside of you*, subject to conscious direction.

Sample Fear Level Chart

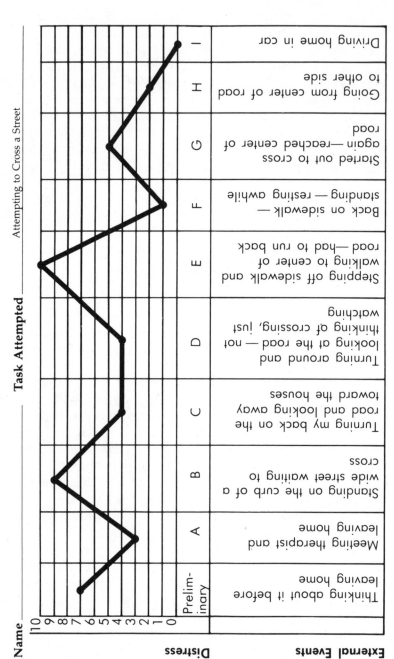

Name _____

Task Attempted _____ Attempting to Cross a Street

	Prelim-inary	A	B	C	D	E	F	G	H	I
External Events	Thinking about it before leaving home	Meeting therapist and leaving home	Standing on the curb of a wide street waiting to cross	Turning my back on the road and looking away toward the houses	Turning around and looking at the road — not thinking of crossing, just watching	Stepping off sidewalk and walking to center of road — had to run back	Back on sidewalk — standing — resting awhile	Started out to cross again — reached center of road	Going from center of road to other side	Driving home in car

Distress scale: 10, 9, 8, 7, 6, 5, 4, 3, 2, 1, 0

Concomitant Internal Events (thoughts, feelings, images, impulses, bodily sensations)

A. Feeling of comfort in having someone with me. Glad to be actually starting to do this after thinking about it for so long. Perspiring, rapid heart beat, and anxious feeling.

B. Feeling I can't do it — I may get run over — die. More rapid heart beat, palpitations, wobbly legs, perspiring. Panic feeling — wanting to run away.

C. Thoughts of safety in seeing the houses. I feel much calmer.

D. Surprised my level didn't go up — I didn't seem so frightened. After waiting, I thought I could cross.

E. Felt alright until nearly reached center of road. But nearing point of no return — sudden panic — had to run back — wobbly legs, thought I might fall down.

F. Felt exhausted and limp.

G. I labeled my fear level and kept my thoughts on getting to the middle of the road, and not on the confusion of all the traffic. Sweating hands, but palpitations not as bad as before, legs not as wobbly, felt I had control of them.

H. I felt much better, since I was on my way to safety.

I. Felt exhausted, but also a feeling of accomplishment. Next time I think I can cross the street by myself.

You decide what to do instead of being controlled by unknown forces.

As a result of your deliberate and conscious efforts every step of the way, guided by contextual therapy, a process of relearning has been taking place. Your automatic, spiralling fear reaction to the products of your imagination are being replaced by a new type of response, a response related to reality, not to imaginary dangers.

After this, another important change is going to take place. You will find that as you enter and learn to stay in the phobic situation, your subsequent fear levels will improve—tend to be much lower—*automatically*. The realistic reaction which you have been coaching and coaxing along through your conscious intervention is now beginning to come spontaneously.

It is the same sort of thing that happens when you are learning to ride a bicycle or learning a speech by heart. At first you practice each movement or each paragraph, consciously and deliberately. After a while the reactions become implanted in your nervous system and the smooth, finished response begins to come automatically, without any conscious effort.

At this stage, instead of responding automatically with frightening thoughts, images, and bodily reactions to *imagined dangers* in the phobic situation, your nervous system is now beginning to respond *automatically, without fear*, to the objective reality in the phobic situation, a reality devoid of real danger.

The instances will now come more and more frequently, where you enter the phobic situation with little or no arousal of fear, validating and proving the correctness and effectiveness of your new approach. With this, your confidence will grow, and you will become ever more comfortable with each successive experience. Now you will no longer need to try to control your external environment—to deal with your phobic fear by avoiding the phobic situation or by having someone there with whom you feel certain and safe. You will have mastered your phobic reaction.

The stage-by-stage development we have just described is a generalization, a picture of what would be expected to happen in the "average" case. There will be some differences from case to case, but not so far as the basic processes are concerned. What *will* differ from case to case is the amount of time each person will have to spend in each of these stages. In some cases, the movement will be smooth and quick from one stage to another. In other cases, some stages may take just a little time, while others persist for much longer. And in still other cases, the entire process may stretch out over many months or even years. This is understandable since the paths and processes of learning do differ from person to person.

These individual differences should be anticipated, so that in case you are progressing a little more slowly than you think you should at any particular stage, you will know not to be disappointed or disheartened. Your background and experience with the phobic situation and your expectations of yourself may be very much different from that of other people, so it may take much longer for you to identify and control your old patterns of reaction, and to acquire new ones that will work.

CHAPTER EIGHT

Recruiting Your Helper

IF YOU HAVE BEEN GETTING IMPATIENT about starting on your own contextual therapy, you may put your impatience aside. We are ready to begin, *right now*!

The first major step will be to enlist the person who is going to be your helper. We are proceeding on the assumption that you want to work with a helper and that you can find someone able and willing to fit into this role. It is not absolutely essential that you have a helper; it is possible to practice contextual therapy without one, but we think it will be easier with one. If your circumstances should be such that you either want to or have to do this by yourself, there will be special instructions for you to follow and we'll get to those later on. Meanwhile, we suggest that you move along with us as we discuss working with a helper. You'll find that some of this will apply to your situation, too; and it may be that by the time you are ready to start, your situation or preference may have changed.

Why a helper? What does the helper do?

Basically, the purpose of the helper is to assist you to undertake systematized, organized activity in the phobic situation; to think and act more realistically; and in that way to control the phobogenic process.

The helper will work along with you from the very first day that you make your plans to go into the phobic situation until the time when you feel you can manage by yourself. Here are the things a helper would be expected to do:

1. Go over the specifics of your phobia and then discuss it with you.

2. Discuss and plan with you, before each work session, just what and how much you think you ought to try that day, in confronting the phobic situation. The final decision in each instance will be yours, but it is very helpful to have someone involved with you, someone with whom you can discuss your ideas, your hesitations, your feelings, and your concerns, and who might, in addition, have some useful suggestions to offer.

3. Discuss and plan with you what specific things (we call them the "tools") you are expecting to do to keep your attention focused on those elements in the phobic situation which are familiar to you and with which you feel comfortable and safe.

4. Accompany you, when you want him to, each time you move into the phobic situation. It will be comforting, reassuring, and stabilizing to have someone with you as you take the step you have been avoiding so long.

5. Stay with you, if needed, throughout the entire time that you are in the phobic situation. Later on, you will be trying certain moves by yourself, for brief intervals, with your helper waiting nearby. We will go into greater detail about that when we get to the session-by-session instructions.

6. Your helper will not be there in just a passive role. There are positive, active things he/she will be doing to help you: reassure you when you are frightened; encourage you as you move along and make progress; ask you to talk about what you are feeling and thinking; ask you to label the levels of your fear on a scale of 0 to 10; remind you of reassuring things you can do, at times when you become confused and cannot remember those things you had planned; help you to keep focused on safe realities by a reassuring "pat" or by offering a hand or an arm to hold.

7. Remind you about filling out your Fear Level Chart for each session and help you with it if that should be necessary.

WHO SHOULD YOUR HELPER BE? A RELATIVE OR A FRIEND?

You have undoubtedly been turning over in your mind some ideas about the person you would want for a helper, and wondering whether we have any suggestions. Would we suggest that it be a relative, or do we think you'd do better with a friend?

There are advantages and disadvantages to choosing a relative and there are advantages and disadvantages to choosing a friend. We will discuss some of the pros and cons on both sides and it will be up to you to weigh them and decide what is best for you.

Significant progress in contextual therapy may take several months, and in some cases even longer. It is going to require at least one work session a week with your helper, more if possible. Each work session should require several hours of your helper's time. While some flexibility is necessary, consistency and regularity are preferred. Optimally, your helper should be a person who will have that amount of time to spare and who will be able to follow through with you, week after week.

With these requirements, the chances are that you will be more likely to find a suitable candidate among your relatives than among your friends. Yet, there are exceptions and we are acquainted with situations in which a good friend stepped into the role of helper with as great a devotion—or even greater— than one might expect of a relative.

There is another factor you might want to think about when choosing between a relative and a friend. This has to do with excessive emotional involvement and "investment," both of which could stand in your way.

Here is what we mean.

It is desirable that in the relationship between you and your helper, there should be a certain amount of objectivity and emotional detachment. You, the one with the phobia, are going to have the responsibility for what you do or do not do in the phobic situation, how conscientiously you practice in between sessions, the pace that is set, and the progress you make. The helper will be there just to guide, assist, remind, encourage, suggest, oversee, and protect. If your helper is too involved with you emotionally, he or she is likely to "suffer" too much with you as you experience distress, yield too readily if you should be hesitant about taking the next step in confronting the phobic situation, sympathize and go along with you when you choose to back away from a problem or miss a session because you are more comfortable staying at home.

A close relative—mother, father, husband, or wife—with whom you have a strong emotional attachment—is more likely to behave this way than would a relative who is more remote— sister, brother, cousin, aunt—or a good friend. However, there are exceptions. Deeply caring relatives can be excellent objective helpers when they understand the basic processes that are at work in the phobia.

Excessive emotional involvement might follow another course. Your helper may feel so charged up, enthusiastic, and excited about the next step in confronting the phobic situation that he might charge ahead and pull you along with him. That might do something for him, but it would not be of very much use to you. This might happen with either a relative or a friend.

Emotional investment—generally concealed—is something different. Some people who are themselves unfulfilled just love to have someone dependent on them, someone for whom they can do things—run errands, cook, clean, wash, entertain. This can be a genuine feeling, sincere and well-intentioned. A phobic person, by the very nature of the ailment, is a "natural" subject for this kind of service and attention, and consequently this kind of relationship is found very frequently in a family in which there is someone with a phobia. It serves the hidden interests of both—the person who is being taken care of and the care-taking person. But when the person with the phobia goes into therapy, this comfortable balance is often disturbed. As the dependent person becomes more and more independent, the care-taking person may feel unwanted and afraid and may be reluctant to let go. A parent or spouse who happens to feel this way could very easily, without even realizing it, become overly permissive and careless about encouraging the phobic person to keep up with regular work sessions and practice. If the person with the phobia should also be lackadaisical about holding to a schedule and pushing ahead for progress, the contextual therapy might easily come to a halt.

"Emotional investment" of a relative could also work in the other direction. Not everyone enjoys having a person with a phobia dependent on him. Some people may resent it very much. They may feel—and understandably—that they're being imposed upon, that their own life is being restricted and disturbed because of all the things they have to do to help the phobic person and all the things they are prevented from doing because of the phobic person's difficulties. They may even think that the phobic person is only acting phobic in order to manipulate and control them. A relative who feels this way might be inclined to push you beyond your own comfortable pace, criticize you, scold you, or ridicule you for not moving ahead more quickly, and even threaten to quit unless you follow orders and meet his expectations for progress. This approach will not only interfere with your therapy, it may even make your condition worse.

Certainly, if you do have a relative who feels that way, he is definitely not a good candidate to be your helper, unless, of course, you can help him to understand the condition better. If not, it would be wiser to select a friend or a more disinterested relative who, though he may have less time to spend with you, will not have this kind of excessive emotional investment in your getting better.

Good Qualities in a Helper

After you have thought through the questions of obstructive emotional involvement and investment, there are a number of other qualities you should look for in a helper, be it a relative or a friend.

Sincerity. This person should be one who is sincerely interested in your welfare, sincerely interested in wanting to help you be free of your phobia. You'll find such a person among those who have stayed close to you these months and years of your trouble, who have come forward with help, and who have shown some pleasure in your gains and concern about your deprivation and suffering.

Kindliness. Your helper should be one who is by nature a kindly person, one who senses what you are going through and is sympathetic with your hurt. This does not mean that he or she needs to be gushy or maudlin, or make things out worse than they are; in fact a supersentimental attitude could be a detriment because it might deter you from the objective, practical approach required in contextual therapy. The kindliness we are talking about stems from human experiences which make us appreciate how much we need others when in trouble. It may be indicated by no more than a look, a touch, a word, a nod, a smile. You'll know!

Tolerance. This quality has to do with acceptance of differences, of thoughts and feelings and behavior that are not always consistent with a set notion of what is "right," "correct," or "normal."

Tolerant people accept others as they are, with their faults, their imperfections, their weaknesses, their failings—all human qualities. They do not reject or turn away from people who do not measure up to their standards. They are more tolerant and easy with themselves, and so are tolerant and easy with others.

You will know, by your own experience, who the tolerant people have been among your family members and friends. They are the ones who did not think you were "strange" or "weird" because of your phobic fears, behavior, and avoidance; who saw your phobia as an affliction that you yourself were eager to be rid of; who kept on liking you and thinking well of you, even after the onset of your phobia.

Patience. Learning anything—riding a bicycle, driving an automobile, speaking a foreign language, trigonometry—can be a drawn out, wearisome process. Where a teacher is involved, the kind of person students find most helpful is the patient person—one who knows you are going to make mistakes, lets you make them, and helps you learn from them; who knows that different people move at difference speeds and makes allowances for the pace which is most comfortable for a particular student. A patient teacher works right along with the individual student, permitting him to stumble, pointing out the error patiently, and helping the student, with encouragement, to try that step again.

Contextual therapy is a learning process, too, and at times a distressing one. Patience on the part of your helper will be a very important factor. As you review the people you have in mind for your helper, think of their patience with you in the past, in relation to things other than your phobia. Then try to make your choice accordingly.

Some Traits to Avoid

Since we have identified objectivity, sincerity, kindliness, tolerance, and patience as traits you should look for in the person you would choose for a helper, it follows that you would try to avoid choosing someone who is too narrowly involved or invested emotionally, unkind, intolerant, and impatient.

There are some other traits about which you should be wary. Some people think they are helpful to others when they criticize, scold, or ridicule them for their mistakes. Someone like that will do you no good at all. The last thing you need is being punished for having a phobia and for being hesitant and tentative about taking the measures required for getting rid of it. Beware also of the person with a "know-it-all" attitude who would likely be more interested in showing you how smart he is than in helping you with your problem. Another trait that would not be too useful is that of casting oneself in the role of a "martyr." People with this trait too readily let you know how much of a sacrifice they are making in giving up so much time and in going to so much trouble to help you with your phobia. This would impose an additional emotional burden that you surely do not need.

Having said all this, we realize that the requirements we have set for a helper might well constitute the job qualifications for a saint. We, ourselves, do not know of a single human being who meets all these requirements, and we certainly do not think that you, either, are going to find anyone who is perfect.

What we would like you to do, then, is to regard the qualifications we have discussed as constituting the "ideal." The closer your helper approximates this ideal the better. But do make allowances. Be flexible. You may have to "trade off" some personality traits for availability and willingness to serve. If you do have to do this, you will at least be forewarned about what to expect and what not to expect of your helper. That way, you are not as likely to feel disappointed and resentful when your helper does not quite measure up in every respect.

Make allowances, also, for the possibility that even though your helper may not meet some of your high expectations at the outset, he or she could change and mature while working with you. This often does happen. Personality characteristics are not immutable. Being a helper is a new and challenging experience and it may bring out some very positive characteristics which may not have been in evidence before. So much the better for you if something like this does happen.

In summary, what is most important is that you find someone

who will listen and try to understand what you are experiencing. It is that sort of person who is most likely to possess the desired qualities of sincerity, tolerance, kindliness, and patience.

APPROACHING YOUR PROSPECTIVE HELPER

We are hoping that you have already told some of your relatives and friends about your phobia and that you will be ready to approach your prospective helper without still having that bridge to cross.

If you have not, and if you are still hesitating about doing so, we will sum up here, quite briefly, some of the things we have already said about the importance of being as open as you are able to be about your phobia.

Obviously, you cannot recruit a helper without letting him or her know about your phobia. But, aside from that—even if you are not planning to work with a helper, we need to remind you that keeping your phobia to yourself will stand in the way of getting rid of it, no matter how you plan to proceed. Unless you communicate with others about your imaginary fears and dangers in the phobic situation, you will miss the opportunity of checking these out with others and learning how baseless they are. Even as you talk about them to others in the clear light of reality, you yourself will get a different perspective on them, a more objective perspective, and that will already be a start in getting them under control. The more you keep them locked up inside yourself, the more exaggerated and terrifying will those feelings become.

Perhaps you are still concerned that your relatives and friends will not understand, that they will think there is something "different" or "abnormal" about you because of your phobia, that they might turn away from you because of your "peculiar" and "weird" ideas and behavior.

If that is the case, then let us assure you again that public attitudes about phobia have changed dramatically in the past few years and that most people who read a newspaper or magazine, or who listen to radio or watch television, have heard about phobias and no longer regard phobic people with suspicion and rejection as they might have in the past. They might not fully understand all that you are experiencing and going through, but they surely will understand that what you have is a *problem*, not a *fault*. There is probably not a single family in this country which has not had someone with an emotional ailment of one kind or another—depression, anxiety, psychosomatic illnesses, alcohol problems, and the like. Most people are already used to this type of disorder, and your disclosure of your phobia is hardly likely to come as a great shock. Patient after patient has come back to report that when they told their relatives and friends about their phobia, they were surprised by the sympathetic and understanding reaction, acknowledging that their apprehensions had been greatly exaggerated and unwarranted.

The problem may be that it is you who has not yet accepted your phobia as just a different kind of emotional problem—rather than some kind of a "weird disease," and that it is you who is still seeing yourself as someone "different," "unlikable," an outcast. Your task then would be for you to work with yourself, in changing your own attitude about yourself. When you have come to terms with this issue, and have finally accepted yourself with your phobia, you will find that you will be much less hesitant about revealing your phobia to others.

WHAT TO SAY TO THE PERSON YOU WANT TO RECRUIT AS YOUR HELPER

When you approach a relative or a friend to ask if he or she would become your helper in your contextual therapy, you are going to have to explain what it is you are planning to do, and what you would like his or her role to be in it. We are going to provide you, now, with a list of the most important things you ought to cover. It is not essential that you cover all of these points at one time, or that you cover them in the exact order they are given. It is not necessary for you to go into deep explanations at the time of the first approach. In fact, the more simple and brief your explanation, the better. You can go into greater detail later on if necessary. Here are some of the points you ought to cover.

About the Helper
Start off by explaining that
- You have been reading this book and that it is offering you what sounds like an effective way to get over your phobia.

- This is something you might be able to do by yourself, but it would be much better if you had someone to help you.
- You would like that "someone" to be he or she. (To avoid saying "he or she" over and over again, we are just going to say "he" from now on, and assume that you know we mean "he or she.")
- The helper doesn't have to be an expert or know anything about phobias. You and the book will be telling him all he will need to know in order to be of help to you.
- All that is required is that he be willing to try to spend a few hours a week working with you, on a regular basis, for at least the next two or three months, possibly longer. The hours will be arranged between you.
- People are different; some take longer than others. You hope that in your case it will be "shorter" rather than "longer," but that you cannot make any promises, because you yourself have no idea how it is going to work out.
- If things go really well, you may not be needing his help on a regular basis, *later on*; you might be able to carry on by yourself a good deal of the time.

About Contextual Therapy
Explain to your helper that

- The method is called contextual therapy.
- It was the method used in probably the first phobia clinic in the United States and that it was introduced by the clinic's founder and director, Dr. Zane. It is now being used in many other treatment centers.
- Contextual therapy is a form of "exposure therapy," meaning that the phobic person goes into the phobic situation, confronts his phobic dread, and works there on bringing it under control.
- There are different kinds of exposure therapy. This one, contextual therapy, concentrates on getting the phobic person to shift the focus of his attention from the imaginary dangers in the phobic situation and the automatic, frightening response this arouses, to the realities in the phobic situation which are familiar and reassuring.
- There are many different kinds of things you are going to plan to do which will keep you focused on the familiar and reassuring realities (and give a few examples of the kind we have listed previously).

What the Helper Will Be Expected to Do

Explain to your helper that

- You are going to have one work session a week—or more, if possible—and that each work session will consist of a single trial in which you, accompanied by the helper, will move into the phobic situation.

- The idea will be to start with a small, simple, not-too-difficult step, master it, and then move on to one that is a little more difficult, and then to one that is more difficult than that, right up the scale.

- You and the helper will meet first and discuss the long-range plan, in a general way. Then you will both sit down before each work session and plan out just what and how much you think you will be able to do that day.

- You and the helper are going to go over the things you will try to do to keep yourself focused on the familiar and reassuring realities and jot them down.

- The helper will stay with you in the phobic situation, offering reassurance and a sense of safety just by his very presence. Later on he will not stay with you in the phobic situation every minute of the time, but may wait outside or out of sight at a designated place and for a designated amount of time.

- The helper will do more than "just be there." He will ask you to talk about what you are feeling and thinking, ask you to label your fear on a scale of 0 to 10 (explain briefly what that means, without going into too great detail), remind you of the reassuring things you need to do in case you become confused or forget, and help you fill out a fear-level chart for each work session.

Throughout your discussion, you should reassure your "prospect" that there is no need for him to try to remember any of this now, that it is only necessary for him to get a general idea so that he can decide about becoming a helper. Later on, there will be ample, detailed instructions for you and for him to follow. He will have all that information in front of him, in printed form, and he can study it as thoroughly as he wants at that time. If your prospect is still a little vague about what the procedure is going to be and about what is going to be expected of him, it would be a good idea to let him read the illustrations of two work sessions (Dave and Sally) on pages 157–161 of Chapter Seven.

When you have gotten an agreement from your prospect that he is willing to be your helper, arrange to have your first planning meeting as soon as it is convenient for both of you. It would be a good idea for the two of you to meet at a place and time where you will be by yourselves with plenty of leisure and without the restraint that might be imposed by the presence of somebody else. When you have made that arrangement, tell him you would like him to take something home to read before this first meeting. This "something" will be a memorandum written specifically for your helper and addressed directly to him. It starts on the following page. (You will not need to mutilate your book to give him these pages. Simply take your book to a photocopy service and have them copy these pages for you, or make the copies yourself at your local public library. It should not cost very much.)

You should also read through this memorandum yourself, since it is basically a concise summary of everything that has been discussed about phobias and contextual therapy to this point. This review of the causes of phobia and the techniques of contextual therapy will help prepare you for your first meeting with your helper, which is covered in the following chapter.

A MEMORANDUM

To:

The helper of _____

(name to be filled in)

From:

Manuel Zane, M.D., and Harry Milt, authors of *YOUR PHOBIA: UNDERSTANDING YOUR FEARS THROUGH CONTEXTUAL THERAPY*

In accepting the role of "helper" for your relative or friend, you are rendering a laudable, humane service. We know that you are doing this out of a personal concern and that you have no need for special recognition or thanks. Nevertheless, it is an act of great generosity. You are going to be giving not only your time, but also your devotion to the person you are helping to be rid of a distressing ailment, one that has been the cause of considerable hardship and deprivation.

We know that you have already been informed, in a general way, about what you are going to be doing, and what your role will be. The precise, detailed instructions will be spelled out in the following chapters. In the meantime, we would like to give you a little information which should help you understand better what the phobias are, and how they affect the people who are afflicted with them.

WHAT IS A PHOBIA?

A phobia is an irrational (unrealistic) dread of a particular place, object, animal, or insect, resulting in avoidance. This is a capsule definition. Let us expand on it a little further.

The central emotion in phobia is fear, but it is not ordinary fear; it is much stronger, more like terror and dread. In addition, the person with the phobia experiences a wide variety of physical reactions, such as racing heart; palpitations; shortness of breath; nausea; trouble in breathing and swallowing; perspiring; dizziness; imbalance; feeling faint and weak; pains in arms, head, legs, and chest; shakiness of hands and trembling of the limbs; ringing in the ears; blurred vision; pallor or flushing; stomach cramps and diarrhea; and urinary difficulties. These physical reactions are activated by the body's mobilization to deal with what is perceived to be a danger or threat to survival.

That is what the person with the phobia experiences when he enters the "phobic situation," or anticipates entering into it.

WHAT IS THE PHOBIC SITUATION?

This is a general term, meaning the place, object, animal, or insect which triggers the reaction we have just described—the feelings of terror and dread, together with the physical sensations.

The phobic situations people have heard most about are heights, closed-in places, wide open and exposed places, some animals, and some insects. But the phobic situation could be anything—these and many, many others, depending on the individual's experience and whatever it was in that experience that made him sensitive to that particular situation.

The phobic situation could be elevators, automobiles, airplanes, tunnels, bridges, highways, shopping malls, stores, streets, churches, classrooms, meeting halls, theaters, barbers' chairs, beauty parlor chairs, dentists' chairs, waiting rooms, waiting in lines in a supermarket or bank, tall buildings, towers, mountains, high-rise apartments, cats, dogs, snakes, birds, spiders, or bugs of any kind.

It could be a phenomenon of nature such as snow, rain, wind, water, fire, lightning, or thunder. It could also be the act of writing, speaking, or eating in front of other people, or urinating in a toilet when somebody else is present.

All of these that we have mentioned are among the more common phobic situations. But some rather rare ones can also be included: balloons, clocks, traffic lights, melon seeds, newspapers, dolls, foam baths, ships, radio music, high-pitched sounds, fuzzy objects, or the colors purple, black, and red.

Many phobic people have a phobia for only one specific type of phobic situation. These are called "simple phobias." For example, there are people whose phobia relates only to closed-in places; others, only to open, exposed places; others only to heights. People with an animal phobia are, generally, phobic only for a particular species of animal—birds or dogs or snakes or spiders or bees, etc. Some people have only a phobia for fire; others only for water; others only for lightning and thunder; others only for hypodermic injections, doctors, and dentists.

But there is another type of phobia—agoraphobia—which is complex and includes a wide variety of phobic situations. Formerly the word "agoraphobia" (from a Greek word) was employed to mean "dread of wide open places." Today it means something quite different. A person with agoraphobia could be phobic to many situations: heights, closed-in places, wide open places, storms, water, and any other specific thing. Generally, this condition starts with phobia for one specific situation, such as elevators or bridges or mountain roads. Then it spreads—sometimes gradually, sometimes quickly—to many other situations, each of which arouses the phobic reaction—the terror, dread, and accompanying physical sensations.

WHAT TRIGGERS THE PHOBIC REACTION?

What is there in the phobic situation which arouses this phobic reaction—this reaction of terror and dread? Everyone, including the person with the phobia, knows there is no real danger there to life or limb. What kind of bodily harm could possibly come to a person standing in a supermarket line, sitting in a barber's chair, riding at slow speed in an automobile crossing over a bridge, riding in an elevator in a busy office building, watching a kitten romping at play, a spider spinning a web, or a bird perched on a tree limb? None! Yet, for people who have a phobia, such situations are enough to trigger a reaction much more intense than ordinary fear.

What is it that they're afraid of?

For the person with a phobia for cats, it may be the thought of the cat—any kitten or cat—touching him, or climbing up on his lap, or staring at him that strikes terror into his heart. The person with a phobia for elevators may visualize himself trapped in a solid steel box without any exit, suffocating for lack of air. The person with a phobia for heights stands in front of a window and may see himself hurtling through the air and plunging down into the street below, his body smashing on the pavement. The person with a phobia for bridges may visualize losing control, smashing through the rail, and plunging several hundred feet into the dark depths of the river below. The per-

son sitting in the waiting room may have a feeling of being
trapped, not being able to get enough air, and fainting in the
midst of a "bunch of strangers" who wouldn't know who he is
or where he lives and wouldn't bother to get him to the hospital. The "scenario" may differ from person to person and from
situation to situation, but all these scenarios depict something
terrible happening, something from which there is no escape,
something irreversible and final.

So, what triggers the dread reaction is not any real danger to
life or limb, but some "terrible thing" that the phobic person
imagines is going to happen.

But the body does not make the distinction between "imagined" and "real" dangers. It reacts to what is in the person's
mind—what he perceives as dangerous. If a person sees a
holdupman approach him with a gun, he is frightened for his
life. His mind conjures up scenes of danger, and his body responds with a fear reaction and physical mobilization to escape
this danger or fight back. If a person hears a noise and *imagines*
there's a robber in the house, his mind conjures up some scenes
of danger to himself, his wife, his children. His body responds
with a fear reaction and physical mobilization, *just as though* a
burglar was actually there (even though the noise was just a
harmless creak). When a person, standing before a window and
looking down at the street below, conjures up scenes in his
mind of himself plunging through the window and hurtling
through the air to the street, his body responds with a fear
reaction, and a physical mobilization as well.

The only difference is this: Where there is a real danger, the
fear reaction and bodily mobilization lead to a realistic practical
life-saving maneuver. But since there is no possible life-saving
maneuver to a totally *imaginary threat*, the body responds not
only with fear, but feelings of terror and dread together with a
physical response which is chaotic and directionless—the racing
heart, shortness of breath, weak and trembling limbs, dizziness,
and faintness. Furthermore, this chaotic fear reaction is itself an
additional source of fear. In a situation in which there is a real
danger, as in the case of the man who is being threatened by a
robber, the danger is identifiable and the fear reaction to this
danger is understandable and acceptable to the person experiencing it. When the danger passes, the fear reaction recedes. But
in the case of the person reacting with fright in a phobic situation which actually poses no real threat, the automatic fear

reaction comes as a shock. The phobic person has no idea why he is reacting this way, and since he cannot understand it, the fear reaction itself becomes a source of additional danger and threat, triggering new thoughts and images of frightening things that might happen. This fear process escalates quickly into a panic attack.

The person with the phobia experiences all of this as happening in a flash, all at once. But it does not, in fact, happen that way, as those who experience it are able to testify when they have the opportunity to examine it in the course of contextual therapy.

What does actually happen is something more like this: Let us take the instance of a person with agoraphobia. That person—a woman—is seated in a train, occupied with her thoughts, when suddenly, "out of the blue," she senses a stab of intense fear. So far as she knows, she has been thinking of nothing that would be really frightening, nor was anything happening on the train that could frighten her. This itself—not being aware of any cause—makes the reaction even more frightening. Immediately, the body responds with a variety of internal activities, as it mobilizes to deal with a danger or threat. It does not matter that no real danger is apparent. It matters only that this woman *feels fright*, and it is to this that the body reacts. Becoming aware that her heart is racing, her hands trembling, her breath failing, this woman becomes even more alarmed and thinks, with accompanying imagery, "Oh my God, I can't catch my breath. I'm going to faint. What is happening to me? Am I going to die?" These frightening thoughts and images trigger off another round of bodily responses which terrify her even more. Now she thinks: "I am really dying. I have to get out of here so I can get to a hospital. What is going to happen to my poor children if I die"? She visualizes herself dead, her children alone and desperate. These frightening thoughts and images trigger another volley of bodily reactions. This continues in an accelerating and expanding spiral, culminating in total panic. At that point the woman's feelings are so terrible and unendurable that she thinks, "I am going to go berserk. I am going to go out of my mind"— anything, even dying, in order to find relief from this unendurable feeling as one might wish to die to get relief from unbearable pain.

But she manages to hold on to herself until the train comes to the next station, and the moment the train door opens she flees.

From that point on, she will not get on a train again, fearing that if she does, she will have this horrible experience again. This is what is called avoidance. From that time on, she avoids getting on any train. After a while (with some this comes very quickly, with others it may take longer), she finds that she is frightened even to get on an elevator, thinking: "What if the same thing happens to me on an elevator? I'd be trapped there and have a heart attack and die." She does try going on an elevator two or three more times, but the experience is so distressing—she is in such a state of tension and fright all the time—that she decides to cut out—avoid—elevators, too. This process continues inexorably, adding one phobic situation after another—shops, bridges, automobiles, meeting rooms, churches, gatherings of all kinds—until the only place where she feels safe, where she feels that the horrible panic attacks will not occur, is her home.

DOES AVOIDANCE ALWAYS OCCUR IN PHOBIAS?

Although we consider avoidance to be a basic criterion for phobias, there are some instances where the person with the phobia struggles with the impulse to avoid the situation and manages to enter and stay in it, occasionally suffering intense anxiety and tension throughout. This is likely to occur in cases where entering the phobic situation is critical for business or for the health and welfare of a member of the family. In many such cases, however, the strain becomes so great that it leads, eventually, to total avoidance of that particular situation.

Avoidance results in the ultimate elimination of any activity which might bring the individual into his or her phobic situation. In the case of specific, simple phobias—such as a phobia for cats or dogs, for elevators or heights—cutting out of these activities may result in only a limited interference with living. But in phobias involving many phobic situations, as in agoraphobia, a person's whole life may be shattered.

WHAT CAUSES A PHOBIA?

What causes a person to become sensitized—phobic—to a particular situation and to react to it with terror and avoidance?

There are many different explanations for this and we will

touch briefly on a few of them. The purpose in our doing this is to provide a broader understanding of the phobias and to reduce some of the mystery which still surrounds them. But we need to stress that, so far as contextual therapy is concerned, our emphasis is not going to be on what might have happened in the past, but on what is happening in the present, as the person with a phobia reacts to the situation to which he is phobically sensitive.

Some experts say that people develop a phobia for a particular place or object after having had a frightening or terrifying experience. For example, some people with a phobia for heights say they themselves had fallen from a height, or had seen someone killed in a fall from a height. A person with a phobia for dogs might recall having been attacked by a fierce dog. A person with a phobia for fire might have been hurt in a fire or had known a person burned to death in a fire. This is called the "trauma" explanation.

However, most phobic people say they cannot recall ever having had a traumatic or frightening experience related to their phobia. This could be because they had had such an experience and forgotten it. Or it could be that they had been told frightening things about their particular phobic place or object as a child, and stored this fear away in their "memory storage," where it lay until something triggered it off later in life.

There is another theory which holds that a particular object or animal or situation triggers a phobic reaction, not because it itself is frightening, but because it was associated with a traumatic, frightening experience in the long forgotten past. The following incident has been offered as an illustration of that kind of occurrence. A little boy of six was playing in the street one day when he saw his little friend run into the path of an oncoming truck. The truck was unable to stop in time and it ran over the little friend and killed him. The child who was killed happened to be playing with a toy balloon and the balloon came to rest alongside the child's body. The incident was so terribly frightening that the little boy observing it quickly forgot about it in its entirety, including the presence of the balloon. Later in life—when this child had grown up—he developed an unexplainable phobia for balloons. A psychotherapist to whom he went for help tried to find out what there was about balloons that had significance for this patient, but this man was unable to come up with anything at all. Then the psychotherapist tried hypnosis and the patient was able to recall the traumatic incident of his childhood, the one in which his little friend has been killed. He also recalled that one thing stood out aside from the accident—the friend's red toy balloon. The terror which has been aroused by the accident had been transferred to an innocent object—the balloon—and this innocent object later became the trigger for a phobic reaction.

This might explain why phobic reactions appear to be so irrational. A balloon or cat or storm might have no meaning, in the present, as a cause of the dread. But it might have been the "innocent element" in a traumatic event which happened long ago and was forgotten.

The psychoanalytic explanation of the phobias had been the one most commonly accepted, until about twenty years ago, when newly emerging theories from the behavioral school of psychology began to overshadow it. In essence, the psychoanalytic explanation is as follows:

When a person—a child or an adult—has a painful conflict between two competing emotions, the conflict is pushed out of the conscious mind and "repressed into the unconscious mind." For example, a child might feel hurt and angry because his mother has shifted her attention and affection from him to a newborn baby. The child begins to hate the mother and wish the new infant would die or "go away." However, these strong feelings frighten him. He knows they are "wrong" and "bad," and he is afraid his mother will find out about them and punish him or "send him away." The conflict between the "bad" wish and the fear are too painful to endure, and so both are banished from consciousness—repressed into the unconscious. But that does not put an end to them. They continue to strive for expression, and since they are not "permitted" to emerge in their frank form, they emerge in a disguised form, generally as the symptom of some emotional disturbance. In a child this disguised expression might come out as nightmares, night terrors, bedwetting, or an unexplainable phobia for a dog or horse or other animal or object. Adult phobias would be explained in the same way: Repressed conflicting emotions emerge in disguise, as the symptoms of various emotional disturbances, including phobias.

The psychoanalytic theory does not explain why one particular phobic object or situation is chosen, rather than any other, to be the target of the disguised emotion.

The final explanation to be discussed is one that is consistent with contextual therapy. The central idea in this explanation is this: Some people become phobic because they have never learned how to make the distinction between the real and imaginary fears which are a normal part of human experiences, starting with childhood.

Children have fears about such imaginary things as witches, monsters, demons, the "boogeyman," and the like. They also have realistic fears about being hurt, getting sick, being lost, or being separated from a parent. Given the chance to express these fears with screaming or weeping (or whatever their mode might be) and then to talk about them to their parents, children are able, slowly and gradually, to distinguish imaginary dangers from real ones, and to stop reacting to imaginary dangers as though they were real. (This development may take as long as ten years.) They also learn how to deal with real dangers and insecurities in life; to guard themselves to the extent possible from injury and illness, and from losses, frustrations, and failures; and not to be shattered by them when they occur, as they inevitably must in everybody's life.

Not all children develop this sort of realistic approach to fears and dangers. For various reasons, they do not find it possible or easy to express their fears about imaginary and real dangers, to talk about them and to put them into perspective. As a result they do not ever learn, fully, to distinguish imaginary dangers from real ones, nor how to deal with real ones in an effective way.

Then, when they grow up and are faced with difficulties and responsibilities—as might occur in graduation from school, romantic involvements, marriage, getting a new job, having a baby, illness or the death of a close relative—they are unprepared to handle them. They react instead with fright, panic, and despair. It is in just such situations that a phobia—with all its imaginary dangers—is likely to erupt. Not having mastered the complicated art of distinguishing imaginary dangers from real ones, they react to the imaginary dangers in the phobic situation as though they were real. This is most likely to happen with people who are exceptionally imaginative to start with.

The task of contextual therapy is, therefore, to reorient the phobic person so he can distinguish imaginary fears from real ones, and to deal with imaginary fears for what they are so they can no longer dominate and control him.

Some forms of therapy make the assumption that phobias

come from personality problems, and that by straightening out these problems, you can cause the phobia to disappear. These methods, based on the psychoanalytic approaches, may have been successful, in general, in correcting personality problems, but have not had too much success in eliminating the phobias.

Other therapies try to get the person with the phobia to move back into the phobic situation—to expose him to it—a step at a time, with the anticipation that the phobic terror and dread will diminish by themselves with each successive exposure. This "passive" form of exposure therapy does work fairly well with some cases of simple phobia, but it has not proven to be too effective with more complex types, such as agoraphobia. In our opinion, passive exposure is not enough. It is also necessary for the phobic person to learn what goes on within him while he is in the phobic situation and to undertake certain, specified measures to regulate and control his phobic reaction.

Contextual therapy does not concern itself with the presumed original causes (as do various kinds of psychotherapy), nor does it rely on change taking place passively, by itself. Contextual therapy concerns itself with the phobic reaction itself. That is where the trouble lies and that is where the work has to be done. Contextual therapy moves into the phobic situation with the person who has the phobia and observes directly and painstakingly what goes on within him *in the context* of his phobic reaction, at the place and at the time it is happening. It observes (1) his internal reaction—his feelings, thoughts and imagery, and (2) his external reaction—the way he behaves in the phobic situation. It involves the phobic person as a participant in this observation, so he himself can be aware of what is going on. He learns that his fear does not stay at a constant level, but gets better and worse. He learns also that the rise and fall of his phobic fear is controlled by what he is feeling and thinking at the time, that his impulse to flee from the phobic situation is directed and controlled by the dangers he imagines and senses to be there.

He begins to understand that if he is to free himself from this control, he is going to have to learn how to stay in the phobic situation and shift his attention from preoccupation with these frightening thoughts and imagery to elements in the phobic situation which are familiar to him and which he finds comforting and reassuring.

This shift in focus compels his body to reorganize its reactions in response to the safe realities instead of to imaginary dangers. This automatically undercuts the spiralling phobogenic process. It does not wipe out the fear reaction entirely, at first. It does enable the phobic person to cope with the fear without running away, and then gradually to bring it under control. As he learns, through experience, no longer to regard the situation as dangerous, the fear diminishes and eventually disappears.

When we say that the person with the phobia is going to have to move into the phobic situation, we do not mean that he is going to have to plunge in all at once. On the contrary, we expect that he will take it in small steps which he can handle. Once he has mastered the first step, then he will be expected to try one that goes a little further, and the next one that goes even further. For example, if his problem happens to be agoraphobia and he has been homebound, the first step might be just to come out of his apartment and walk down the corridor as far as the elevator; or if he lives in a private house, to come out and walk as far as the sidewalk. What that first step is going to be and what the following steps are going to be will depend on your partner. He might be able to ride down the elevator on the very first try; or he might (if he lives in a private home) be able to walk up to the corner, or around the block, with you by his side. You are going to plan the steps together, but the final decision will be his. You don't need to be concerned about planning these steps right now. We are going to work out a schedule for your partner and you, and you will be able to follow it quite easily. Right now, all we are asking is that you get a general idea of what the process is going to be, so you can be thinking about it, and be prepared to discuss it with your partner when you have your first planning meeting.

Your role in the phobic situation is not going to be a passive one. You will be doing more than just being there for your partner to "lean on." Here are some of the other things you will be doing:

1. Reminding your partner—in case he becomes confused or too upset to remember—to do some of the things that will keep him focused on the reassuring realities.

2. From time to time, asking your partner to tell you what he is feeling and thinking.

3. From time to time, asking your partner to "label" his fear—to assign a number to it according to how strong it is.

Number 10 will mean it is so bad, he almost can't stand it. Number 0 will mean he feels no fear at all. The numbers in between will be for the different levels of intensity. Number 2 might mean, "Hardly any fear at all," number five might mean, "It's fairly strong but I can handle it without too much of a problem." Number 8 might mean, "It's really bad, and I don't know whether I can stand it much longer." You will find that after a while, your partner will be able to "label" his fear at various levels quite easily, and that you will quickly get to know the intensity of his fear at these various levels.

4. Helping your partner fill out a Fear Level Chart for each of the work sessions. You will be getting a sample chart, showing you how this should be done.

We suggest you read this memorandum a few times, until you feel that you've really got "the hang" of the procedure. If you have any questions, jot them down and discuss them with your partner at your first meeting. Your partner has the book in which all of this is discussed in great detail. If necessary, you can both look at the book and try to find the answers to your question.

Your partner has instructions about working out a date with you for your first planning meeting, as well as about the things you should discuss there. The next signal will come from your partner. If he does not get in touch with you after you have waited a few days, it would be a good idea for you to call him, just in case he has gotten "cold feet."

Before leaving you this time, we would like to go over a few additional points about phobias, some things you should know.

1. Phobias are very common. Many millions of Americans are suffering from this affliction and many of them are getting treatment in various clinics or other treatment facilities around the country. In addition to those who have been identified as having a phobia, there are estimated to be millions of others who have a phobia but have not done anything about it yet. When you start to ask around, it seems that everyone you talk to either has a phobia or knows of somebody else who does.

2. Phobias do not reflect any lack of intelligence. Professionals who treat people for phobias are in general agreement that these people rate high in intelligence and do very well in their studies, professions, or businesses.

3. You hear people say to a phobic person, "How can such a smart person as you believe those ridiculous things you think could happen to you? Why can't you use good sense and reason? You'd get over it in a minute."

If reasoning and good sense could solve a person's phobia, there probably wouldn't be a single person with a phobia today. Phobic people know their fears are absurd, that they do not fit with reality. They know it is "ridiculous to be afraid of a tiny little kitten," or to think "that the snake in the picture is moving," or that they are in any real danger looking out of a window in a high-rise apartment. They work very hard trying to prove to themselves that their fears are absurd. But this does absolutely no good; in fact it makes the fears worse. There is no way a phobic person can "reason himself" out of a fear reaction. It comes on automatically and is entirely out of his control. Phobic people would give anything to be able to suppress their fears and make them go away, but they cannot.

4. You hear people say, "Your phobia is just a weakness. If you wanted to, if you used your willpower and really tried hard, you'd get over it." No one in the world is more anxious to get rid of a phobia than the person afflicted with it. But the dread that phobic people anticipate or experience in the phobic situation is so powerful and so unendurable that they are powerless to combat it. Telling a person with a phobia: "Go on. Do it. Get into that elevator." Or, "Pick up that cat." Or, "Drive across that bridge," is the same as telling another person to plunge into a fire, or jump out of a window, or stab himself with a knife. The terror aroused by the imaginary dangers can be even greater than that aroused by real dangers, and you can no more expect a phobic person to ignore his terror than you can tell a non-phobic person to ignore his.

Contextual therapy and other types of exposure therapy *do not* tell the person with the phobia "Go on, use your willpower. Jump into the phobic situation and you'll conquer your phobia." On the contrary, they recognize the immense power of the terror and dread which are holding him back from doing this. They offer him various strategies to deal with and overcome this resistance, a little at a time, and in that way to gain control of his phobic reaction.

If it were true that people with phobias do not have any "willpower" or are not using it, then we would not be witnessing what we are witnessing today—thousands upon thousands of people with phobias flocking to every kind of treatment facility. The fact that so many are eager to undertake any sort of therapy which offers even the slightest glimmer of hope is proof enough of their desire to get better.

5. People with phobias find it very hard to talk about their problem, or even to let others know that they have it. They are concerned about being seen in an uncomplimentary light, being ridiculed and rejected. It has taken a great deal of courage for your partner to talk to you about his problem and to invite you to take the role of helper. It is taking even more courage for him to decide to move into his phobic situation, confront his phobia, and "stay the course" until he can control it.

But we know that with your help, this "impossible task" will be reduced to manageable proportions.

6. Does contextual therapy get results? Will it work for your partner? Answering the first question first, contextual therapy has been in use since 1971 at the White Plains Hospital Phobia Clinic and in other treatment facilities which have adopted it. It has proven to be very effective.

The White Plains Hospital Phobia Clinic has conducted a study of progress made by several hundred patients who had been treated there. In one phase of this study, these patients were contacted six months after they had completed their eight-week treatment program at the clinic (one practice session a week) and asked whether their phobic condition was better than when they started, and if so, to what extent they had improved. About ninety percent said their condition was improved, and six out of every ten said they were very much better or totally set free of their phobia.

In the second phase of the study, these same patients were followed up again four years later. The great majority responded, and of these, about ninety percent said they had maintained their gains.

It is not at all unusual to hear patients at the clinic say such things as the following, after only a few weeks of treatment: "I hadn't been out of my house for two years, but yesterday I walked all around the block." "I got on the bus last night and rode about a mile, all by myself. That was my first time on the bus in five years." "I was able to sit in the same room with a cat without getting hysterical." "We took a drive over the George Washington Bridge and we had to drive over an expressway to get there. Before I started treatment, you couldn't have dragged me there with wild horses." "I thought I would never go up in a plane again, but last Saturday I flew to Washington and on Monday I flew back again. My helper was with me, both ways, but in a few weeks I'm going to try it alone."

Now to answer the second question: "Will contextual therapy work for your partner?" We expect that readers of this book will have similar success as those mentioned above just a few weeks after putting into practice what they have learned in this book.

But you must remember that each person is unique, and that the problem to be dealt with is complex. Hence, for most people, much more work and practice will be needed. Nor should anyone expect a smooth course. There will be ups and downs, which are normal in any learning process. But over the long run the trend will be toward continued improvement, the rate depending on the individual and his practical life situation. For the great majority, the outlook is very definitely for substantial improvement, including, for many, total freedom from their phobia.

CHAPTER NINE

The First Meeting
with Your Helper

THIS CHAPTER, while addressed to the person with the phobia, is meant for the helper as well. You might both read it together a few pages at a time and discuss what you have read, or you might want to read it separately and discuss it afterward.

If you have not already set a date for your first meeting—a planning meeting—do so now. You can meet at your home, your helper's home, in the park, a community center, church, or synagogue meeting room—wherever you will be able to talk freely without being disturbed. Naturally, if your phobia makes it difficult for you to get out of your home, the meeting will have to be where you live.

WHAT SHOULD YOU DISCUSS AT THIS PLANNING MEETING?

Your phobia. Your helper should have a clear idea about your phobic condition. Are you phobic for cats, automobiles, bridges, elevators, or what? Tell your helper what happens to you—what you feel, think, and do—when you see a cat, ride in an automobile, go to a party or meeting, ride in the subway, get into an elevator, or whatever your particular phobic situation might be. If you are phobic for more than one situation, object, animal, or insect, let your helper know all about these different situations. If you haven't been in or near your phobic situation for some time, tell him what happened when it first began. (Again we are faced with the editorial problem of saying he or she, since your helper may be either male or female. To avoid this awkward problem we will only say he, but you will know that when we do, we mean he or she.)

As you get into giving an account of your phobia, you and your helper should be warned about something that is likely to happen, something that should not be encouraged. People with phobias may be burdened down with problems and difficulties relating to their personal lives, their relations with others, their feelings about themselves, their problems on the job or in their profession or business, their marriage, their children, and other things which do not have to do directly and specifically with their phobia. It is natural to want to discuss these things, and there is nothing wrong with that so long as it does not distract you from the main task at hand—to concentrate on your contextual therapy. (If your problems are so upsetting as to interfere with your concentration on contextual therapy, it might be wise to seek some other sort of help from a psychiatrist.)

It is also quite natural for a person with a phobia to want to theorize about the "original" causes of the phobia. While this may be of interest to both of you, it will not be of practical value in your planning meeting. Further, contextual therapy does not concern itself with remote causes. It is concerned primarily with the present cause—the same for all phobias—and that is the phobogenic process and its power to dominate and control a person's feelings and behavior in the phobic situations.

Identifying your long-range goal. What is it you want to happen as a result of your contextual therapy? The first answer that is likely to come to your mind is, "I want to get better. I want to get rid of my phobia." That's fine, but it is too general. It doesn't define clearly enough what you're aiming for. A more useful answer would be something like this (taking as an example a phobia for cats, which would be one of the simplest situations): "My cat phobia means I can never visit any of my friends or relatives who has a cat. It means that wherever I go, I am always tense and anxious that a cat might run out from behind a store counter, or jump out from an open doorway, or run out from behind some trees or bushes. I want to be free of this constant tension and worry. I want to be able to see a cat and not have it mean anything more to me than seeing a bicycle or chair. I don't particularly care about keeping a cat for a pet, I just want to get to the point where I am able to see and touch a cat and not have it bother me."

When you have discussed this with your helper, jot down a few notes, and later, when you are alone, write down: "My long-term goal is. . ." and fill in the rest. It would be a good idea to get yourself a notebook because you will need to make notes of other things from time to time.

What do you put down as your goal when you don't have a simple phobia like a cat phobia but a complex one like agoraphobia? The process is the same. It could go something like this: "I want to be able to walk out of my house without giving it a second thought, with the same kind of freedom I had before my phobia. I would want to be able to get into my automobile and drive anywhere and when and how I wanted—right into heavy traffic, over bridges, on expressways, out into the country, across bodies of water, up into the mountains, down into tunnels. I would like to get into an airplane and fly to Florida, San Francisco, Paris. I would like to be able to go to the theater again and see a musical comedy. I want to go to supermarkets and do my own shopping again. I want to be able to drive my children to their football practice and dancing lessons. I want to be able to get together with all my relatives at my mother's house for Thanksgiving and Christmas. But most of all, I just want to be like everybody else, like I was before my phobia—free, independent, to go where I want, when I want, when the mood strikes me, without worrying, ever again, whether my panic is going to strike. I want to feel safe everywhere and anywhere outside my home."

After you have done that, begin to narrow it down. You undoubtedly have, among all your long-range goals, some specific priorities. You may feel that what is most important right now is to be able to drive your children to school; or to be able to go out, once more, to the theater and restaurants with your husband; or to go to work again and regain your sense of independence and self-fulfillment. If so, then choose that one as your first priority long-range goal, and set that as your primary objective for the present, keeping the others in reserve, to tackle when you have achieved your first priority. Then jot these down in your notebook in order of their priority so that you can refer to them as you progress.

Building your graded practice ladder. Now comes the business of planning how to arrive at your first priority goal. This will consist of building a "graded practice ladder" or "ladders." If yours is a simple phobia, such as a phobia for cats or elevators, you will have to build just one ladder. If it is a complex phobia, such as agoraphobia, you will have to build several.

Let us start, for purposes of illustration, with a simple phobia, a phobia for cats. You begin by thinking of the situation, with respect to cats, that would likely cause you great distress and that would be very difficult for you to do, like holding a cat in your lap and stroking it, for example. That would be the top rung of your ladder. In the case of an elevator phobia, the top rung might be to ride in the elevator of an office building up to the thirtieth floor and down again, alone in the car. In the case of a heights phobia, it might be to walk out on the observation platform of the Empire State Building or a similar tall structure.

Having chosen your top rung of the ladder, you now start from the bottom and work your way up to it in steps of increasing difficulty. Your first or bottom rung would be something that would cause you some phobic distress, but not very much. Again, using a phobia for cats as an example, your first rung might be to get hold of a book about cats and look through all the illustrations.

You would then go on to your second rung, and in the example we are using, this might be buying or borrowing a toy stuffed cat, feeling its fuzzy texture, and making yourself look into the toy cat's glass or plastic eyes.

After that, you would continue to add more rungs, each somewhat more difficult than the preceding one, until you reached the top rung.

As you work on the selection of a rung, discuss it with your helper. When your decision is firm, write it down. On completion, you will have constructed your "graded practice ladder." This will serve as the guide for your step-by-step confrontation with your phobic situation. The finished ladder would look something like this:

1. Obtain a book about cats, and you and your helper look at the pictures together.
2. Obtain a toy stuffed kitten, and you and your helper handle

it, feeling the fuzzy texture of the fur and looking into the kitten's glass or plastic eyes.

3. You and your helper walk up to a pet shop and look at kittens in the window.
4. You and your helper walk into an animal shelter and look at cats in their cages.
5. You and your helper sit in a friend's living room, with a cat confined in the kitchen.
6. You and your helper sit in the friend's living room with the cat lying on the sofa, awake, not being held.
7. You and your helper sit in the friend's living room with the cat walking about freely.
8. Repeat rung seven. Then your helper walks over and touches the cat. You follow your helper's example.
9. Your helper picks up the cat, holds it for a minute and puts it down; you follow your helper's example.
10. Your helper picks up the cat and holds it in his lap and strokes it; you follow your helper's example.
11. You pick up the cat and hold it, without your helper being present.

Each of these rungs would be scheduled for separate work sessions several days apart (depending on your comfort and patterns of living, and on your helper's convenience), with practice sessions in between. No matter how well the work sessions go, you will need the extra help that only practice can provide. Practicing is done by yourself, with your helper absent. Practice should consist of repeating the rung the two of you most recently worked on together, until you are able to manage it well. "Managing it" *does not mean* being able to do it without experiencing any phobic reaction at all. It means staying in the phobic situation even while experiencing some distress.

The ladder you construct during the first planning meeting should not be regarded as final. In all likelihood, you will have to revise it as you go along. You do not really know how easy or difficult a particular rung is going to be until you have tried it out. Something you thought would be quite easy might in fact turn out to be rather difficult, and something you thought would be very difficult might in fact turn out to be rather easy. When that happens, you may have to move some rungs further up on the ladder and others further down.

Another thing you may find is that the jump between two particular rungs is too great and that you may have to break it down into a number of smaller steps.

To illustrate this last point, let us go back to the example we have been using—the phobia for cats. In rung 3, "you" walk up to a pet shop and look in at the kittens in the window. In this and the following step, you are separated from the animals by substantial barriers, and you are not afraid that they are going to be able to get out and run toward you. But in rung 5, when it comes to being in the same house as a cat—even though separated by a closed kitchen door—you are afraid that the cat might get out and run up to where you are sitting and crawl up on you. In that case you might refuse to go into the friend's home so long as there was a cat in there. To get through this "resistance point" you might need to break up that step in the following fashion:

a. You and your helper meet your friend outside her house or apartment and talk about your going in with the cat confined in the kitchen.
b. You and your helper walk into the friend's house or apartment, standing just inside the entrance for about fifteen minutes.
c. You, your helper, and the friend go into the living room and go ahead with rung 5 as originally scheduled (cat confined in kitchen).

The two intermediate steps a and b might be taken on separate days, or they could be done the same day. It might even be possible to move onto c the same day, too. But it should not be rushed. Take separate days for all three, if necessary.

Now let us try constructing ladders for several other phobic situations. Instead of working with imaginary examples (as in the case of the cat phobia), we will work with real case illustrations.

Before going any further, we must stress as emphatically as possible that building a ladder and then performing each of the rungs is just the *framework* for contextual therapy. The main idea is *not* going to be to take steps of increasing difficulty and getting "used to" each of them. The contextual therapy idea will be to move into the phobic situation a little at a time, experiencing distress at each step, and learning to cope with it—to remain in the situation while experiencing the distress. The "learning" and the "coping" must positively include the six points of contextual therapy:

1. Expect, allow, and accept that fear will arise.
2. When fear comes, wait. Let it be.
3. Focus on and do manageable things in the present.
4. Label fear from 0 to 10.
5. Function with a level of fear. Appreciate the achievement.
6. Expect, allow, and accept that fear will reappear.

As we proceed to the construction of the several ladders, for purposes of instruction, we are assuming that the reader will continue to bear in mind that each of these is just a structural framework for reaching your goal by putting into practice the tools and techniques of contextual therapy, including the six points.

Driving an Automobile

Ellen's phobia began when she suffered a panic attack while driving across a long bridge spanning the Potomac River between Maryland and Virginia. As soon as she got across the bridge, her panic subsided, only to be aroused again as she continued along the expressway leading away from the bridge. The panic was so severe that she had to stop and wait for a police patrol car to come along. One of the policemen drove her car from the expressway to a quiet side road, and she was able to resume her trip home. The following morning her dread arose again as she prepared to drive her children to school. That morning, and henceforward, she had to make other arrangements for her children's transportation. Also, from that point on, she would no longer drive and would ride in an automobile only when a close relative or friend was doing the driving. This had been going on for ten years when Ellen came for treatment.

At the first planning meeting with her helper, the following ladder was worked out.

1. Helen at wheel, her helper alongside, they drive a block on quiet street.
2. Repeat rung 1, for about five blocks, or longer if possible.
3. Repeat rung 2, driving to edge of downtown business district, but not into it.

4. Repeat rung 3, but continue through business district, off rush hours.
5. Repeat rung 4 during rush hour.

It was agreed that this would be planning far enough ahead for several weeks, and that after this much had been mastered, they would then continue to build additional ladders for crossing bridges and driving on expressways.

Several days later they had their first work session and Ellen started working on rung 1—driving a block on a quiet street. But once she had started the engine, Ellen "froze." She could not get herself to put the car into drive. So she and her helper decided that they would just sit there and talk for the remainder of the session and start again the following day. On her second start, Ellen did not attempt to start out in drive. Instead, she started in second gear and crawled along for about half a block. Then she stopped, and with the engine still running, rested. A few minutes later she started again and crawled another few hundred feet. She repeated this procedure for about an hour. The following work session, she started in drive but did not accelerate beyond a crawl. The session after that, she was able to drive three blocks at about twenty-five miles an hour.

When Ellen had finished her second rung (Ellen drives about five blocks or more with helper seated alongside of her), it was decided to introduce another variation into the schedule. Instead of going on to driving through the business district, it was decided that Ellen would repeat rungs 1 and 2 but without having the helper inside the car with her. Instead, her helper was to follow her in his car, while Ellen worked at these tasks. Several times in the course of these work sessions, Ellen panicked and had to pull over to the curb to wait for her helper to catch up with her. The first time or two this happened, they had to call off the work session for that day. But after that, it went smoothly.

That accomplished, they went on to having Ellen drive through the city streets and business district (rungs 3, 4, and 5). This went more slowly than anticipated, and several times during the following weeks her helper had to move back into the car and accompany Ellen for a number of work sessions. Finally, Ellen was able to drive comfortably by herself. She was now more confident of her ability to control the phobogenic process herself.

Next came the task of tackling expressways. Even though Ellen was quite confident about city driving, she was still completely phobic about driving on expressways. That being the case, she and her helper plotted out a new ladder for expressways, as follows:

1. Ellen driving, accompanied by her helper; drive up to expressway entrance, but do not enter. Repeat several times during the same work session.
2. Ellen driving, accompanied by her helper, ride onto expressway and drive to next exit, and get off.
3. Ellen driving, accompanied by her helper, repeat last rung, but try for two or more exits.
4. Same as rung 3, but Ellen continues driving for as many exits as she can.
5. This time, Ellen is driving but her helper is not in the car with her. Instead, her helper is following her in his own car. She drives as many exits as possible.
6. Same as rung 5, except that, instead of following Ellen in his car, her helper is waiting for her at a designated place up the expressway. First time, her helper waits for her one exit ahead, next time two exits ahead, next time three exits ahead, and then as many exits ahead as Ellen is willing to try.
7. Following that, Ellen is to drive by herself, with nobody waiting for her or following her: first one exit, then two, then as many as she can manage.

That finished, they got down to their work sessions. Ellen moved very quickly through rung 4. Rung 5—the first rung in this ladder at which Ellen was at the wheel alone in the car—did not go smoothly. On her first attempt to drive just one exit on the expressway, Ellen had to pull over to the side several times and wait for her helper to catch up with her. When he asked if she had been working on "keeping focused on comforting realities" by doing some of the "manageable things" she had planned, she answered that she had become so confused and frightened that "everything flew out of my mind." It was agreed that in the next few days she was to practice doing these "manageable things," concentrating more on those than on the actual driving. This she did and when the next work session came along, she drove to the first exit without panicking. She did have some fairly high fear levels, but she was able to cope with them and keep on driving. In short order, she was able to drive for more than fifteen miles on the expressway, with her helper following. Her progress was equally as even and as good with her helper waiting for her at the successive exits.

Then came the day when she was to try driving on the expressway alone with nobody waiting or following. The first time out she panicked and had to pull over to the side. Then she started again, "crawled" to the exit, and got off.

She phoned her helper and asked him to accompany her again, but he thought it might not be too wise to do this. Instead, he offered her a "substitute for himself," a tape recording of his voice, speaking to her and reassuring her. (This was a tape they had made together.) With this device, she tried again by herself, the following day, turning on the tape recorder when she felt the fear levels getting too high in spite of her efforts to do "manageable things." The tape worked, and she was able to make it to the first exit without stopping.

That was the breakthrough, and from then on, she progressed with little interruption and was driving on expressways comfortably. An added and very welcome bonus came along as a great surprise.

> One Sunday, I decided to drive up to the lake, so I could really "try out my wings." I had completely forgotten that the route to the lake included a bridge crossing, across the Delaware River. The big surprise came about five miles beyond that bridge. I suddenly realized that I had driven over that bridge and had not even been aware of it.

Her success in mastering her phobia for expressways had simultaneously erased her phobia for driving over bridges. We continue now with our ladder-building for several other phobic situations.

Getting Out of the House

For a person with agoraphobia, making the first move to get out of the house can be a monumental task—or at least feel like a monumental task—especially if that person had not been out of the house for years. Yet, many have found that having taken the first step—actually venturing out of doors—was not nearly as frightening as they had anticipated, especially when accompanied by a helper with whom they had already worked out a plan of action. Some have even been able, after taking the first move out into the open, to advance very quickly to taking long walks by themselves, even without their helper, or with their helper waiting at a distance.

However, since one cannot know beforehand how quickly he will be able to progress, it is best to plan for small, moderate steps of increasing difficulty rather than for bold jumps. It is better to plan small steps and then be pleasantly surprised, rather than to plan large steps and then be disappointed and demoralized.

Annette P. had not been out of her house, not even once, for four years. Her agoraphobia had started with a panic attack in a large department store during the pre-Christmas rush with its milling throngs, high pressure, and frenetic countdown of the number of "days left to do your Christmas shopping." When the panic struck, she tried to battle her way through the "hundreds of people, all of whom seemed to be intent on pushing me back and not letting me through." When she had finally managed to "bulldoze" her way through to the elevators, she found dense masses of customers gathered there, too, "waiting to pounce on an elevator even before the passengers had gotten out." Annette found she "could not breathe" and became dizzy and faint. "I must have looked real sick and frightened, because a man came over to ask me if anything was wrong." She was escorted to a lounge where she recovered her strength, then made her way out of the store by means of a service elevator.

The phobia then spread quickly, in a course well known to people who have agoraphobia, until Annette was literally homebound. At first, her husband and other relatives struggled to get her to visit a doctor or seek some other sort of help. But Annette was resistant and soon everyone lapsed into acceptance of the fact that she could not and would not go out. Resignedly, they took over those of her tasks which involved doing anything outside the home.

Finally, a member of the family heard about contextual therapy, and it was arranged that a paraprofessional working with the White Plains Hospital Phobia Clinic visit Annette in her home and work out a program with her.

Some people with agoraphobia are able to move about with some freedom in a limited area around their homes when accompanied by someone they know and trust. Annette, too, had been able to do this for a little more than a year after the onset of her phobia. But then she found that even this limited egress was becoming too difficult for her to handle. Consequently, she lapsed into total self-internment.

This being the case, it was decided to start out very slowly and with a limited goal. The goal was set at visiting a friend who lived a few blocks away, spending about fifteen minutes with her and walking back. This is the ladder Annette and her helper constructed.

1. Sit at an open window for about fifteen minutes and look up and down the street.
2. Call in a neighbor's boy, send him on an errand, and watch him as he runs down the street on his way to the store.
3. Walk with the helper to the front door of her (Annette's) house and just open the door without going out. Stand there and talk for about ten minutes.
4. Repeat rung 3, but with the helper moving out the door and onto the sidewalk and walking down the street; Annette standing at the open door and watching.
5. Annette and her helper walk out on the landing in front of the house and remain there for fifteen minutes, talking.
6. Annette and her helper walk down the pathway to the sidewalk and remain there ten minutes.
7. Annette and her helper walk to the sidewalk, and then continue for another hundred feet.
8. Annette and her helper repeat rung 7 and then walk as far as the home of the neighbor whom she is going to visit.
9. Repeat rung 8 and then Annette and her helper enter neighbor's home and stay there for as long as Annette is able to stay.

After this ladder was constructed, Annette and her helper worked out a list of things Annette would be prepared to do when her fear levels were high, and when it was necessary to "keep herself connected with the reassuring realities in the phobic situation."

The nine rungs in the ladder had been scheduled for nine work sessions several days apart, depending on the helper's availability. In between, Annette was to practice, by herself, the rung she and her helper had just worked on.

As the day of the first work session drew near, Annette was filled with mounting anxiety and apprehension. At night she couldn't sleep. During the day she was testy and quarrelsome. She had fallen into the habit of not even going to her window at all, literally immuring herself inside her four walls. So to her, sitting in front of an open window—which to others might seem like nothing—was a gigantic step. But once this hurdle had been taken, the other steps moved more quickly than she and her helper had anticipated, and she was preparing to work on rung 9 (visiting with her neighbor) by the end of the third week.

Once she had achieved that, she and her helper worked on setting up a more ambitious schedule, somewhat as follows:

1. Annette walks out of her house to the corner by herself and back. The helper waits outside Annette's house, watching.
2. Annette walks around the block and returns home. The helper waits for her outside Annette's house.
3. Annette walks to neighbor's house by herself. The helper waits for her there.
4. The helper stays at Annette's house while Annette visits friend and returns.
5. Annette walks to local grocery store by herself (two blocks away). The helper waits in store for her. Annette comes into store and shops for a few items.
6. Annette walks to grocery store and shops, while her helper stays at Annette's home, awaiting Annette's return.
7. The helper stays away altogether (but within telephone reach) while Annette goes shopping at grocery store by herself.

By the time Annette had finished her rung 3 (Annette walks to neighbor's house by herself, helper waiting for her there), she was euphoric. She had been having some fairly strong fear levels but could keep them under control by preplanned strategies ("keeping focused on comforting realities"). Now the fear levels were becoming weaker and weaker. This had to be "the beginning of the end," Annette felt. She was convinced she was now "out in the clear" and the rest would be like coasting downhill.

But when she got to the next rung (Annette goes to friend's house, visits and returns, while helper stays at Annette's house and waits for her), her progress came to a sudden halt. The day before the scheduled work session, Annette developed intense anxieties. She began to feel as she had at the very beginning, that she would never be able to leave her house again. She felt isolated and depressed and did not even want to call her helper.

"I felt," she said, "as though it was all starting to close in around me once more. It was almost like what had been happening in the previous weeks was a fantasy, that it had never really happened, that I had dreamed it all up. I knew this wasn't so. I had my notebook with all the schedules we had made up and all the notes I had taken. I had the charts I had filled out, but somehow it all seemed unreal." Finally, she was able to stir herself sufficiently to call in her helper. Her helper tried to reassure her, told her this was to be expected, that it was not a major setback, just a minor snag from which she could surely free herself. But Annette was not to be consoled. She attempted to cancel the work session, scheduled for the following day, saying she just didn't feel well enough to undertake it. Her helper did not try to push her. She suggested Annette do what she could to get herself absorbed in a book or a television program, do some sewing for her daughter, help her son with his homework when he came home from school, straighten out the drawers and closets.

The following morning, when the helper arrived for the work session, Annette was still feeling anxious and depressed but said she would try, anyway. It did not work well. The helper was to stay at Annette's while Annette walked to the friend's house, remained there a while, and then came back. But Annette had only been out a few minutes when she returned, drawn-looking and tense. She had not been able to get beyond the next corner. Her fear levels were just too high and she felt unable to keep herself from being swept back into her spiralling fears, her frightening thoughts and imagery.

Again the helper reassured Annette that this was a common experience, that most patients go through this sort of thing, especially after a stretch of good progress. No one really knew the reason for these temporary snags in the learning process. But most assuredly, they were temporary. Annette would see that in a day or two. Whatever was bothering her internally would work itself out and her progress would resume, perhaps not at so spectacular a pace, but at a steady, consistent pace, provided she continued to practice and learn from what she had been doing in contextual therapy. There would come a time, not too far away, she was assured, when her effort would not need to be so laborious, conscious, and deliberate, when the process would become more and more spontaneous and automatic.

And so this did in fact occur. Several days later—two days ahead of her regularly scheduled work session—Annette called her helper to say she was feeling real "peppy" and eager to get on with a repeat of the rung on which she had tripped—visiting her friend, while the helper remained at Annette's house. The helper dropped by, and Annette started out. An hour later, when Annette had not returned, the helper became uneasy and telephoned the friend to find out what had happened. She was told that Annette had enjoyed the visit so much, she had lost track of time, and was now on her way back. Just then Annette burst in flushed, smiling, elated. She had gotten over this obstacle and was now ready to move on.

About two months later, Annette had completed rung 7—shopping in a local grocery store by herself. From that point on Annette and her helper continued to work on shopping projects, with a large shopping mall as the final goal. This last stretch took about four months to complete. Suddenly, however, Annette's mother died, and Annette's contextual therapy came to a standstill. When she resumed, she was shaky and frightened, but managed to move ahead at a slow, steady pace. A year later, Annette wrote her helper to say that she "was doing just fine, going everywhere by herself, shopping, visiting friends, 'taxiing' her children." In fact, she had even gotten a job selling in a department store.

In Annette's case, "getting out of the house" meant starting at the very beginning since she had not been out of her house at all for several years. There are many people with agoraphobia who manage to get out for short trips—on foot—so long as they are accompanied by somebody, or in a car with somebody else driving. In such cases, one would not need to start with the goal of "getting out of the house" but rather, with *getting out of the house by oneself* and moving about freely, on foot or by automobile.

If you look back a few pages, you will see this was the goal which Annette had set for herself *after* she had worked her way up to being able to get out of the house and move about freely in the company of her helper. The ladder she and her helper constructed for this second goal may be used as an example for those readers who are not altogether homebound, who have been getting out accompanied by somebody else, and who now want to be able to move about outside by themselves.

For Complex Cases, a Varied Approach

Not all cases of agoraphobia are so clear-cut and straightforward that one can construct a series of ladders, taking one after the other, until all distinct components of the agoraphobia have been solved. A person with agoraphobia may be sensitive to as many as ten or fifteen or even more different phobic situations, including some to which she is only moderately sensitive, others to which she is extremely sensitive, others to which she is only intermittently sensitive. To separate out every single phobic element in this complex and to work on each of them separately would be an enormous task. Fortunately, it is seldom necessary to do so. In most such cases it is possible to single out three or four major phobic situations and work on these. In the process, most of the other phobic situations will simultaneously become "neutralized," without any additional effort. This occurs because the underlying process is the same for all phobic situations, and the gains that are made in controlling the phobogenic process in one phobic situation will generally spread out to the others. The case of Vivian K. will illustrate this.

Vivian, single and twenty-four, lives with her mother. There are no other children. Vivian's parents were divorced when she was a child. Vivian's first phobic attack occurred when she was bicycling with her boyfriend.

> All of a sudden I couldn't breathe. I panicked. I knew I had to get home. We were about two miles away from home, and I made it back in record time. I didn't even say anything to my boyfriend, just turned around and raced for home. I don't know what did it. It was very hot and humid, about ninety-five degrees. I was terrified every second pedalling home that I would not be able to catch my breath and that I would die.

In the following few weeks, the following phobic symptoms developed:

> I used to go to work with my mother every morning—we both work in the same building. Now I've taken off a couple of weeks from work. I can't stand being confined there, not being able to get out if something should happen.

I'm afraid to be alone. When my mother leaves for work, I try to fall asleep again, so it won't be so long before my mother gets home again.

I don't answer the phone unless somebody gives me the code. I've worked out a code with my mother and my friends.

I'm afraid to go out by myself. I just stay in the house and pass the time away by reading and watching TV, or straightening out the drawers.

I can't be confined, even here [the phobia clinic]. The hour and a half is very long. I keep my watch in my pocketbook so I can't see how slowly the time passes. It's torture sitting here, confined.

I can't stand rain or humidity. I can't even take a hot shower because it gets steamy and humid.

My boyfriend and I were going out to restaurants a lot. But the last few weeks, I would order, and then when the food came, I had to leave. So they had to put our food in doggy bags.

I cannot stand being in a line, anywhere, in a store or super-market. I have to run out.

I cannot drive. I can ride in the car with my mother driving.

I can't go to family gatherings anymore. I feel confined. I'm afraid I'm going to stop breathing and pass out. It would be terribly embarrassing in front of my family.

I can't sit in the hairdresser's chair. I tried it but I had to run out just as she was getting started.

One thing was happening after another, and, as Vivian put it when she came for help at the clinic, "My boundaries are getting smaller and smaller. If this keeps up and I don't get help, I can see myself shut away from the world entirely in just another couple of weeks."

It was important to keep these boundaries from drawing in any closer. Hence Vivian and her helper decided that the best strategy would be to pick activities that would keep Vivian in circulation and to work on those first. Vivian felt priority should be given to helping her stay at her job. She liked the work and was highly valued by her employer. This, then, was chosen as the objective of Vivian's first ladder.

The problem of Vivian's driving was to be postponed for a later date. Until the job phobia was worked out, Vivian could continue to ride to work with her mother as she had been doing. Vivian's employer knew about her phobia and was eager to cooperate in whatever plan was worked out. This is the ladder that was constructed:

1. On Vivian's arrival at the office, her helper would be there to greet her and reassure her. Then when Vivian went up to her office, the helper would remain in the lobby for about forty-five minutes in the event Vivian needed help or decided she could not stay and had to leave to go home. At noon, the helper would be there to drive Vivian home.
2. Since the paraprofessional helper could not work with Vivian every day, the help of a friend was enlisted, and for several days the friend would repeat the procedure outlined in rung 1.
3. After that, the helper would come to the office at noon, and Vivian would show her around the office and the office building. This rung was designed to help Vivian overcome fear of moving outside the safe confines of her firm's office suite. Vivian would then stay on the rest of the day, driving home with her mother in the evening.
4. Vivian's friend would repeat rung 3 with Vivian for several days, substituting for the helper.
5. After Vivian felt a little more free about moving around the building, her helper would come to have lunch with her at a cafeteria inside the building.
6. Vivian's friend would come and have lunch with Vivian for several days, substituting for the helper.
7. Vivian would ride to work with her mother, stay all day, and ride home with her mother at night.

The first morning this plan was put into effect, Vivian had a panic attack and had to leave her office shortly after she had arrived. Her helper was still there and drove Vivian home. The following day, Vivian would not go to work. The day after that she tried again, and this time she stayed until the scheduled time of departure, noon.

For the next several days, the schedule worked very nicely, and Vivian was finding that she was able to stay at work with only occasional brief surges of intense phobic fear. Otherwise, she experienced "low levels" of fear a good deal of the time, but she was able to function in spite of them, utilizing the tools of contextual therapy.

Now that she was able to remain on the job, day after day, with only an occasional interruption, Vivian and her helper decided they could get started on her driving phobia.

This turned out to be a relatively simple matter. By the time she got to working on her driving phobia, Vivian had already gained considerable experience in coping with her phobic fear while remaining in the phobic situation. Because of this advantage, it was possible to leave the paraprofessional out of this process almost entirely, and to use Vivian's mother as a substitute helper.

This is the ladder Vivian and her helper constructed:

1. Vivian drives to and from work, accompanied by her mother, for a week.
2. Vivian drives to and from work for a week, her mother following in her own car.
3. Vivian drives to work, for a week, with no one following her. Drives home that week with her mother following her.
4. Vivian drives both ways with nobody following her.

During the first two weeks, Vivian experienced an occasional surge of intense panic when her car was tied up in traffic; also when she lost sight of her mother in the rearview mirror (second week). The third week she was driving quite comfortably through traffic, and toward the end of that week was not even concerned about having her mother follow behind her on the drive home.

Since, during that four-week period, Vivian's helper did not need to be involved in helping Vivian with her driving phobia, she was able to concentrate, with Vivian, on another phobic situation—stores. This situation was tackled evenings and Saturdays (since Vivian was working during the week).

First to be tackled were the small stores, using this ladder:

1. Vivian drives to the mall. Helper follows in her own car.
2. Both park and walk to one of the small boutiques. Vivian enters and stays a few minutes, while helper waits outside.
3. Vivian enters, helper stays outside, while Vivian makes a purchase.
4. The first three rungs are repeated with a larger store, with Vivian attempting to browse around in the store for fifteen minutes to a half hour and making several purchases.
5. After that they move on to a department store in the mall. Vivian enters the main floor of department store, with helper waiting outside. Stays there a few minutes, then leaves.

6. Vivian browses around on main floor of department store; helper agrees to meet her at a designated spot on another floor, a half hour later.
7. Vivian walks through several floors of the department store, makes some purchases, and meets helper at the entrance.
8. Vivian goes into the department store and shops on several floors. Meets helper in coffee shop a block away.

By the end of the eight-week clinic program, Vivian was not yet able to go shopping in the department store by herself. She had managed to get only as far as the sixth rung and was working on the seventh. But this did not end her efforts in contextual therapy. When the clinic program was over, she and several other members of the clinic group joined a mutual-help group conducted by one of the clinic's paraprofessional helpers, but outside the clinic's auspices. In the final chapter of this book, we will tell you how you can organize such a group in your own community and continue to work in that group to reinforce what you will have achieved through the guidance of this book. But, getting back to Vivian: During the eight-week period at the clinic she had made splendid progress mastering three of her basic phobic situations—her job, driving, and shopping. In addition, she had made a number of additional gains even though no special efforts had been made to deal with them.

The fear of being alone. Several evenings when her mother had gone out and left her alone, Vivian had suffered intense bouts of phobic anxiety. Now, however, she no longer had to suffer in solitude. She could telephone her helper, as well as a friend and some of the other people who were attending the phobia clinic with her. Without realizing it, she had established a telephone network, to which she could "plug in" whenever she needed. The helper would also telephone Vivian when she knew Vivian would be alone. What Vivian had been most worried about was that she would not be able to catch her breath and that she would "pass out and die" with nobody there to help her. By the time the clinic program was finished, she was no longer afraid this would happen. In fact, this fear of not being able to catch her breath had gone entirely, as had her hyperventilation—the conscious, deep breathing she did in order to avoid being left without breath.

Telephoning. This fear, too, had gone as a result of the fact that Vivian had to keep in touch with her "network" whenever she felt a panic attack coming.

Going to the hairdresser. About five weeks into the clinic program, Vivian decided she was going to have her hair done in a different style, and one evening she walked into a hairdresser's shop and asked to be served. After waiting an hour, she became anxious and left. The following morning she walked into another beauty parlor, sat down and had her hair cut. "It wasn't until I got to my grandmother's that night, where we were having a family gathering, when I realized that I had had my hair cut and that I hadn't had any 'levels' at all."

Family gathering. During this family gathering, Vivian felt a brief surge of fear only two or three times during the evening, but resisted the urge to flee and ended up by "having a really enjoyable time."

Humidity and rain. Hot showers with their steaminess were no longer much of a problem. Vivian remained apprehensive about showers for some time, but when her fear of "losing her breath" went, so did the fear of humidity which she had associated with not being able to breathe. The fear of rain, too, had gone. In fact, Vivian said, she was now enjoying it when it rained. "There was this young man who would make fun of me because I was afraid of the rain. Now I'm happy when it rains because it means that fellow can't play golf."

Again we draw attention to the fact that during all these weeks of working on her various ladders, Vivian was not just passively "getting used to" one situation after another. She was working assiduously at combatting her anxiety and phobic fear at each step and in each situation by practicing the techniques of contextual therapy. Here are some excerpts from Vivian's accounts of these experiences:

When I was eating lunch with Susanne [her paraprofessional helper] at my place of business, it was like having lunch with a friend. I wasn't even aware that this was a work session. But after she left and I had to walk back to my office, I began to have levels. ["Having levels" has become a shorthand expression at the phobia clinic for "experiencing phobic anxiety at high levels."] I started to feel that I couldn't breathe, I became lightheaded. I started to have phobic thoughts. My first impulse was to run after Susanne and get her to stay. But I fought off that impulse and, instead, I pulled out a poem that I had found in a magazine and read it to myself as I walked down the corridor. Then when I got inside my office, to my desk, I pulled out an article I had clipped from the *Wall Street Journal* and started to read it. To tell you the truth, I really didn't know what I was reading, since I was still having such high levels, but I kept on just the same. Then I made myself call the secretary of one of my clients and asked her to return some papers she had borrowed. This brought the levels down to about four or five, and they kept up that way a good part of the afternoon, until it came time to go home.

. . . .

I had been in that store two or three times without any levels, but this time they came on when I didn't even expect them. I became frantic. I thought everything was slipping. So I started doing what I had done before—I read the labels on the dresses, I felt the materials, I started to count dresses on one rack. None of these things worked the way they had before. I still had enough presence of mind to try something new. So I approached a woman standing next to me and asked her if she knew the difference between polyesters and rayon and nylon or were they all the same thing. It happened she did know and she explained it to me. By this time, I was able to listen and pay attention. My levels were going down. So I stayed a little longer.

. . . .

My mother had to go out bowling that night, and I thought I would be alright being alone. I knew I could call up Susanne if I got frightened, or some of the other people. For a while it was alright, but then I started to feel scared and helpless. I started hyperventilating and thought I would pass out. I called Susanne. She wasn't home. I called a friend and she wasn't home. I felt so helpless, like I was going to die. But I remembered to pull out the card of reminders I had prepared for myself. I said to myself, "Concentrate—concentrate—concentrate," and looked at the card. I picked out the first thing that caught my eye. "Type something on typewriter." So I went to my desk and started copying sentences out of a book. I didn't even try to understand what I was copying, just making myself do the mechanical things of copying one word after another. That helped a little, but I was still terribly nervous, so I looked at the card again and read: "Smell your different perfumes and see if you can tell the differ-ence." I did that. The smell of the perfumes made me sick to the stomach, but even that got my mind off the fear that I was unable to breathe, and then I realized that while smelling the perfume I was breathing and that I wasn't going to pass out.

After a while, it got a little better and I was able to get myself to sit down and watch television until my mother came home.

. . . .

I was driving to the office with my mother driving behind me. I kept her in my rearview mirror. Then someone got between us and I started to panic. I couldn't pull my reminder card out of my bag because I was afraid to let go of the wheel. So I looked for license plates and started to read them out loud. Then I bit my lip and scraped off some of the lipstick with my teeth and wiped it with some tissue I had in my hand. I flipped on the radio and tried to listen to the music. I started to recite the first names of all my cousins. Then a traffic light stopped the traffic and I could look back and see my mother's car, and I saw her and she was waving at me. That made me feel better. Then she caught up with me and we drove all the way to the office and I had hardly any levels at all.

Not a Cut-and-Dried Affair

As you can see from this rather detailed account of Vivian's work with her helper, setting up a "ladder" or "ladders" to deal with a phobia in the phobic situation is not a simple cut-and-dried affair. The sample ladders we have constructed for you give you a general idea of what needs to be done and how to go about doing it. But you should not rely on these, and those that are listed below, as exact models to follow exactly. You and your helper will have to work up your own ladders according to your individual situation. Then, having constructed your ladders, you will need to be prepared to make adjustments and changes as you move along. It will take just a little bit of learning and getting used to, but you will find that you can master the technique rather easily, since most of it is largely common sense. Naturally, people working with paraprofessional helpers in the phobia clinic have an advantage, since most of the helpers have been "through the mill" themselves as phobic patients, and have subsequently been trained and guided by professionals. However, we know that, as a rule, phobic people are imaginative, intuitive, and creative, and that these qualities should stand you in good stead.

But we urge you to remember that fluidity, flexibility, and adaptation should come later on—not in the beginning. Build your ladder first, even though it may appear somewhat stiff and artificial at the outset. These rungs will be your basic guides. They will give you something solid to start with. Then if you need to alter them, you are free to do so. It is better not to rush into your first work session on impulse, with the idea that you will make the rest up as you go along. If you do this, you may find yourself confused and frustrated at a time when you will be needing to concentrate your wits and energies on coping with your fear in the phobic situation and bringing your phobic reaction under control. Don't rush. Think, discuss, prepare, plan, work, and rework your starting ladder. Then, when you are satisfied you have it the way you think it should be, that'll be the time to start.

LADDERS FOR OTHER PHOBIC SITUATIONS

We have already covered the construction of ladders for several phobic situations: cats, driving an automobile, leaving your house, shopping in small stores, shopping in a shopping mall, staying in your work situation. We will now provide sample ladders which may be used as general guides, in the manner that we have just demonstrated, for a number of other situations.

The number of rungs in each ladder may be too many for your personal situation and your capabilities, and the distance between them too minute. In that case, eliminate the rungs that may be superfluous. On the other hand, the number of rungs may be too few and the distance between them too great. In that eventuality, do the opposite: Insert additional rungs and narrow the distance. Also, you may need to change the order of some of the rungs, since some steps that we might think are easy you may find difficult, and vice versa.

The following are sample ladders for you to use as a basis for constructing ladders of your own.

Buses
1. You and your helper stand at bus stops and watch passengers get on and off.
2. You and your helper walk along bus route and stop for a few minutes at successive bus stops, watching buses pull in and out.
3. You and your helper get on bus and ride until the next stop, or as long as you are able to stay on. (Do this during nonrush hours, when buses are not crowded.)

4. Repeat rung 3, but with you and your helper seated at opposite ends of bus.
5. Repeat rungs 3 and 4 during rush hours.
6. During midmorning (after the rush hour), you get on bus alone; helper following you in automobile. You ride one stop (or more) and get off. Your helper picks you up.
7. Repeat rung 6 except that your helper is waiting for you at a designated point along the bus route.
8. Repeat rung 7 with your helper waiting for you in a restaurant, rather than at bus stop.
9. Repeat rungs 6, 7, and 8 during rush hours.
10. You ride the bus for a short distance, by yourself, with nobody waiting for you or following you.
11. You ride a long distance by yourself, with nobody following or waiting.

Subways
1. You and your helper go down into subway to coin booth. Buy tokens or get change, but do not enter.
2. You and helper enter subway and go down to train platforms. Stand there for fifteen minutes or longer while watching trains pull in and out of station.
3. During midmorning (after the rush hour), you and your helper go down to train platform, board a local train, sit down together, and ride the train for one station or as many stations as you can manage.
4. Repeat rung 3, but you and your helper sit at opposite ends of the subway car.
5. Repeat rung 4, but you and your helper sit in adjoining cars.
6. Repeat rung 5, but you and your helper sit several cars apart.
7. Repeat rungs 3, 4, and 5 during busier hours, but *not* rush hour. (Rush hour riding should be saved until you can ride alone comfortably.)
8. Midmorning, you ride one station by yourself, with helper waiting for you on platform at the next station.
9. Repeat rung 8, but distance is increased to the number of stations you feel you can manage alone.
10. Repeat rung 9, increasing distance.
11. Repeat rungs 8, 9, and 10 during busier hours.
12. You ride one station alone with nobody waiting.
13. Repeat rung 12, increasing distances.

Trains

1. You and your helper go to railroad station, any morning or evening, and stay there about a half hour watching passengers getting on and off.
2. During midmorning you and your helper get on train and ride one station together.
3. Repeat rung 2, but ride as many stations as you can handle.
4. Repeat rung 3, but you and helper sit apart.
5. Repeat rung 4, but you and your helper sit in adjacent cars.
6. Repeat rung 5, but you and your helper sit several cars apart.
7. Repeat rungs 3, 4, 5, and 6 during a busier hour of the day.
8. You ride one station by yourself; your helper is on platform, next station, waiting.
9. Repeat rung 8, but your helper is waiting for you several stations ahead.
10. Repeat rung 9, but your helper is waiting for you in nearby restaurant, not on platform.
11. You ride one station alone with nobody waiting.
12. You ride as many stations as possible with nobody waiting.

Elevators

1. You and your helper go to lobby of busy building and observe passengers getting on and off elevators.
2. Get into an elevator car with your helper, remain a few seconds, and then exit.
3. You and your helper get into an elevator car and ride up one floor or as many as you feel you can manage.
4. You and your helper go to lobby. You get into the car, stay a few seconds, and then exit.
5. Your helper rides up one floor, gets out, and waits for you. You ride up one stop and get off. You and your helper ride down together.
6. Repeat rung 5, increasing the length of the ride.
7. With your helper waiting in the lobby, you ride up one floor and exit. Ride down.
8. Repeat, increasing distance to the extent you can manage.
9. You ride up alone one floor, and then down. Nobody is waiting.
10. Repeat rung 9, increasing distance.

Note: Some people with an elevator phobia dread being in an elevator alone. For them, the problem is the fear of being closed in. Others cannot tolerate being in a crowded elevator. Their phobia is the dread of not being able to get anough air. For those in the first category (dread of riding alone), rungs 9 and 10 should be executed first in elevators with other passengers, and then riding alone. For those who cannot tolerate crowded elevators, the process should be reversed.

Airplanes

Because of restrictions by airlines and air terminals, it is virtually impossible for *individuals* to have access to airplanes for the purpose of getting over their flying phobia by means of graded exposure. Many airlines and airports do have arrangements for *groups* functioning under auspices of a clinic or other professional facility. Hence, this ladder has as a prerequisite the formation of such a group, if none exists, or the joining of a group that is already formed. If you join a group that is already formed, then you will need to ignore this ladder and follow the progression worked out by the group. You will have the advantage of knowing about contextual therapy and being able to practice it while the others are following the group's techniques (which may not be contextual therapy as we have described it in this book). If you cannot find a group to join, then you may be able to form your own under the auspices of a church, temple, university psychology department, or local community mental health center or clinic. If you can persuade the director of any of these institutions to form a group, they will probably conduct the publicity to attract the prospective members. Otherwise, you can enlist the help of a local newspaper editor or radio station program director. If you are able to form such a group, then you will need to contact the airport management or airline to set up arrangements for your group to have access to a plane that is not in active service at the time.

Assuming you are successful in forming such a group, here is a basic ladder you can use.

1. Group (led by group leader, who takes the place of the individual helper) goes to an airport, walks around the lobby and ticket counters, and then goes on to "gate" lounge to watch planes taking off and landing.
2. Individual members of the group go to different ticket counters and ask for information about different flights, prices, etc.
3. Group and leader go to gate lounge and go through the

motions of waiting for a particular flight, stay there until after boarding of passengers is completed, and then leave.

4. Group and leader board a vacant plane, take seats, buckle seat belts as though the plane were actually going to take off. Airline personnel may also close plane's doors for the group.
5. Group and leader arrange to take a short flight together. (At this point—that is, after you have taken a flight with the group—you will need to enlist a helper, since your next rung will be performed without the group.)
6. You and your individual helper take a short flight together.
7. You take a short flight yourself. (An additional plane trip with helper accompanying you may be necessary before you are ready for your "solo" flight.)

If forming or joining a group presents too many difficulties, you may want to proceed, working with your helper alone, as with any of the other phobic situations. Under these circumstances, your ladder would be constructed as follows:

1. You and your helper go to the airport, walk around the lobby, shops, and ticket counters.
2. You and your helper go to the airport; you walk to several ticket counters and make inquiries about plane schedules, fares, etc.
3. You and your helper go to the departure lounge and watch planes taking off and landing. Watch passengers waiting for arrival of their flight. "Accompany" them, *mentally*, as they line up for boarding and board the plane.
4. Go to lounge windows (or observation platform) and watch planes as they land and take off. (In some airports, it may not be permissible for non-passengers to go beyond security check point. This may necessitate your getting special permission to do so.)
5. You and your helper take a short flight together. (An additional plane trip with your helper may be necessary before you are ready for your "solo" flight.)
6. You take a short flight alone.

It is important that you and your helper prepare, in advance, the different kinds of things you are going to do to keep yourself "in the present" and involved with reality during your joint flight. Your helper should keep you involved in conversation, explain to you each step in the procedure. ("We are now taxiing to the runway. We're going to be waiting until the other planes take off. There are three planes ahead of us. Now it is our turn. He is going to rev up his engines and you'll hear a throbbing sound. Now he's picking up speed.") Hold onto the helper's hand or arm if you need to. Keep reporting your levels. Tell your helper what you're feeling and thinking. When the plane has reached its cruising altitude, try reading a magazine, doing a crossword puzzle, or playing a card game with your helper. Expect to have varying levels of fear and don't be upset when they come. Work at keeping yourself involved with reality, using the various tactics we have discussed.

It might be advisable on your first trip without your helper to let the stewardess know you have had a flying phobia and that you are now making your first flight alone. You need not be hesitant or embarrassed about telling this to the stewardess. They have had considerable experience with this kind of problem, and airlines instruct their flight personnel about helping passengers who have had a phobia or who are still phobic. Even without training, the stewardess will know to sit near you, if there is a seat available, or she may even ask your permission to inform the person sitting next to you of your problem. You may wish to inform that person yourself and ask him or her to reassure you in whatever way is comfortable for you.

Many people who have had a phobia for flying have reported that they approached their first flight with great apprehension, but that once they were there and started to put their contextual therapy techniques into practice, their fear was not nearly as strong as they anticipated and faded once they were in the air.

Heights

There are ever so many height situations which arouse phobic reactions in those who are susceptible that it would not be practical to cover them all. Therefore, we will cover a few which happen to occur with a fairly high frequency and assume that these can serve as models for other situations.

The upper stories of a tall building. Some people have a phobic reaction to being on the upper stories of a tall building even if they have no view out of a window. Just the knowledge that they are "way up there" is enough to arouse the phobic reaction. Others become phobically distressed only when they are looking out of a window on an upper story of an apartment building or office building.

For the former—those who are phobic even when in the interior of the bulding—the ladder would be built as follows:

1. You and your helper walk up one flight together.
2. Your helper walks up ahead one flight and waits for you.
3. You both walk around inside hallway of that story.
4. You repeat rungs 2 and 3, going higher and higher. If you are able to manage the initial increments without too much distress, skip a few floors at a time, using the elevator. (For example, you've made it to the fifth floor and feel you can skip a few. You and your helper ride to the eighth floor. Then you both walk to the ninth floor. After that, your helper walks to the tenth floor and waits for you.)
5. Start where you left off last time, if you're comfortable doing it. If not, start at a lower story and work your way up as high as you can go, each time entering into the hallway and walking around for a few minutes.
6. Start all over again, from bottom, but make larger jumps. For example, your helper rides up to fifth floor and waits. You follow. Both walk around hallway. Your helper rides up to tenth floor, waits. You follow. Both walk around hallway. Go as high as you can, following same system.
7. Your helper waits down in lobby, while you try riding up to the fifth floor and walking around. Your helper rides up and meets you. Your helper stays on fifth floor, you ride up to tenth floor. Your helper follows and meets you there. You both walk around in the hallway. Continue the same pattern until you can go to the highest floor and cope with your phobic fear there.
8. You repeat the entire process, but entirely by yourself, without your helper.

If your phobic reaction is aroused, not by being on the inside of a tall building, but by looking out the window high up, then your ladder would be built exactly as the one we have just finished except that, instead of walking around the hallways at each of the floors at which you stop, you would look out the window at that floor, staying there, each time, until you can cope with your phobic fear, and then moving on to the next height.

Expressways

1. You and your helper drive around together for a while and then up to expressway entrance, but do not enter. Repeat several times during the same day.
2. With your helper driving, you ride onto expressway up to the next exit, or further, if you can continue.
3. With you driving, you and helper ride onto expressway and continue to next exit, if you can manage it; if not, pull over to the side for a while. Then continue, making as many stops as necessary, until you get to exit.
4. Repeat rung 3, extending distance to two exits.
5. Repeat rung 4, extending distance as far as you can.
6. Repeat rungs 3, 4, and 5, with your helper in a separate car, following you.
7. Repeat rung 6 with your helper waiting for you one exit ahead, two exits ahead, and then as many as you can manage.
8. You drive alone with no one waiting and no one following for one exit, then two exits, and then as many exits as you can.

Crossing Over a Bridge

Some people with this phobia are sensitive only to crossing an overpass that spans a very wide expressway. Others are sensitive only to crossing a bridge that spans a body of water. Some are sensitive to both. We will build separate sample ladders for each type of situation, and the reader can use either, or both, depending on the nature of the phobia.

Bridge Over Expressway

(This ladder assumes that you do not have a problem with driving in general, but do have a phobia for crossing bridges that go over wide expressways.)

1. You and your helper drive to a small bridge that crosses over a narrow roadway. With the helper driving, you cross this bridge up and back several times.
2. Repeat rung 1, with you driving, but with your helper accompanying you in your car.
3. Drive to the same bridge and park. You and your helper walk across the bridge and back several times together.
4. Drive to the same bridge and park. Your helper walks across

bridge and waits for you. You walk across to meet him. Your helper then walks back and waits for you. You recross.

5. Drive to same bridge and park. With your helper waiting you walk across and recross bridge by yourself.
6. Drive to same bridge. You drive across and back by yourself; your helper follows you in his car.
7. Repeat rung 6, but your helper does not follow you in his car. Your helper waits for you at the starting point as you cross and recross (you driving) several times.
8. You drive to bridge by yourself; your helper is absent. Cross and recross until you can do so with your fear levels under good control.
9. Repeat rungs 1 through 8 with an overland bridge that crosses a wide expressway. If this is too great a jump, you move on to a somewhat wider bridge than the first, and after that, go on to the bridge crossing a wide expressway.

Bridge Across a Body of Water

1. You and your helper drive up to approach of the bridge a few times, without driving across. Just park and watch other automobiles driving across the bridge.
2. With your helper at wheel, you ride up and back across bridge several times.
3. If there is a walkway on this bridge and walking across the bridge is permitted, you and your helper walk across a segment of the bridge, which only passes over the land. Do this several times until your fear levels become manageable.
4. With you at wheel and your helper alongside, you drive over the bridge and recross several times.
5. You drive your own car. Your helper drives a separate car. Your helper drives onto bridge with you following, right behind, keeping him in sight.
6. Repeat, with you driving ahead and your helper following.
7. Your helper drives ahead, crosses bridge, and waits for you on the other side. You drive over bridge and meet your helper. Repeat the process coming back across the bridge.
8. You drive across bridge by yourself; your helper is absent.

Restaurants

This ladder is mainly for people who have agoraphobia and want to give priority to this particular phobic situation.

1. You and your helper go to busy downtown area and get some "fast food" from a street vendor.
2. You and your helper go to a luncheonette or drugstore where you can get counter service and order something that will not keep you waiting or eating too long. Should you feel uncomfortable, it will be possible for you to make a quick exit. If you do have to exit, repeat this step several times until you can manage to stay until you have finished eating.
3. You and your helper try to find either an open "garden type" restaurant or possibly a sidewalk cafe, where you can sit down and eat at leisure, and not feel too enclosed. Order something a little more elaborate so you can get used to waiting to be served and to staying there a little longer. If necessary, take a seat near the exit.
4. You and your helper go to a fast-food restaurant such as McDonald's or Burger King (or someplace similar, depending on what is available in your neighborhood). Waiting on line to be served will be part of your learning to cope in the phobic situation. If necessary, take a seat near the exit.
5. Repeat rung 4 in a small, uncrowded restaurant, one that is well-lighted and bright, while you are seated near the exit.
6. Repeat rung 5 in a larger restaurant, while seated near the exit.
7. Repeat rung 6 in a large restaurant, while seated in the interior, away from the exit.
8. Repeat rungs 4, 5, 6, and 7 by yourself, without your helper, but with the helper agreeing to meet you outside the restaurant at about the time you expect to be finished.
9. Repeat these same steps, but without your helper waiting.

Enclosed Places of Assembly (Church, Temple, Theater, Classroom, Meeting Halls, Movies)

If you are phobic for one of these situations, you are very likely phobic for the others since all are enclosed places in which sizable groups of people assemble. As you develop control over your phobic reaction in one, you should simultaneously be developing control of your phobic reaction for the others. Therefore, select the one to which you will have easiest access for purposes of practicing contextual therapy. In building the sample ladder, we will use the general term "hall" to cover any of these situations you may select.

1. With your helper, come to the hall when it is unoccupied and spend some time sitting and standing around in it.
2. Return with your helper when the hall is occupied and stand outside while the people enter. Enter and stand at the back a few minutes and then leave.
3. Return to the hall when it is occupied; you and your helper sit at the rear. Stay as long as you can manage, then both leave.
4. Return to the hall. You sit in rear, and your helper waits for you outside. You remain there as long as you can manage. If you have to leave after only a short while, return and repeat until you can manage to cope with your fear while you remain fifteen minutes or longer.
5. Return to the hall. You and your helper take seats further down, but on the aisle.
6. Return to the hall; you take a seat further down, on the aisle. Your helper waits outside. You remain as long as you can manage. If you have to leave after only a short while, return and repeat until you can manage to cope with your fear for fifteen minutes or longer.
7. Repeat rung 6 until you can remain for a half hour or longer.
8. You return alone, take aisle seat back of hall, near the exit, and stay there as long as you can manage. If you have to leave after a short while, repeat until you can stay there for a half hour or longer.
9. Repeat rung 8, taking a seat further down, but on the aisle.
10. Repeat rung 9, but four or five seats in.
11. Repeat rung 10, but with a seat in the middle of the row.

Eating in Public

This ladder is for people with a social phobia, specifically the dread of eating anyplace where they are being observed.

1. Your helper meets you at your home. You serve coffee. You watch your helper drink the coffee. You need not participate unless you are able to. If you are afraid to lift your filled cup to your mouth for fear your hand will shake and that you'll spill it, go through the pantomime of having your coffee, but with an empty cup.
2. Go to a small coffee shop or diner with your helper. Your helper orders coffee and a light snack. You order coffee. If

you can manage to have a spoonful of coffee at a time, do so. If not, wait with your helper while helper finishes, and then leave.

3. You and your helper are at your home. You serve coffee. You go as far as you can in drinking your coffee, either a spoonful at a time or from a cup. If your hand shakes and you spill some coffee, that's alright. You're learning.

4. Continue to repeat rung 3 as many times as necessary until you can manage to finish a cup of coffee without too much shaking and spilling.

5. You and your helper go to the helper's home. Your helper serves something light. You do your best to eat and drink, repeating this effort until you eat at the helper's house without too much difficulty (shaking and spilling).

6. You invite a friend to your house and, with your helper there and you, serve all three something to eat. You go as far as you can in consuming your food with others there. Repeat this rung until you can eat in presence of the friend and your helper without too much difficulty.

7. Repeat rung 6 in the helper's home if your helper happens to be a friend or a relative who is not of your immediate family. If your helper is a member of your immediate family, this rung should be executed in the home of a friend or a more distant relative.

8. Repeat rung 7, eating in a different friend's or relative's home and increasing the number of people present.

9. Repeat rung 8, with larger gathering of family and friends.

10. Your helper, you, and a friend go to a small restaurant, order, and eat.

11. Repeat rung 9, but in a larger, busier restaurant.

12. You eat alone (nobody else present) in a small restaurant.

13. You eat alone in a large restaurant.

14. You buy a ticket to an organizational luncheon or dinner, where you will be sure to be seated at a table with seven or eight other people.

Writing in Public

1. You and your helper meet at your home. Your helper writes a check in your presence, then writes a note to you in your presence. You take out your checkbook, but do not attempt to write (unless this is no problem for you in presence of helper).

2. You and helper go to a place where helper will be required to fill out some forms or write a check. (For example, purchases something in store; waits in line and then pays by check; applies for library card and has to fill out forms; or goes to bank to make deposit, filling out deposit slip). You stand in line with your helper and wait, but you do not write anything.

3. You and your helper are at your home. You go into another room and write a note to the helper. You bring the note in and give it to the helper.

4. Sitting at same table as your helper, you write your name on a piece of paper. Let your hand shake, it doesn't matter. Even if what comes out is unreadable it doesn't matter. Repeat this several times until your writing begins to be legible.

5. Repeat rung 4, but this time write a note to your helper, with the helper watching. Repeat this several times until what you write can be read.

6. You and your helper go to a place where you will be required to fill out a form or write a check. If it is a place where you need to fill out forms, just ask for the forms. You do not need to fill them out there. If it is a place where you have to write a check, fumble around with your checkbook, then put it away, take out cash, and pay.

7. You go to another place where you need to fill out forms and wait in line with your helper to get the forms. Then take the forms aside where no one can observe you and fill out the forms. Turn them in.

8. You go someplace where you need to pay for something with a check. Select your item, wait in line, with your helper alongside. Write out your check, with helper observing. It may come out a scrawl; that's alright. Just say you have a problem writing. You will not be the first one. Most cashiers have had experience with this sort of thing before.

9. You repeat rung 8 in two or three other locations (with helper present).

10. You make a purchase or a bank deposit or withdrawal doing the necessary writing. Helper is absent. Repeat in different places until you can do it with little difficulty.

Social Gathering

1. You, your helper, and one good friend meet at your house and you host a tea or coffee-and-cake for them.

2. Your helper hosts similar event for you and a good friend or two. If you think you may need to leave suddenly, explain in advance.
3. You ask a close friend or relative to host a similar event for you, your helper, and one or two friends. If you think you may need to leave suddenly, explain in advance.
4. Repeat rung 3, but with slightly larger group. Same instruction about leaving.
5. Ask a relative or friend to host a somewhat more formal and structured event, such as luncheon for a small group, which you and your helper attend.
6. Repeat rung 5 with a larger group. (If you find yourself imposing too much on one friend or relative, ask another person to take on one or more of these hosting tasks.)
7. Find out if your church, temple, or community center is holding a social event for a small group. You and your helper go. Seat yourself near the exit in the event you have to leave suddenly.
8. Repeat rung 7, but attend without helper.
9. Seek out large social gathering; you and helper attend. Situate yourself near the exit, if you should still need to.
10. Repeat rung 9 without helper.
11. Repeat rung 10, but do not seat yourself near the exit.

Crawling Bugs (Ants, Crickets, Spiders, Beetles)

1. Go to library or bookstore and get a book on insects, with illustrations. Look through the book, with helper present. Find "your" bug, and continue to look at it, until it no longer upsets you too much.
2. Your helper then buys a toy or rubber imitation of your bug, or the nearest thing to it. Your helper gives you the toy or rubber article and you handle it.
3. Ask someone to find some live bugs—of the kind that you dread, if feasible—and put them in a small vial or bottle of alcohol. You hold the bottle, look at the bug, and continue to do so. (Your helper is present.)
4. If there is a museum or high school biology class where insects have been preserved, you and your helper go there and spend some time studying the specimens.
5. Go with your helper to where you can find one or more of the bugs you dread, alive in their habitat (ants and beetles in the yard, spiders outside your window, house-dwelling bugs in a basement, bathroom, or under a sink). You and your

helper stay there and watch them; stay there as long as you can. If you have to leave, leave when you have managed to reduce your fear levels somewhat through the contextual therapy techniques.

6. Repeat rung 5 with your helper at some distance.
7. Repeat rung 5 without your helper.

Flying Insects (Bees, Wasps, Moths, Butterflies)

If you are allergic to the sting of bees and wasps and you are careful about avoiding places where you are likely to encounter them, this is not to be treated as a phobia. Your fear is realistic. However, if you find yourself being on guard against bees and wasps in places where there isn't the remotest possibility of their being there, your problem should be treated as a phobia, even if your fear of an allergic reaction is realistic. We suggest, entirely apart from contextual therapy, that you might consult your doctor for desensitization of your allergy.

1. Get a book about insects with lively illustrations, and concentrate on photographs of the insect to which you are phobic.
2. Find toy or rubber replicas of the insect (or have helper locate them) and handle them to the point where you can manage the fear reaction.
3. If there is a museum or laboratory where you can find specimens of these insects preserved, go there with your helper and become accustomed to looking at the specimens. Butterfly and moth collections are more likely to be available than the others. If you have any problem about locating preserved specimens of your insect, inquire at the biology department of your university or a natural history museum.
4. Take a walk with your helper into an area of fields and trees where your insect is not too likely to be found, and become accustomed to moving about in such areas while managing your fear.
5. Take a walk with your helper to the same type of area, but have your helper remain at the outskirts while you wander about.
6. Take a walk with your helper to an area where you know your insect can be found. Move about in that area, accompanied by your helper. Then move about in that area, with your helper at the outskirts.
7. Move into that area alone.

CHAPTER TEN

Gaining Control
Over Your Phobia

NOW IT'S YOUR TURN. Armed with an understanding of your phobia, it's time to act. With the assistance of your helper, you are now ready to begin the process of gaining control over your phobia. This chapter is addressed to the person with the phobia, but it should be read by the helper as well.

We assume that by this time, the following things have already been done.

1. You have enlisted your helper.
2. Your helper has read our memorandum at the end of Chapter Eight and is well acquainted with its message.
3. Your helper has gained a clear idea of what his role is going to be and what he is going to do (and not do) to help you.
4. You have had your first planning meeting where you have reviewed the method for constructing your first ladder. (You understand that the ladder is not the be-all and end-all but only a framework for your contextual therapy.)

Now it is time for another meeting, the meeting at which you and your helper are going to do three things. First, you are going to review the ladder or ladders you constructed during your first meeting, and make adjustments if necessary. Second, you are going to decide on all the different things you can do while in the phobic situation to keep your attention *focused on* the reassuring realities and *away from* the frightening thoughts, images, and feelings generated in the phobogenic process. Third, you are going to review the six points of contextual therapy. These six points should be your constant guide, and to save you the trouble of looking them up, we are going to review them briefly here. Before we do, we would suggest that, during your second meeting, you write down on one index card some of the things you are planning to do to keep yourself involved with comforting realities, and on another, the basic headline of each of the six points. Arrange to have these cards handy each time you confront the phobic situation.

With these in hand—your ladder, your "things to do," and the six points—you will be ready to venture forth, to take on rung 1 of the ladder you and your helper have constructed together. Here is a summary of the six points of contextual therapy:

Point One.   *Expect, allow, and accept that fear will arise.* Your phobic reaction is automatic. It is going to be triggered spontaneously when you step into your phobic situation. Don't try to keep it from happening; you won't be able to. Know it is going to happen and be prepared for it to happen. Remember—and this is most important—our objective is to *control* the process by which the fear intensifies. It is not to *stop* fear from appearing.

Point Two.   *When fear comes, wait. Let it be. Take one step at a time.* When your fear does come, let it come. It isn't going to be pleasant. Neither, in most instances, is it going to be as bad as you expected. The idea behind Point Two is to slow down your automatic involvement with fear-generating thoughts and expectations, and to shift you toward involvement with more realistic and comforting thoughts and actions. Remember, the whole point in contextual therapy is not to *avoid* phobic distress, but to *experience* it according to your ability and to *learn to cope* with it. If you do not experience it and learn to deal with it, you will continue to regard it as dangerous, focus on it more intently, and remain unable to bring it under control. If the distress becomes too painful and too frightening, you always have the option to move out. But try, if at all possible, to resist taking this option, and stay until the intensity goes down. If this proves too difficult, back up a step so that you can recover enough to be able to study the situation and then attempt to identify what caused your fear level to climb, and prepare yourself with things to do to keep control the next time that you try.

Point Three. *Focus on and do manageable things in the present.* This point has been made before, but it cannot be stressed too strongly. You do not just move into the phobic situation and "get used to it." On the contrary, there are things that you do actively to put you in control of your phobic reaction. You perform various little tasks and routines rooted in the "here and now" that compel your attention to focus on present and comforting realities instead of permitting it to be swept toward your frightening thoughts and images. This process moves you from disorganization to mental and behavioral organization. You will be surprised and relieved to see how effectively this technique can work. Once you have been able, as a result of your experience, to see this for yourself, you will lose your feelings of helplessness and develop a growing sense of confidence and hope. This in turn will reduce the intensity of your fear reaction, overall, and make the next step easier.

Point Four. *Label your fear from 0 to 10 and watch it go up and down.* This is an essential part of the contextual therapy technique. You monitor your fear levels and take "readings" from time to time. This does two things for you. As you monitor your fear you objectify your experience. You become an outside observer, able to report something that is happening inside of you. Putting yourself in the position of observer and reporter takes some of the fright out of the experience. Second, you will see for yourself that your fear levels change dramatically from moment to moment and that you can make them go down by shifting the focus of your attention and involvement from your frightening thoughts and images to the reassuring elements of reality. It is important that you keep this connection constantly in mind—the connection between the focus of your attention and involvement and the level of your fear. To help you keep aware of this relationship and to identify the elements affecting the changes in your levels of fear, you should fill out your customized Fear Level Chart (a Sample Fear Level Chart can be found on pages 170 and 171).

Point Five. *Function with a level of fear and appreciate the achievement.* Naturally, your most earnest desire, after such a long time of suffering, is to be rid of your phobic fear in short order. We would want that for you, too. But, unfortunately, this would be an unrealistic expectation. Because the fear reaction is based on your past experience and on your way of perceiving things, it has become quite firmly entrenched and cannot yield that quickly. Your task is going to be to learn to function in the phobic situation at low and even moderately high levels of fear for several weeks at least. The levels of fear should begin to decrease gradually as you gain greater confidence in the techniques for controlling your fear. The control you obtain will lessen your sense of danger, which will in turn lessen your fear. After a while, as your confidence grows, you will be able to function in the phobic situation, remaining there for considerable stretches of time even while experiencing fear. This is an essential part of the process by which fear levels are kept from going out of control. Therefore, when you find yourself being able to stay in the phobic situation for even a short time while experiencing varying levels of fear, you may consider this a positive and encouraging achievement and know that your progress toward recovery has begun. The time will come, after that, when you will be able to stay in the phobic situation for increasingly longer periods.

Point Six. *Allow and accept that fear will reappear.* It may take a little while before you will need to be concerned about this point, but you may as well get it set in your mind now, at the beginning, so you will be prepared for it when it occurs. No matter how quickly and well you progress, there will come a time, almost inevitably, when you experience what you may think is a setback. You may be moving about in the phobic situation with considerable ease and confidence and having very little fear, when, all of a sudden, you experience a return of intense fear, even panic. If and when this happens, you will in all likelihood think that you are back where you started and that contextual therapy is not working for you. You may even think that you are never going to get better. Be prepared so that when it happens you will not become too upset. Remember that these setbacks are only temporary and that you have not lost what you have learned. You can get over this in a short time and start to make progress again. These temporary setbacks are natural parts of the ups and downs of any learning process. It would also be wise to use such an event as an opportunity to study what happened and to review your application of the other five points of contextual therapy.

NOW, YOU TAKE YOUR FIRST STEP

The reading and the discussion and the explanations are done. Your ladder has been built and all your preparations have been made. Now there is nothing left to do, except to take your first step, to tackle rung 1 of your ladder. Set the time and the place and then . . . *Go!!!* What happens now is up to you and your helper. This book will be available to you all the time for guidance and for encouragement. Let us hope that after a very short while you are not going to need it at all, that you will have mastered the concept and techniques of contextual therapy so well that you and your helper can carry on alone.

We, the authors, wish we could accompany you as you take your first and second and third steps, standing there by your side to encourage you and lead you on. But the truth is that you are not going to need us. This is something you and your helper are going to be able to manage on your own, knowing that you have our deepest, most heartfelt wishes with you, for ultimate recovery from your phobia.

Before leaving you we would like to set down a number of additional suggestions for things to do and to remember.

Take the easiest phobia first. If you have a number of phobias, the one you might work on first is the one that is least frightening to you. We are not suggesting that you take the "easy way out." The purpose of taking the easiest phobia first is to give you some experience and help you learn about the process, and to build up your confidence in what you are doing. When you find that "it isn't so terrible after all," you will be able to tackle the next rung in your phobia ladder with a greater degree of assurance.

Take a small step at the beginning. When you are deciding on how difficult a step your first move should be, you will probably be feeling somewhat upset as you consider such things as "How far should I go?" "How long should I stay?" and "How close by should my helper be?" Our recommendation would be to accept the disturbing feelings and take a small, relatively easy step for a starter. There is no particular advantage in "trying to be a hero" or trying to do it all at once. You will probably find that even a tiny first step will take a great deal of courage and determination. This step, no matter how small, may be the biggest and most difficult step you will have to take, because this will be the first time you are choosing to go *toward* rather than *away from* dread. The effort it takes you to walk just five feet outside your door (for example) may be more than it will take to walk a mile weeks later.

Remember, the first thing you are seeking to achieve is to break, for the first time, the understandable but destructive phobic pattern of running away. If, on the very first try, you stay in the phobic situation even for two or three minutes while experiencing intense phobic fear, you have made the most important breakthrough of all. Beyond that, the task will be to expand the breakthrough and advance it farther and farther. When you have succeeded in making this first breakthrough, you can congratulate yourself on having had the strength and courage not to turn away, and this can stand you in very good stead in the steps you take after that.

What to do about your physical symptoms. It is likely that your phobic experiences involve suffering from one or more of a variety of such physical symptoms as disturbed sleep, sleepiness during the day, excessive and persistent tiredness, headaches, poor appetite, diarrhea, constipation, acid stomach and heartburn, jitteriness and tension, palpitations, night sweats, and others. Some of these *may* be associated directly with your phobia and may disappear as you progress through your contextual therapy. However, this should not be taken for granted. It is better to go to your doctor and have yourself examined. That way you will not only be reassured about your symptoms but you will also be helped to apply yourself to the task of dealing with them. Phobic people also tend to worry about physical reactions they get in the phobic situation—pounding heart, weakness in the limbs, pains in various parts of the body, difficulties in swallowing and breathing, dizziness and loss of balance, flushing—and think these may be indicators of a serious illness. An examination by your doctor should reassure you on these, too. Typically, such symptoms are transitory and harmless.

Use of tranquilizing and antidepressant drugs. People entering contextual therapy frequently ask whether they should continue to use their tranquilizer or antidepressant. If you have such a question, this book cannot give you the answer. We suggest that you consult your physician and then make your own decision. We can, however, inform you of a viewpoint derived from much experience with phobic people. This may be of help to you in coming to your own decision.

Because fear and distress build up so quickly from endangering thoughts and imagery which arise during anticipation, phobic people typically resist going into the phobic situation. Our goal in contextual therapy is to help persons to enter the phobic situation so they can learn by realistic experience that the actual threat is considerably smaller than that which is felt in anticipation. Anything that makes it easier for a phobic person to enter the phobic situation helps to attain that goal. This would include the helper. It would also include various tranquilizing drugs that are in common use. In ways not yet fully understood, these tranquilizing drugs reduce the levels of fear and anxiety and, when used in connection with contextual therapy, can make it possible for the user to enter the phobic situation, apply the techniques of contextual therapy, and thereby gain this invaluable fear-reducing experience. Many people have found it helpful in approaching their phobic situation just to have some of these pills in their pocket, as a kind of "security blanket" should the dreaded fear and panic emerge. It would seem that merely having these pills available allows the individual to pay greater attention to the realistic task than to the anticipated dangers.

These drugs do not, however, work with equal effectiveness in all people. In some, they are not very helpful in reducing anxiety, and hence cannot be useful in the fashion suggested.

How many work sessions a week? The frequency of your work sessions—the times when you and your helper work together on a specific rung of your ladder—is up to the both of you, but we think it should not be less than once a week. Two sessions a week, we think, is even better, and if you can manage three, that would be even better still—provided you find this pace comfortable. How many hours should you allow for each work session? That, again, is up to you and your helper, but it would be good to have it last for at least an hour, and longer if possible.

The frequency and length of your practice sessions—the efforts you make in between the work sessions with your helper —are also up to you. We realize that you will have other responsibilities and demands on your time, but we would urge you to practice every day and to put as much time into your practice as you can.

The payoff from frequent and regular work sessions and practice sessions should be speedier and more lasting progress.

The importance of holding to schedule. When contextual therapy is directed by a psychiatrist or a paraprofessional working with the support and guidance of a psychiatrist, work sessions are scheduled and observed with a high degree of regularity. However, when the helper is a relative or friend (nonprofessional), there may be a tendency on occasion for laxness to creep in. You may feel on the morning of a work or practice session that you are too weary and worn out and would rather postpone the session for another day. Or you may have a stomach upset or headache and feel that you would do better to stay in bed that day. Or you may suddenly remember some unrelated chore that you've been putting off and decide that this would be the day to do it. You need to be aware of these tendencies to continue to avoid the phobic situation, and try not to let such excuses as these—while legitimate and realistic— stand in the way of your contextual therapy efforts. If you give in the first time, you are likely to give in a second and a third time, and your intentions to undertake contextual therapy may go by the board. Naturally, if you are genuinely sick, you do need to stay home. And if there's a truly pressing family obligation, it needs to be taken care of. It is you, however, who will always be the judge of how serious or urgent it is, and what should be given priority that day.

Having said this, allowances need to be made for those instances when putting off practicing one day instills a feeling of "having let yourself down" and increases the resolve to get to work the following day.

The helper has responsibility in this, too. He should anticipate that there may be times when you, the person with the phobia, will be frightened or upset about going into the phobic situation that day, and may try to find a way of getting out of it. Should the helper suspect this to be the case, it would be up to him to do a bit of friendly prodding. Generally speaking, when the reason given for staying home is not too realistic, a little gentle encouragement is enough to overcome the resistance. But there should be only encouragement and persuasion; never ridicule, scolding, or threats.

Again, we reiterate that in the final analysis it is the person who has the phobia who has to decide when and how he wants to work and practice in order to get rid of the phobia. But we do urge strongly that work and practice be as regular as possible. If you decide you do not want to keep regular work and practice sessions, that is up to you. But you need to remember that without work and practice sessions, in which you confront your phobic fear, nothing is going to happen, and with infrequent and irregular sessions, very little is likely to happen. Contextual therapy is a learning process and, as we know from every other type of learning, regular drill and practice is required. There is no easy way. Reading this book—even memorizing and understanding it intellectually—is not going to help you get rid of your phobia, unless you also work and practice.

Communicating with your helper. Phobic people have found that contact with the helper is more important than anything else in helping them to enter the phobic situation. The contact takes various forms at various times. At first, you may need to hold on to your helper's arm or have him hold on to yours. Later, physical contact may not be necessary and talking to each other may take its place. Still later you may separate deliberately, so that you can move into the phobic situation without your helper's physical presence. But even though he is not actually there, you still know that you will be able to reestablish contact in some fashion. You may make arrangements to separate for a short while and to meet at a certain place at a certain time. Or you may decide that the helper will stay away from the scene but will be available by telephone. In either situation, punctuality and reliability are mandatory. The helper should be there, at the agreed-upon place and at the agreed-upon time, earlier if possible, never later. If the arrangement is for contact by telephone, the helper should be at the designated number throughout the time that you are making your move.

If you are going to be out of each other's sight, a walkie-talkie could prove to be a very useful implement. You'll be surprised how reassuring the helper's voice can be even though you are at a considerable distance from each other. A pair of walkie-talkies with good power and range should not be financially prohibitive.

Another device that has proved helpful is a tape recording of your helper talking to you and reassuring you. You can decide between the two of you what message would be most helpful.

Then, when you are in the phobic situation and feel the need for reassurance, you can just flip the recorder switch and listen to your helper's voice. Eventually, you won't even need a tape recording. You will be able to "hear" your helper's voice "in your head," and that, for many of you, will be enough. Even the sound of your own voice, tape-recorded, can be reassuring. People who have tape-recorded messages of reassurance and listened to them when in the phobic situation say it has the comforting effect of feeling the presence of another person.

The role of the helper. It is essential to remember that the role of the helper is to *help*, not to *decide*. The helper is there to give reassurance and emotional support, to help construct the ladder, to keep in contact with the partner (the phobic person), to remind the phobic person, when necessary, of things to do to keep in touch with reassuring reality, to query the partner about his fear levels, to help fill out the Fear Level Chart, to encourage the partner to "stay the course" and move ahead with more difficult steps. But it is the person with the phobia who decides what each successive step should be, how long to stay in the phobic situation, and whether to work with or without a helper present. Each person has to move along at a pace that is most comfortable for him. A particular move may appear very easy to the helper, yet be terrifying to the phobic person. In his eagerness to move the phobic person along, the helper may become insistent and try to put on excess pressure, or even to shame the person into taking that step. This can do more harm than good and actually interfere with progress. One person may be able to move at only one-half or one-tenth the speed of others with the same kind of problem. But if that is all he is able to do, then it has to be accepted. What matters in the end is how the individual evaluates what he can and cannot do. He has to be permitted to move along and learn, at his pace, to perceive more realistically that the danger is not as great as he thinks, and ultimately, that there is not any realistic danger there at all.

Make a detailed plan. This reminder has to do mainly with the days when you are practicing a move by yourself. On those days you will not have the reassuring presence of your helper. Being on your own, it is possible you may get rattled, frightened, and confused and have a panic attack. One good way to avoid this is to work out a fairly detailed plan for controlling your level of fear in the event of unpredictable developments. Here is an illustration:

Suppose you are going to try that day to spend thirty minutes in a shopping center and do a little shopping. Your plan for that day might include the following:

1. Decide, in advance, whether you want to get to the shopping mall when it is least or most crowded, and schedule the hour accordingly.
2. Map out a route that you feel is best for you.
3. Map out alternate routes for those streets where traffic might be too heavy and where a traffic jam is likely to occur.
4. If you still feel uneasy about being out of contact with a trusted person, arrange, if necessary, to telephone your helper, a relative, or a friend at any time that you might feel the need, while en route or at the mall.
5. Decide whether you will want to take a tranquilizer, and if so, have it handy in your pocket, to take it as you feel the need.
6. Decide, in advance, where you are going to park, taking into account such things as the distance between parking place and mall entrance, possible complications in getting from the parking place to the mall and back, etc.
7. Make a map of the route from parking place to the mall so that you can refer to it in the event you get flustered or frightened.
8. Plan ahead as to what you will do if the store elevators are too crowded and you feel too phobic about getting into one. Will you wait there until the crowd thins out? Will you back up and go into a street-level store for a while? Will you use a stairway? Decide this in advance so that you will feel better prepared to deal with the eventualities.
9. Decide in advance how long you will stay in the store once you enter, how much shopping you will do, what you will buy, and whether you will charge it or pay by check.
10. Map out your route home as well as alternate routes.
11. Write down all the routes you have mapped out, the various locations where you will be, and all other specifics so that you can refer to them easily.
12. Write down and keep handy a list of the manageable things you may need to do in order to keep you focused on reassuring reality.

The idea in working out a plan for the day is *not* to keep you from experiencing phobic anxiety. It is taken for granted that

you are likely to feel some fairly strong levels of fear in your
phobic situation, especially if you are just venturing into that
situation alone for the first time. It is assumed that you will be
prepared to deal with these by the customary techniques you
have been using to keep yourself involved with reasuring realities. The purpose of making the kind of plan we are suggesting
is to reduce the possibility of a panic attack in an unanticipated
eventuality, one that is not part of your practice session for the
day. Without a plan, such an attack may impel you to abort
your practice session and run home, ruining your program for
the day.

Try to be open about your phobia. On days when you are
practicing alone (without your helper), you may have a tendency to shrink into yourself and avoid making contact with
other people, still out of a fear that others may think you're
"abnormal," turn away from you, and regard you with suspicion and loathing. If so, we urge that you try not to do so. You
might, in fact, use this as an opportunity to reach out to other
people, and if possible, to involve them in helping you. Phobic
people who have tried this have found, according to their own
witness, "an amazing response of kindness, cooperativeness,
and helpfulness." Let us relate a number of experiences of this
kind.

> **Henry M.** (elevator phobia): I had not yet been able to go back to
> my regular job because of my elevator phobia. But a friend let me
> come in several days a week, for half a day, to do some of the
> same type of work in his office. There was still a problem of
> elevators, but I had gotten to the point where I could ride up in
> the elevator provided someone else was in the car, and was
> going up as far as my floor (the fifteenth) or further. So I would
> wait until about 9:30 A.M. when the crowds had thinned out and
> when just one or two people would come along every few min-
> utes, I would wait in front of the elevator cars, and when some-
> one would come along I would stop him (or her) and say: "I beg
> your pardon. Are you, by any chance, going up to the fifteenth
> floor or further? I have an elevator phobia and I can't ride up in
> the elevator by myself." They would either say, "Yes," or "No,
> I'm sorry." I seldom had to wait more than five or ten minutes at
> the most. Not a single person ever made a nasty remark or was
> in any way discourteous. They didn't particularly fall all over me
> with sympathy (which I wouldn't have wanted), but neither did
> they turn away from me or insult me by word, look, or gesture.

Then one day, the elevator starter came over to me and said, "Mister, I hear you asking people about going up to the fifteenth floor. Would you want to try it alone, and I'll talk you up over the intercom?" I told him I thought that was one of the nicest things that had ever happened to me and gladly accepted his offer. The first time was a little scary, but I did hear his voice and that was reassuring. He would say, "Hey, how is it going? I see you're getting right up there. You'll be there in another moment. That's great." And I would talk back to him on the intercom telling him I was doing fine. On the way down, I waited until someone on that floor was going down, and then got into the car with them.

The elevator starter kept this up for a whole week and then, the following Monday, he asked if I would like to try it without his talking me up. I did and felt just a little scared, but I didn't panic. I knew that if I got really panicky, I could push the alarm button and that would get him to the intercom. Besides, I practiced my contextual therapy tasks and stayed connected to reality. By the end of that week, I was riding the elevator alone, even when the elevator starter was not there. And that was the end of that problem. After riding the elevator became routine, we would just nod to each other politely, just as though nothing had ever happened. He certainly didn't act as though it was any big thing in his life; just a routine courtesy, not warranting further mention. And this was not an intellectual with an academic background. He was just a nice human being, a working man who had probably not gone far beyond grade school. And they say New Yorkers are not friendly!

Elsie G. (storms, lightning, thunder): I was out in Dallas visiting my sister and decided one day to go shopping at Neiman-Marcus. It was a bright, sunny day, humid and hot, but there wasn't even a hint of rain. Not a cloud in the sky. No one had bothered to tell me that in this part of the country it can be like that one minute, and a half hour later the sky can come down and it can rain two inches in an hour. But I guess they had no reason to warn me, not knowing that I had this phobia, and assuming that as far as rain was concerned, I would not need to be told how to keep from getting wet. Well, I had finished my shopping and was making my way to the exit. Then I saw one or two people carrying umbrellas and thought, how strange, carrying umbrellas on a perfectly clear day. But my mind was busy with other things and I didn't give it a second thought. Then, as I came around a corner, within ten or fifteen feet of the exit, I looked out through the glass doors and it was as black as night outside. A flash of lightning that must have come within five feet of the building lighted up the street and the other buildings with an eerie blue light, like something out of a science fiction movie. I was petrified with panic. My arms were loaded with gifts I had bought for my sister and her husband and children, and I dropped them and started to run. I had completely lost my bearings and didn't even know how to get to the interior of the store away from the storm. Instead, I found myself near another bank of doors, and just then a clap of thunder exploded that shook the building to its foundations and the rain came down in a deluge. I turned around and ran in the other direction, pushing people and almost knocking them down. I knew I was weeping and talking to myself, but I couldn't help it. I couldn't control myself. I thought surely I was going to die right then and there.

Then, out of nowhere, there was this man, an elderly gentleman, and he put his arm around my shoulders, and spoke to me in a nice, quiet, gentle Southern voice. He asked me what was wrong, and I told him I had a phobia, that I was frightened to death of storms and thunder and lightning. He said he understood, and for me not to worry. He had been watching me and saw that I had a problem and said that he would help me get to the interior of the store. I clung to his arm and started to get hold of myself. Then he called over a young man and told him to go find the packages I had dropped. But by this time, three or four other people were making their way over to where we were standing, and they had my packages in their hands. They handed them to the young man and then the two men escorted me to the lounge where they put me in the charge of a woman attendant. They told her what had happened and she said to them, "Don't you worry. I'll take care of her." Then she sat me down in the lounge, and for the next fifteen minutes she talked to me and quieted me down. She told me she knew exactly what I was going through, that she had a sister who hadn't been out of the house for more than three years and a brother who had a deadly fear of planes. In no time, we were telling each other about our families, and it was so wonderful and reassuring.

I told her that I was visiting and had to return to my sister's home, but that I was terrified to take a taxi there, because it was storming and, even if it stopped, it might start again. You will never believe what happened next. She said she had to leave me for a few minutes, and would be back right away. After she returned, we sat and talked some more. In a little while a young man, about seventeen, came in, and she introduced him as her son and said that he had come with his car and that he would drive me to my sister's home. I said I couldn't put them to that trouble, but they insisted.

Gina T. (driving on expressway): This is something that I have had off and on for several years. Sometimes I could drive on an expressway and feel only slightly tense and nervous. Other times, it would grab me all of a sudden, and it would be so bad, I had to pull over to the side and then crawl along on the shoulder —you know, the emergency parking strip on the side of the highway—until I came to an exit. This thing that I'm telling you about happened while I was in therapy for the driving problem. I had already had several good work sessions with my helper and a few good practice sessions by myself, so I was getting pretty confident. I was on the Connecticut Turnpike moving along at about fifty miles an hour in the middle lane when it hit me without a second's warning. It felt like a rush of blood into my head, dizziness, loss of control. I could feel my hands grabbing the wheel and trembling, and I was sure I was going to swerve and smash into another car. It felt like the car was racing along at a hundred miles an hour out of my control. I started to slow down, and the car behind me started honking and honking, and that frightened me even more. I don't know how I got out of it, but somehow I did manage to sidle over to the outside lane and then I drove onto the shoulder and stopped the car. I was so shaken, I put my head on the wheel and started crying hysterically.

Then I saw a car pull over in front of me and stop about fifty feet away. A man came running out of the car to where I was, pulled open the door, and asked me was anything wrong. He must have seen me with my head on the wheel and maybe thought I was dead or something. Anyhow, I just knew I couldn't tell him about my phobia; I was too ashamed. So I just told him I had started to feel faint, and had to pull over until I felt a little better. He offered to stay with me for a while until I felt better, but I told him it wasn't necessary, figuring I could do what I had done those other times, crawl along until I got to the exit. I noticed that he was looking at me a little suspiciously, and I wondered why. Then he said, "Ma'am, have you got a driving phobia? If you do, please don't be ashamed to tell me. I know all about phobias. My wife used to have the same problem herself." Was I ever thankful and relieved to hear him say that. So I broke down and told him that I did have this phobia and that I was getting therapy. Then he said, "Ma'am, would you like my wife to drive you off the expressway and onto a side road? It'll be no trouble for us at all, and we'd be glad to help you." This time, I did not feel ashamed any longer and I accepted. So he went back to his car, and his wife came out and got behind the wheel of my car, and we drove off to the other road with the man following us in their car.

Vincent (speaking in public): I've always had a problem about speaking in the company of a large group of people. I would be very shy and never say anything, and when anybody pressed me, I would blush and blurt out a few words and run away. I could manage this in social groups, just by keeping quiet and staying out of group discussions. But in school, when I had to get up and recite, it was something different. I would freeze and nothing would come out of my mouth. The instructors would think I was stupid and move on to the next student. The only thing that saved me were my high grades on written tests. Not one single instructor ever tried to investigate this discrepancy—stupid recital, top grades on the tests. But I was satisfied. I didn't know that what I had was a phobia, but I didn't like the idea of anybody prying into what I thought was my basic inadequacy.

Then after I graduated from college and went to work as a junior economist with a banking firm, I decided to go on with getting my M.B.A. [Master of Business Administration] in the evenings. Once these courses started, I found myself in the same bind—freezing when I was called upon to recite. But I decided I wasn't going to let this go on any further. I would find out what my problem was and try to do something about it. That's how I got into psychotherapy and that's how I found out I had a social phobia. After a few months I quit psychotherapy when I learned about contextual therapy and started at the White Plains Hospital Phobia Clinic. When I told the people in the group about my difficulty, several of them urged me to tell my school instructors and fellow students about it and ask for their understanding. I was just too embarrassed to do this, and I never would have except for one of my classmates who had become a very good personal friend. Charles—that was my friend's name—knew about my phobia. I had told him but I had sworn him to secrecy. But after watching me get up and sweat and blush and stammer in class two or three times, he threatened that if I didn't tell the teacher and the class, he would tell them himself. I told him I would kill him if he did, but he said I would just have to kill him; he was going to do it. He said he would just give me three more classes. If I didn't get up and tell the class by the fourth session, he would get up and make an announcement to the class about my phobia. I waited two classes, and then the third class I came to class a little earlier and told the instructor that I had a speaking phobia and that was why I was having a problem reciting. I also told him that I was getting contextual therapy at the clinic and he asked me to explain what it was. When I told him, he was very interested. Then he asked me whether I minded if he told the class about this. I told him I didn't mind.

When class started, the instructor said he would like to discuss something concerning one of the students, and he told them about me and about my contextual therapy. He then did something which was a complete surprise. He asked if the class would like to join in giving me a five-minute practice session each class, for the next few weeks, as part of my contextual therapy. They all applauded and said it was a great idea. And so they did. For the next four classes, they would sit there quietly while I gave a two- or three-minute talk on a subject we were taking up in class. It was very difficult for me, and I had to prepare my talks by writing them out verbatim, and looking at the cards. But the fifth time, I spoke for about five minutes and I had to look at my cards only three or four times. [Vincent reported back, several months later, that by the end of the term, he was speaking freely in front of the class, with hardly any tension at all.]

Communicate your thoughts and feelings. In your first encounter with your phobic situation, you may tend to turn inward, absorbed with your frightening thoughts and feelings. You should try very early to counteract this tendency by keeping in verbal communication with your helper. Take the opportunity to tell him what you are feeling, thinking, and expecting. Tell him about your fright and distress. Report to him, by "labelling," how your levels of fear rise and fall. Communication has two important purposes. One is to keep you attached to comforting reality. A verbal exchange with your helper will help to do this. The very fact of his listening to you, hearing you, and responding to you will reassure you and keep you organized and oriented as you struggle with your fear. Second, in communicating what you are feeling and thinking, you automatically become an observer and reporter of your inward reactions, giving you some "distance" from them and enabling you to begin to control them. Through this process, you will ultimately gain an understanding of what goes on in your phobic reaction, leading toward more stable and lasting *voluntary, conscious control.* Especially during the first several work sessions, the responsibility for keeping you communicating is going to rest with your helper. It will be up to him to ask you questions, to encourage you to report your thoughts and feelings, and to label the changing levels of your phobic fear.

Don't underrate your gains; don't be troubled by slow progress. It is a characteristic of many people who are phobic that they tend to underrate themselves, to make little of their successes and to make a great deal of any shortcoming (or what they may believe is a shortcoming). This tendency can be expected to show up also as they evaluate their progress in contextual therapy. It is not unusual to hear some of these people make little of truly remarkable advances. One woman, for example, who had not driven for more than five years, was able after only four weeks of contextual therapy to drive by herself for a few blocks. Instead of exulting in this advance, she said she felt that "it didn't really amount to much." A man who hadn't been able to attend any social or business gatherings for more than ten years because of his dread of crowds and enclosure, and who was able after six weeks of contextual therapy to attend a lecture in an evening course and remain for more than thirty minutes, felt "terribly disappointed" because he found it too difficult to remain for the remaining forty-five minutes. He could not be convinced that what he had achieved really amounted to a major advance. A woman who hadn't been out of her home for more than two years was able, after only a few weeks of therapy, to go by herself to a little neighborhood store. She couldn't see this as very much progress toward her ultimate goal, to "be able to go shopping in a department store, or to go anywhere I wanted without any fear." All three lacked a realistic perspective in their objectives and accordingly were unable to credit themselves with having done something worthwhile.

Going along hand-in-hand with this inability to recognize achievement is the exaggeration of little setbacks and the tendency to become easily demoralized. An occasional, minor failure is blown up out of proportion, overshadowing important and impressive gains. The failure is remembered, the successes forgotten.

A third tendency that goes along with these two others is that of comparing oneself with people who are not phobic. A woman might say, after leaving her house for the first time in several years and walking a block or two, "My sister goes all over the country. She's an important businesswoman and travels thousands of miles to business meetings and conventions. So, look at me. I can walk three blocks from my house. What's so wonderful about that?" This is like hearing a patient who has suffered a stroke and is beginning to regain use of her legs say, "My niece just ran in the twenty-six-mile marathon. So what's so great about my walking ten steps with a walker?"

Progress in contextual therapy—or any other creditable therapy for phobias—is made by little steps, at the beginning at least. Every little step forward should be seen as an important gain. Just being able to enter or even to think about entering the phobic situation, something that was impossible before, is a very great gain. Staying in the phobic situation two minutes longer today than you did yesterday is a great gain. Being able to lower your level of fear just two or three points, or even to keep it steady by performing one of the little tasks that keep you involved with reality, is a great achievement. Being able to cope with your panic a minute or two longer today than you did yesterday—that's a great achievement. These are real advances because they become the solid basis for recognizing that you are able to acquire control over what you had thought to be an uncontrollable process.

In the beginning, measure your success in "baby steps." You can start thinking about "giant steps" later, when you have gained control over your phobic reaction and you are ready to move into wider arenas.

How to deal with anticipation. Panic reactions can occur when you are nowhere near the phobic situation. They can come anywhere, even at home. They can come even when you're just *thinking* about going into the phobic situation. Your imagination can work even more powerfully than it does in an actual encounter. You can expect this to happen most intensely in the days preceding your first move into the phobic situation. You may be at home reading a book or at work performing some routine task, or you may wake up suddenly during the night, and there it is, the terror and dread which you have always associated with your phobic situation. You see yourself entering the train, automobile, elevator, tunnel, observation platform, or stadium. Your heart begins to race. You feel the lightness, dizziness, tightness in the head and throat, or the sinking feeling in your stomach. You try to get hold of yourself and say to yourself, "This is insane. I'm not there. I am here!"

You try to stop the thoughts and the imagery from coming, but they keep on coming just the same.

This is the business of anticipation, of frightening yourself with the thoughts and images of how terrible *it is going to be* and trying to stop the fear by suppressing the thoughts and images. What to do? First, you might try a tactic used by other people who have been in the same situation. Many phobic people find that they can go into the phobic situation better when they do not have the time to think and anticipate, and so, when their anticipatory anxiety comes on, they say to themselves, "That's something I don't have to deal with now. I'll deal with it when I get to it. The chances are that when I actually get to it, it isn't going to be as bad as I anticipate." This happens to be one situation in which putting off worrying about something can serve a useful purpose. Should you be unable to put it off as suggested, then don't try to fight off this surge of fright and all that comes with it. Don't try to reason yourself out of it. Deal with it as though you were actually in the phobic situation. When fear comes, wait. Let it be. Instead of hopelessly trying to get rid of the fear or escape, think of this as an opportunity to cope with your fear in a phobic situation. Recognize that this is an automatic response to your mental processes. Get involved with one of the activities you have been preparing to use, some activity which will pull your attention back to the reassuring present and away from the frightening future. And begin to practice labelling the levels of your phobic fear. You will see, even before any actual encounter with the phobic situation, that you are capable of controlling this reaction, lowering the levels of fear by the things that you do. Then you will see how the surge of fear passes like a wave. But don't think this won't happen again. It will, but you'll be prepared for it. It should happen less and less in the weeks when you're already involved in your work sessions and practice sessions, because by that time you should already have been having some success in bringing your phobic reaction under control. Spontaneous fear arousal outside the phobic situation should then occur less and less frequently.

What to expect.   You can definitely expect to make progress as you move along in contextual therapy, but remember: The rate of progress varies from person to person. As a rule, the more diligently you practice, the better your progress will be. But even though you practice as diligently as somebody else, your progress may not be as quick as his. This happens because people are different; they learn differently; and they react differently. Some may be more resistant to some changes than others. Some are less free to try a different approach. Keep that in mind as you try to evaluate, "How am I doing?" Aside from that you can expect these things to happen as you work on your contextual therapy:

1. Your progress will not be consistent. You may experience a fast initial surge, then slow down, then speed up again. Or it may start slowly, move quickly, then slow down again. There will be ups and there will be downs and there is no way of knowing when the change in direction is going to come. But it must come as your experience in the phobic situation changes.

2. Your panic attacks may come quite frequently at the beginning, then diminish considerably for quite a while, but then they may come back for a short while even worse than before. Expect that to happen, so that when it does, you won't be frightened or discouraged.

3. There will be times when, anticipating strong surges of phobic fear, you will experience none at all. And there will be times when you will not be expecting to have any phobic fear, and a surge of panic may come on all of a sudden.

4. Little by little your perimeters of safety will get wider and wider, adding places and activities that your phobia had forced you to exclude from your daily life. But even in those places that have once more become safe, expect to have an occasional panic attack. This is so because old patterns of response tend to recur under certain conditions, even after they have been displaced by new ways of perceiving the situation.

5. The longer you continue practicing contextual therapy, the fewer will be these recurring attacks, and the time should come when you will be having none at all. That may mean, for you, that you are free of your phobia forever. Or it may be that you could have a recurrence of your phobic reaction. But if you do, you will be prepared to deal with it, limit its intensity and duration, and increase your control.

Take the offensive against your phobia. Anyone who has been phobic for any length of time is, without a doubt, "frightened to death" of the phobic experience. If that weren't so, avoidance would never have occurred. But you have to realize that in this process, another destructive thing has taken place. You see the phobia and the phobic fear as a monster which has you in its terrifying grip. You see yourself as helpless, the phobic "monster" as all-powerful. You cannot visualize how anything at all can break its life-squeezing hold. You may be too frightened and discouraged even to try. Now try to think of it another way. Your phobia is not a "thing." It is a reaction of your body and mind to assumptions and expectations derived from past experiences in these situations. Just as it came into existence because of your erroneous reactions to imaginary dangers, it can go out of existence as you learn to correct these misconceptions. This "monster" is something *you* have created without realizing it. You have the power, now, through contextual therapy, to "un-create" it, to dismantle it and destroy it. Visualize yourself as going on the offensive. Think of yourself as venturing out to "hunt down" the phobogenic process so you can rob it of its power to do you any further harm. Think of each venture into the phobic situation as a sortie against your enemy, with the certain knowledge that you now have the weapon in your hands—contextual therapy—with which to vanquish your "monster."

Reward yourself. When you have mastered the first rung of your first ladder, reward yourself. Give yourself a treat. You may have been wanting a sweater, a blouse, a tie, a shirt, a record, a chess set, a video game, a meal at your favorite restaurant. Go out and get it for yourself. Or see if you can entice someone who appreciates your achievement to treat you. Maybe you've been wanting to see a special movie or theater show, or hear a special concert. This is the time to go, or to get someone to take you. If you can't get out, movies, theaters, and concerts are obviously out (for now, anyway). But you can still have someone bring in one of the other treats you've been wanting.

When you've done this after mastering the first rung of your ladder, do it again for every additional important gain you make. See, too, if you can involve some of the members of your family in fixing up a little surprise for you, when you've been making good progress. If it embarrasses you to do this, let your helper be the one to get the word around. There's a lot more to this than just pampering yourself. What it does for you, say the psychologists, is to "reinforce" your gains, to "stamp them in." So, you get a double benefit each time you reward yourself. You get pleasure out of your treat, and you also reinforce your gain.

CONTEXTUAL THERAPY WITHOUT A HELPER

All of our instructions, thus far, on the practice of contextual therapy are based on the assumption that you are going to try to enlist a helper.

But what if you cannot enlist a helper, or prefer to work by yourself? What do you do then?

Basically, contextual therapy is directed to the phobic person himself. All of the tools and techniques, including the six points, are intended for the person with the phobia. It is he, and nobody else, who has the responsibility for going into the phobic situation, using the tools to stay connected to reassuring reality, learning about and understanding the nature of the phobogenic process, and through these measures, bringing the phobogenic process under control. The helper is there only to assist you in achieving these goals. Certainly—and we have emphasized this point strongly—the helper performs many important functions. His very presence is comforting and reassuring. He helps plan the steps you take in confronting the phobic situation. He enters into the phobic situation and stays as long as you find it necessary. He reminds you, in case you become confused, about the little tasks that will keep your attention focused on the present and not on the frightening things that "might happen." He reminds you to label the intensity of your fear and to fill out his fear-level chart.

All these are very important, and for some phobic people they are essential and indispensable. There are some people who find it impossible to go into the phobic situation and to undertake contextual therapy without a helper. But that is not true for all phobic people. Many can get along without a helper and can do all the things that are required in contextual therapy by themselves. It is possible that you, yourself, are one of those people. The only way to find out is to try. Without any doubt, it will be more difficult. And without any doubt, it will be more frightening *at the outset*.

But let us assure you that if you can get yourself just to take those one or two tiny first steps, while fighting back the powerful impulse to run, you will learn, at the very beginning, the basic lesson of contextual therapy: that you can control your phobogenic reaction and keep it from spiralling, and that the power and control needed to do so is in your possession. Once you have experienced even the slightest success in staying in the phobic situation without running away, deliberately doing those things that will keep your attention focused on the familiar and reassuring elements in the situation, you will *know* that you can do it, you will be confident about pursuing it further and gaining even greater control.

The important thing, therefore, is to gear yourself to take just the first small step—remaining in the phobic situation for one minute, two minutes, five minutes, or longer without running. The rest is not going to be easy (no more than it is for those who work with a helper), but it should be *easier*, and the next step *easier* than that, and you will be on your way. There may even be a benefit in working alone—you will have the feeling that you are able to do it by yourself, without any help, except the guidance of this book, which can stand in the stead of a helper. Think of this book as representing many professional and paraprofessional people who have worked with thousands of phobic individuals and who have applied this method for many years in many places and have seen it work. Think of these instructions as coming to you out of years of successful experience. Think of the thousands of phobic people who have been freed from their suffering through the use of the tools and techniques of contextual therapy. And know this: If you yourself apply them, you, too, will likely succeed in overcoming your phobia. You may notice that we qualify; we don't say "positively" or "absolutely." We do not know you and your personal traits and characteristics. We would rather postulate on the basis of averages and probabilities, and thus we can say that the probabilities are high that contextual therapy will work for you, even without a helper.

There are times in everyone's life when steps have to be taken that will result, temporarily, in suffering and pain, but which will ultimately bring about a resolution of what appears at the time to be an impossible problem. This is the kind of choice that faces you now. Would you prefer to remain enslaved by your phobia, suffering for the rest of your life, or will you try to make a decision, to endure the initial pain and difficulty, and then embark on a program that holds the promise of freeing you of your phobia? Think of the things you have been missing. Think of the deprivations your phobia has caused you. Think of the ways in which your phobia has impoverished the personal relationships in your life. Think of all the things that you could regain, or even gain for the first time, by taking these steps and then overcoming your phobia. And then resolve that you are going to use contextual therapy to master your phobia, with the guidance of this book.

The things you do will be just the same as though you had a helper, only you are going to do them by yourself.

1. Decide on your long-term goal, then narrow this down into a number of specific, practical goals.

2. Build your first ladder, following the instructions detailed in Chapter Seven.

3. Prepare a list of all the little, manageable tasks you are going to perform in the phobic situation to keep your attention focused on comforting reality and the present, and away from the frightening thoughts, images, and feelings about what "might happen to you" in the phobic situation.

4. Practice labeling your fears from 0 to 10, while you are not yet in the phobic situation but just thinking about entering it.

5. Keep a list of the six points before you at all times at home, and on a little card which you can carry with you in the phobic situation, and practice them. Let us repeat them here, although we have already listed them several times:

- Expect, allow, and accept that fear will arise when you enter the phobic situation or when you even think about it.
- When the fear comes, wait. Let it be. Don't run. Make yourself stay there one minute, two minutes, three minutes and you will be able to see how the fear will reach a peak and then pass over like a wave, becoming less and less intense.
- Focus on manageable things in the present. Be sure to perform the little tasks you have written out for yourself to do.
- Label your fears from 0 to 10, reciting the figures to yourself as you might recite them to a helper if he were there. Observe how these levels go up and down, and observe how they are governed mainly by what is going on in your mind at the time.
- Function with a level of fear. Appreciate the achievement. The only way you are going to be able to bring the phobogenic process under control is to learn to function with a level of fear while in the phobic situation and to gain confidence in your controls. The more frequently and the longer you are able to do this, the more certainly will you be on the way to mastering your phobia.

- Expect, allow, and accept that your fear will reappear. No matter how well and quickly you progress, there will come a time when fear will reappear, and even surges of panic may suddenly come back. Don't let this throw you. This is part of the learning process. It is only a temporary phase.

6. Reread the list of "things to do and to remember" that we have just gone over in this chapter. Only two or three have to do with working with a helper. The rest are basic and apply to anyone undertaking contextual therapy—with or without a helper.

NOW YOU ARE SET TO GO

The explanations and the instructions have been given—both for those who will be working with a helper and those who will be working without one. The guidelines and the rules have been set down. The principles and the processes are the same. All that has been preparation. Now the preparation is finished. Now it is the time to START.

Our congratulations to every one of you who is going to confront your phobia using contextual therapy. You have our assurance that significant gains will come; for many they will come quickly. You have our assurances, further, that as you continue to learn in the phobic situation and continue to apply what you have learned, your progress will broaden and deepen and, ultimately, the very great majority of you will be liberated from your phobia. It is a tried and tested method. It has worked for thousands of others. It should also work for you.

CHAPTER ELEVEN

Organizing a Mutual Support Group

WHEN PATIENTS FINISH their eight-session course at the White Plains Hospital Phobia Clinic, they are encouraged to join a mutual support group so they can continue working on their contextual therapy with other phobia patients, until they feel they can manage well alone without further assistance. There are several such groups operating at the White Plains Hospital Medical Center and in the surrounding community.

With the same thought in mind, we strongly recommend that the readers of this book organize mutual support groups of their own. Experience has shown that these groups are highly beneficial in supplementing and consolidating the gains made through the individual practice of contextual therapy.

This may seem like a difficult task to undertake without the direct help and guidance of a person who is trained in contextual therapy and knowledgeable about mutual support groups. However, the experience of others has shown that the formation of mutual support groups is entirely within the capability of intelligent, determined people.

What follows is a step-by-step plan for organizing a mutual support group, worked out with the guidance of Mrs. Fern Overlock, a paraprofessional at the White Plains Hospital Phobia Clinic. Mrs. Overlock has herself organized several such groups with great success.

How to Organize Your Own Mutual Support Group

There are four major objectives in starting and conducting a mutual support group:

1. To enable the group members to share and compare their own experiences with their phobias.
2. To acquaint the members with the theory and tools of contextual therapy and specifically with the six points of contextual therapy.
3. To help the members to develop short-term and long-term goals for the control of their phobias.
4. To help the members to take the specific steps toward achieving these goals, using the concepts and techniques of contextual therapy.

There is no one best way to fulfill these four objectives. The format and structure you work out will depend on your own ideas and creativity. We will, however, suggest a basic plan which you might wish to use as a model for the development of your own group.

You, yourself, will be occupying two roles in the mutual support group. One role will be that of group organizer and leader. The other will be that of group member. This will mean that, when members of the group choose immediate and long term goals, you, too, will do that. And, when members of the group report about their progress during the week, you, too, will report on your progress. Even as you help the others, you will be helping yourself as well. As you attempt to explain to the group the meaning and practice of contextual therapy, it will help to clarify your own understanding of the concepts and techniques, which will give you an even better grip on the process than you had before. Now, for the suggested plan:

Step One. Find a place to meet. Your first inclination may be to have the group meet in your own home. While this may be convenient for you, it has some potential drawbacks. For people with phobias, a home setting may be more intimate and enclosing than they would like, at least at the beginning, and so they are less likely to respond willingly. A meeting room in a church, temple, mental health association, YMCA or YWCA, or other community center is much less intimate and more open, making it easier to come and go as one wishes. Also, the host institution is likely to be helpful with recruitment of group members through public announcements, newsletters, or even advertisements. Further, an institution may have its own counselling or social work staff and may be willing to offer some professional help in organizing and conducting the group.

Step Two. Recruit your group. If you have arranged for the group to meet in a church, community center, mental health association, etc., ask whether the agency or institution would be willing to publicize the group and solicit membership through its regular channels of communication (such as an announcement from the pulpit, on a bulletin board, or in a newsletter). In addition, you may want to advertise in your local weekly newspaper. If you do, the rate should be nominal, and you may wish to ask the group, once it is formed, to "chip in" for what the ad cost you.

If the experience of others is any indication, you should get a very enthusiastic response both to the announcements by the institution and to your advertisement.

Step Three. Plan your first meeting. Once you have found a place for regular weekly meetings, and perhaps enlisted the help of the professional staff of the institution, you should plan the program for your first meeting in detail. We advise against jumping in and "playing it by ear." Even those with considerable professional experience in organizing and conducting groups do not do this. Hence, you, as a beginner, should certainly avoid going in to the first meeting without a plan. Here is what your plan could include:

• You introduce yourself to the group and explain the purpose in bringing it together. You tell them that you have learned about contextual therapy through this book and have been practicing it, and that you have made progress in controlling your phobic behavior through the application of the principles and techniques of contextual therapy. You would now like to continue working on your contextual therapy with the support of other people with phobias, and at the same time, impart to them the benefits of this method through the functioning of the group. You tell them that you will leave the detailed explanation about contextual therapy for a later session, after you have all gotten to know each other a little better.

• Then you tell them that, in a group, phobic people can help each other, can give each other emotional support, can share with each other the techniques for dealing with their phobias, and can encourage each other in taking the steps necessary to overcome their phobias.

• After that, you tell them about your own experience with your phobia and the difficulties and problems it has created for you. Tell them also about the progress you have made in coping with and controlling your phobia by means of contextual therapy.

• Next, you ask the members of the group, one at a time, to tell about their own experiences and struggles with their phobia. If anyone wants to "pass" for the time being, you tell them it is perfectly alright to do so and that he or she will be able to take a turn at a later session, that everyone will understand.

• The session should last about ninety minutes, or a little longer if you and the group would like to extend it. But it should not be allowed to run more than two hours. Before ending the session, ask the members of the group to comment on how they liked the session and if they would like to continue on a regular basis. After some brief discussion, ask the group to agree on meeting at the same time and place the following week. It is assumed, of course, that you have already arranged for permission from the host institution to continue on a weekly basis.

• Pass around a sheet so that each member can write down his or her name, address, and phone number. Offer to make duplicate copies so that each member can receive a copy at the next meeting. Explain that an important part of group support is being able to call each other when going through a panic attack, or for any other kind of help related to contextual therapy. Some members may not wish to give out this information, so reassure the group that this is entirely voluntary and optional. Ask for a volunteer to act as "recorder." The recorder keeps notes on attendance, meeting changes, program events, and the like.

This, basically, is the format for a first meeting. Outline it for yourself on index cards or in your notebook, and use the outline as a guide during the meeting.

Step Four. Hold your first group meeting. Follow the plan you have already prepared.

Step Five. Your second group meeting.   Continue the process of having each member tell about his experiences with his phobia. This will probably take up the full meeting.

Step Six. Planning your third meeting.   Well in advance of your third meeting, prepare a brief information sheet on the concepts, tools, and techniques of contextual therapy. You can use as a guide for this information sheet the "Memorandum to the Helper" at the end of Chapter Eight. This information sheet should certainly include the six points of contextual therapy, in addition to whatever else you may want to include. Plan to discuss the contents of the information sheet, item by item, at your third meeting.

Step Seven. Hold your third group meeting.   You may find that by the time of your third meeting your attendance has fallen off some. Don't be discouraged if it has. Some members may be experiencing practical difficulties in getting to the meeting. Others may have found that this is not what they had expected. Others may be timid or may have become frightened after hearing the others tell about their own fears. When this meeting begins, note the absence of those who have previously attended and ask members of the group to volunteer to call the absentees (one member for each absentee, so as to spread around the feeling of mutual support). Once this has been arranged, follow the plan you have already worked out for this meeting; that is, hold a point-by-point discussion of contextual therapy, with emphasis on the six points. You will probably need at least one more full session to complete this.

From time to time as you explain the concepts and techniques of contextual therapy to the group, you will be referring to this book, perhaps to read aloud a case description or some passage which clarifies a question that comes up in discussion. Some of the group members may wish to borrow your copy so that they can read for themselves a fuller explanation of some point in which they are interested. The group may want to "chip in" to buy some additional copies to circulate among the members, or some participants may want to obtain a copy for their personal and exclusive use. YOUR PHOBIA: UNDERSTANDING YOUR FEARS THROUGH CONTEXTUAL THERAPY has been written to fill those needs. If your local bookstore doesn't have enough copies to meet the demand among the group members, you can special order as many copies as you need through a bookstore, or you can even order directly from the publisher (whose address is listed on the title page).

Step Eight. Hold your fourth group session. Continue and complete the discussion of contextual therapy and review the main concepts and the six points. If you have not gotten through all of the points by the end of this session, explain that the discussion will continue in the course of the following sessions. However, explain that you will be ready to start on the practice of contextual therapy in the following session. Tell the group that each member should be prepared to select a specific goal he would like to achieve during the next few months.

Step Nine. Hold your fifth group session. Have each member identify the short-term goal he has chosen as his first, immediate objective (for example, driving the children to school, shopping at a local supermarket, eating at a cafeteria, etc.) and the first small step he plans to take in working toward this goal. Include yourself as one of those who has to report. (Naturally, your goals will be further advanced since you have already been using contextual therapy for some time.) Explain the concept of starting with just a very little step, one that can be managed without excessive anxiety. Explain, again, the importance of staying in the phobic situation through the use of the tools and techniques of contextual therapy, and point out the importance of mastering that first little step—and how this will open the way for much larger steps later. If the individual who is speaking has a problem in deciding on a first step, ask the group members to help out with their own suggestions. When one member has finished deciding on his "first step," move on to the next, staying involved with him until he, too, has decided on his first step. Continue in the same way with the third member of the group, and then the others, until you have gone all around. Try to complete this process in this session, so that all will be able to work on their first "step" or "rung" during the week. Ask everyone to be prepared to report on his or her progress at the following meeting.

When this discussion is completed, try matching up the members so they can serve as each other's helpers.

Here is what we mean by "matching up the members." Let us say that one member of the group might not be able to go to the store, while another might not be able to drive. These two would make a good "match." Each could become the helper for the other. One might have a bus phobia, the other an elevator phobia: These two would make a good match to be helpers to each other. One might not be able to drive over a bridge; another might have problems about driving in heavy traffic; these two could team up. One might be afraid to stand in line at a supermarket or to go to a movie or a bingo game, while the other might be afraid to go to the beach or to the park. You should be able to get some good matchups with situations such as these.

If you have a problem making matchups, or even if you do not, try to enlist friends or relatives of some of the group members to serve as helpers. Ask the members if they would prefer a friend or relative as a helper rather than a matchup from the group. If they do, ask them to invite the friend or relative to attend the meetings regularly. However, the participation of the helper from outside the group should be limited to attending, listening, observing, and learning. These helpers should not be asked to participate in the discussions; it should be pointed out that the sessions are intended for the people with the phobias and that the friends and relatives are there to learn the ways in which they can be of most help to the phobic person they have agreed to help. Of course, questions from the helpers about their role in contextual therapy should be welcomed. Refer back to Chapter Eight for guidance on the recruitment and use of friends or relatives as helpers.

Step Ten. Hold your sixth session. At your sixth session, you are going to begin to ask the members to report, one at a time, what they did during the week in working with their phobia. Give each member plenty of time to express his enthusiasm, fears, or disappointments and encourage the group to help out with suggestions. When each individual is finished, ask what he plans to do the following week. He may want to continue to work on the same step or may feel that he has already mastered it and may want to start on one that is a little more difficult. Continue in the same way from member to member. Try, if possible, to give every member a chance to report on his progress, so that no one feels neglected or left out. This may mean shortening the reports so that all can be included. Explain, however, that fuller discussion will be allowed, once you are all in the swing of it, and after each member is moving along more or less on his own initiative.

Step Eleven. Further sessions. The sessions after the sixth will pretty much shape themselves, since they will basically consist of reports from the members on what they had achieved the previous week and on what they are planning for the following week, together with helpful suggestions and discussion from other members of the group.

As word gets around about your mutual support group, you will find that additional people will ask to join the group. Many phobic people, particularly those with social phobias, are not natural "joiners." They are not likely to join a group when it first gets started, but once they hear some positive things about your group—perhaps through publicity or a newsletter—they may express an interest in joining after the group has been established for some time. As new members join the mutual support group, they will need an "orientation" about the concepts and techniques of contextual therapy, the goals of the group, and how they will be expected in participate in the mutual support process. Regular review of the six points of contextual therapy at group meetings will help to reinforce these important concepts for all members of the group, but particularly for those who join after the group has become established.

SOME HELPFUL POINTERS

Here are some suggestions that should be useful to you in planning and conducting your meetings:

1. When you ask people to tell about their phobias, there will be one or two who will want to tell all about their personal problems with their relatives, children, neighbors, ailments, etc. You should not try to shut them off. They have felt terribly burdened about these things, and this is probably their first opportunity to get these feelings off their chests. You need to be concerned and sympathetic, but do not let it run on for too long. You need to explain that while these matters are important, they cannot be dealt with at these meetings, and that everybody is here to work on his phobia. It may be necessary to be a little firm; otherwise the meetings will run out of control.

2. When you ask the members to tell about their phobias, they will tell you about their particular phobic problem, but they may not want to call it a phobia. They would rather think that the problem is something physical, like hypoglycemia, chemical imbalance, poor nutrition, or something else in a similar vein. It may be frightening to them to think that the problem is "in their head," because people tend to associate that with being mentally ill. You have to assure them that phobias are not related to serious mental illness, and that phobias happen, naturally, because a person can become sensitized to a particular situation as a result of some previous experiences that give that situation the power to arouse frightening feelings and thoughts in him. To reassure them further, tell them that, on the average, phobic people are very intelligent, capable, and successful. This should relax them and allay their concern about identifying themselves as a person with a phobia.

3. If members are concerned that theirs is a physical rather than an emotional problem, advise them emphatically to seek a consultation with their physician. This suggestion—that each member get a medical evaluation—would be advisable under any circumstances. This should help to allay unfounded concerns, or may even identify a medical problem if there is one.

4. Set up a telephone "hotline." We have already mentioned telephone support briefly, but we think it needs to be reemphasized. After the members of the group have gotten to know each other, ask them if they would be willing to give their phone numbers to each other so they can call one another when they feel frightened, when they have a panic attack, or for any other kind of appropriate mutual help. Most should be willing to do this, since a strong sense of comradeship and a desire to help each other develops very quickly. The hotline will serve another purpose, too. After the group has been in operation for a while, some of them might tend to call you only, because you are the group leader, and some may want to lean on you as a "personal therapist." This could become quite a burden. If this does happen repeatedly, we advise that you listen to the member patiently for a minute or two, and then suggest in a kindly manner that it would be better if he or she called some other member of the group in the telephone network. But be careful about giving the caller the feeling that he is being rejected. Phobic people have enough of a problem in that respect already, and this feeling should not be reinforced if at all possible.

5. You may be able to use volunteers as helpers. They may be recruited through a church, a local mental health association, a college, or through newspaper articles in which the help of volunteers is solicited. After you have recruited them, ask them to sit in for half a dozen sessions or so, so they may get the hang of contextual therapy and mutual support. Then they can begin to serve as helpers.

6. How long should an individual member stay in the group? Since there is no fixed time limit in a mutual support group, people who join like to know how long they ought to remain part of the group. We cannot give one answer that applies to everyone, because every person is different. We have found, for instance, that as a rule, young people of high school and college age seem to get hold of the basic ideas of contextual therapy more quickly and progress more quickly than do people who are older. This may be because their phobia has not yet become so firmly entrenched. They haven't been avoiding contact with their phobic situation for as long. They are often more assertive and more willing to take risks. With older people who have had their phobia for a long time, phobic behavior has almost become a way of life; it is something to which they have resigned themselves, and so it is more difficult to stir up the interest, enthusiasm, and courage to take some action which may be painful at first. Of course, there are exceptions. Some young people find it very difficult to move and to change, and some older people throw themselves into the struggle with spirit and courage.

Leaving aside the age differences, a person who has joined a mutual support group should stay in it for three or four months at least, and for as long as a year or more, if possible. Some group members make the mistake of quitting early. They come in, stay a few weeks, and make rapid strides. This gives them the feeling that they have mastered the concept and techniques of contextual therapy and so they quit. Actually, they often have just begun to get the hang of it at that point. They may find that, after a few tries, they can enter their phobic situation and stay in it without experiencing too much fear, and so they think, "This is it. I've got it licked. I'm ready to quit." They don't know that reducing phobic fear by using the tools of contextual therapy is only the beginning of the process. It is a complex process and it takes time, for some much longer than for others. That is why we urge members to stay with the group for four months at minimum, and to continue, if possible, for a year or longer.

Under any circumstances, even if they quit, they know the group is there, and they come back again whenever they need it. Often people will come back after having been away two or three years. They may have a temporary recurrence and decide they need the support of the group to deal with it.

7. Start a newsletter. After the group has been in existence several months, it would be a good idea to start a newsletter. The newsletter would contain little articles from individuals telling about their own experiences. It could also serve to review the basic principles of contextual therapy and list the six points of contextual therapy. Issued every few months, the newsletter would be helpful to people who are no longer members of the group but who want to keep in touch, to others who might have an interest in joining the group, and to still others who cannot join but who would like to benefit from the feeling of mutual support they get from reading about the experiences of group members and from learning about contextual therapy. A mental health association or other community agency might help with the preparation, financing, and distribution of the newsletter.

Index

Acrophobia. *See* Height phobias
Agoraphobia
    case examples, 2–3, 11–12,
        22–23, 78–81, 83–86, 89–
        100, 212–25
    definition, 36, 76
    dependency on parents and,
        85–88
    depersonalization, 95–97
    depression and, 94–95
    description, 75–77
    graded practice ladders, 212–
        25
    life change factors, 89–94
    male-female, mix, 78
    obsessive, 97–101
    personality characteristics,
        81–85
    progression of, 77–78
Airplane phobias
    description, 38
    graded practice ladder, 229–
        31

Animal phobias
    birds, 54–56
    cats, 57–59, 206–208
    description, 50–52
    dogs, 59, 159–61
    insects, 4, 52–54, 239–40
    snakes, 56–57
Anticipation, 259–60
Arieti, Silvano, 110–11
Avoidance response, 11–13

Beck, Aaron, 119–20
Behavioral therapy
    phobia cause theory, 111–15
    phobia treatment, 123–28
Bird phobias, 54–56
Blood phobias, 49–50
Bridge phobias
    contextual therapy case, 145–
        48
    description, 37–38
    graded practice ladders, 233
Bus phobias, 226–27

Cat phobias
    description, 57–59
    graded practice ladder, 206–
        208
Causes
    Arieti theory, 110–11
    behavioral theory, 111–15
    "cognitive" view, 118–20
    contextual therapy theory,
        104–108
    instinctive fear, 117–18
    psychoanalytic theory, 108–
        11
    trauma, 115–17
Childbirth, 91–92
Claustrophobia. *See* Enclosed
    place phobias
"Cognitive" therapy
    phobia cause theory, 118–20
    phobia treatment, 128–30
Conditioning theory, 111–15
Confrontation stage 149–51
Contextual therapy
    agoraphobia case examples,
        212–25
    confrontation stage, 149–51
    control stage, 151–68
    description, 25–26, 132–33
    development of, 31–32
    driving case example, 207–12
    effectiveness, 28–29
    goals, 29–31
    helper's memorandum, 186–
        201
    phobia cause theory, 104–108
    phobic reaction approach, 27–
        28, 145–48
    planning meeting, 203–209
    outsiders' involvement, 252–
        57
    self-directed, 263–66
    understanding stage, 168–73
    See also Graded practice

ladders; Helpers; Mutual
    support groups
Control stage
    expectation of fear, 152–53
    guidelines, 245–52, 257–62
    labeling fear, 156–61
    personality trait problems,
        164–68
    progress recognition, 161–62,
        258–62
    reality activities, 154–56
    self-directed, 263–66
    setback attitudes, 163–64
    subsiding of fear, 154
    summary of points, 242–45
    See also Graded practice
        ladders; Helpers

Depersonalization, 95–97
Depression, 64–66, 94–95
Depth phobias, 44–45
Dog phobias
    contextual therapy case, 159–
        61
    description, 59
Driving phobias, 207–212, 220–
    21, 233, 255–56
Drug treatment, 130–31, 246–47

Eating phobias
    case examples, 68, 73–74
    graded practice ladder, 236–
        37
Elevator phobias
    case examples, 252–53
    graded practice ladder, 228–
        29
Emotional investment, 178–79
Emotional involvement, 177–78
Enclosed place phobias
    description, 38–44
    graded practice ladders, 235–
        36

Exposure therapy, 24–25, 124–26, 150
See also Contextual therapy
Expressways, 211–12, 233, 255–56
Eysenck, Hans, 117–18

Family traits, 120–21
Fear Level Chart, 169, 170–171
Fear reaction
children and, 104–108
description, 6–7
family patterns, 120–21
Feather phobias, 55–56
Flooding, 125–26
Freud, Sigmund, 108–109, 121–22

Gift giving phobias, 70–73
Goal setting, 204–205
Graded exposure. *See*
Contextual therapy;
Participant modeling;
Reinforced practice
Graded practice ladders
agoraphobia case examples, 212–25
airplanes, 229–31
alteration of, 225–26
bridges, 233–34
buses, 226–27
development of, 206–209
driving case examples, 209–12, 220–21
eating in public, 236–37
elevators, 228–29
enclosed places, 235–36
expressways, 233
heights, 231–32
insects, 239–40
restaurants, 234–35
social gatherings, 238–39
subways, 227

trains, 228
writing in public, 237–38

Height phobias
case examples, 2, 3
description, 36–38
graded practice ladder, 231–32
See also Airplane phobias;
Bridge phobias
Helpers
communicating with, 249–50, 257–58
explanatory memorandum, 186–201
functions, 175–76
mutual support group role, 272–73
planning meeting, 203–209
qualities of, 179–82
recruitment, 183–86
revealing phobia to, 182–83
role, 250
selection, 177–82
session cancellation and, 248–49
Hypnosis, 131–32

Imaginal therapy, 124–26, 128
Insect phobias
case examples, 4
description, 52–54
graded practice ladders, 239–40
Instinctive fear theory, 117–18
In vivo therapy, 24–25, 124–26, 150
See also Contextual therapy

Job phobias, 219–20

Ladders. *See* Graded practice ladders

Learning theory, 111–15

Marriage, 92–94
Mutual support groups
  development model, 268–74
  guidelines, 274–77
  objectives, 268

Natural element phobias, 4–5,
  45–47, 253–55
Newsletters, 277

Obsessive phobias, 97–101
Overlock, Fern, 267

Participant modeling, 126–27
Perfectionism, 164–65
Personality traits, 81–85, 164–68
Pharmacological treatment,
  130–31, 246–47
Phobias
  avoidance response, 11–13
  case examples, 2–5, 8–9, 11–
    12, 18–19, 22–23
  classification of, 35–36
  definition, 16
  description, 5–10
  extent of, 16–18
  family patterns, 120–21
  phobogenic process, 26–27
  reaction characteristics, 13–15
  self-image and, 19–24
  stimuli range, 33–35
  treatment approaches, 24–26
  See also Agoraphobia; Causes;
    Contextual therapy, Simple
    phobias; Social phobias;
    Treatment
Phobic reaction
  attention focusing factors,
    141–44
  case examples, 135–40

contextual therapy approach,
    145–48
  expecting the worst, 140–41
Planning meetings
  goal setting, 204–205
  graded practice ladder
    development, 206–209
  phobia discussion, 203–204
Practice ladders. See Graded
    practice ladders
Pregnancy, 91–92
Psychoanalytic therapy
  phobia cause theory, 108–11
  phobia treatment, 121–22

Reinforced practice, 127–28
Restaurant phobias, 3–4, 234–35

School phobias, 87–88
Self-directed therapy, 263–66
Self-statement, 130
Separation anxiety, 85–88
Simple phobias
  animals, 50–59, 159–61, 206–
    208, 239–40
  blood, 49–50
  definition, 36
  depths, 44–45
  enclosed places, 38–44, 235–
    36
  heights, 36–38, 145–48, 229–
    34
  natural elements, 45–47, 253–
    55
  water, 47–49
Snake phobias, 56–57
Snow phobias, 45–47
Social gathering phobias, 238–
    39
Social phobias
  cluster pattern, 66–69
  definition, 36

depression and, 64–66
description, 61
eating in public, 68, 73–74, 236–37
gift giving, 70–73
speaking in public, 68–69, 256–57
urination, 69–70
writing in public, 67–68, 71, 237–38
Speaking phobias, 68–69, 256–57
Specific phobias. *See* Simple phobias
Spider phobias, 52
Store phobias, 221–22
Storm phobias, 4–5, 45, 253–55
Subway phobias, 227
Systematic desensitization, 123–26

Tape recordings, 212, 249–50
Telephone support, 275
Train phobias, 228
Trauma theory, 115–17

Treatment
behavioral therapy, 123–28
"cognitive" therapy, 128–30
hypnosis, 131–32
participant modeling, 126–27
pharmacological, 130–31
psychoanalysis, 121–22
reinforced practice, 127–28
See also Contextual therapy

Uncertainty, 166–68
Understanding stage, 168–73
Ungraded exposure. *See* Flooding
Urination phobias, 69–70

Water phobias, 47–49
Watson, John B., 111
Westphal, G., 75
Wolpe, Joseph, 123–24
Writing phobias
case examples, 67–68, 71
graded practice ladder, 237

Zane, Manuel D., 31–32